SOFTWARE-DEFINED NETWORKING FOR FUTURE INTERNET TECHNOLOGY

Concepts and Applications

T0321102

SOFTWARE-DEFINED NETWORKING FOR FUTURE INTERNET TECHNOLOGY

Concepts and Applications

Edited by

Kshira Sagar Sahoo, PhD
Bibhudatta Sahoo, PhD
Brojo Kishore Mishra, PhD

APPLE
ACADEMIC
PRESS

First edition published 2022

Apple Academic Press Inc.
1265 Goldenrod Circle, NE,
Palm Bay, FL 32905 USA

4164 Lakeshore Road, Burlington,
ON, L7L 1A4 Canada

CRC Press
6000 Broken Sound Parkway NW,
Suite 300, Boca Raton, FL 33487-2742 USA

2 Park Square, Milton Park,
Abingdon, Oxon, OX14 4RN UK

© 2022 Apple Academic Press, Inc.

Apple Academic Press exclusively co-publishes with CRC Press, an imprint of Taylor & Francis Group, LLC

Library and Archives Canada Cataloguing in Publication

Title: Software-Defined Networking for Future Internet Technology : concepts and applications / edited by Kshira Sagar Sahoo, PhD, Bibhudatta Sahoo, PhD, Brojo Kishore Mishra, PhD.
Names: Sahoo, Kshira Sagar, editor. | Sahoo, Bibhudatta, 1967- editor. | Mishra, Brojo Kishore, 1979- editor.
Description: First edition. | Includes bibliographical references and index.
Identifiers: Canadiana (print) 20210188626 | Canadiana (ebook) 20210188715 | ISBN 9781771889865 (hardcover) | ISBN 9781774639702 (softcover) | ISBN 9781003145721 (ebook)
Subjects: LCSH: Software-defined networking (Computer network technology) | LCSH: Internet of things.
Classification: LCC TK5105.5833 .S64 2021 | DDC 004.6—dc23

Library of Congress Cataloging-in-Publication Data

Names: Sahoo, Kshira Sagar, editor. | Sahoo, Bibhudatta, 1967- editor. | Mishra, Brojo Kishore, 1979- editor.
Title: Software-Defined Networking for Future Internet Technology : concepts and applications / edited by Sagar Sahoo, PhD, Bibhudatta Sahoo, PhD, Brojo Kishore Mishra, PhD.
Description: First edition. | Palm Bay, FL, USA : Apple Academic Press, 2021. | Includes bibliographical references and index. | Summary: "The growing usage of networks presents many challenges for network administrators. Network infrastructures are growing rapidly to meet needs of business, but the required re-policing and reconfiguration provide challenges that need to be addressed. The software-defined network (SDN) is the future generation of Internet technology that can help meet these challenges of network management. This book, Software-Defined Networking for Future Internet Technology: Concepts and Applications, includes quantitative research, case studies, conceptual papers, model papers, review papers, theoretical backing, etc. This book investigates areas where SDN can help other emerging technologies for delivering more efficient services, such as IoT, industrial IoT, NFV, big data, blockchain, cloud computing, and edge computing. The book demonstrates the many benefits of SDN, such as reduced costs, ease of deployment and management, better scalability, availability, flexibility and fine-grained control of traffic, and security. Chapters in the volume address: Design consideration for security issues and detection methods State-of-the-art approaches for mitigating DDos attacks using SDN Big data using Apache Hadoop for processing and analyzing large amounts of data Different tools used for attack simulation Network policies and policy management approaches that are widely used in the context of SDN Dynamic flow tables, or static flow table management A new four-tiered architecture that includes cloud, SDN-controller, and fog computing Architecture for keeping computing resources available near the industrial IoT network through edge computing The impact of SDN as an innovative approach for smart city development More The book will be a valuable resource for SDN researchers as well as academicians, research scholars, and students in the related areas"-- Provided by publisher.
Identifiers: LCCN 2021016977 (print) | LCCN 2021016978 (ebook) | ISBN 9781771889865 (hbk) | ISBN 9781774639702 (pbk) | ISBN 9781003145721 (ebk)
Subjects: LCSH: Software-defined networking (Computer network technology)
Classification: LCC TK5105.5833 .S644 2021 (print) | LCC TK5105.5833 (ebook) | DDC 621.39/802855--dc23
LC record available at https://lccn.loc.gov/2021016977
LC ebook record available at https://lccn.loc.gov/2021016978

ISBN: 978-1-77188-986-5 (hbk)
ISBN: 978-1-77463-970-2 (pbk)
ISBN: 978-1-00314-572-1 (ebk)

About the Editors

Kshira Sagar Sahoo, PhD

Assistant Professor, Department of Computer Science and Engineering, SRM University, Amaravati, Andhra Pradesh–522502, India

Kshira Sagar Sahoo, PhD, is currently working as an Assistant Professor in the Department of Computer Science and Engineering at SRM University, Amaravati, AP, India. He received his PhD degree from the National Institute of Technology, Rourkela, India, in 2019. He received his MTech degree from the Indian Institute of Technology Kharagpur, India, in 2014. He completed his BTech from the Institute of Technical Education and Research, Bhubaneswar, India, in 2007. He has authored more than 50 international conferences and journals, including IEEE transactions, Wiley, Springer, and Elsevier. His research interests include Future Generation Network Infrastructure such as Software Defined Networks, Edge Computing, IoT, etc. He is a member of the IEEE computer society and an associate member of the Institute of Engineers (IE), India.

Bibhudatta Sahoo, PhD

Associate Professor, Department of CSE NIT Rourkela, Odisha, India, E-mail: bibhudatta.sahoo@gmail.com

Bibhudatta Sahoo, PhD, is presently working as an Associate Professor in the Department of Computer Science and Engineering, NIT Rourkela, India. He have 25 years of teaching experience in undergraduate and graduate level in the field of Computer Science and Engineering. He has authored in several international conferences and journals, including IEEE transactions, Wiley, Springer, and Elsevier. His technical interests include data structures and algorithm design, parallel, and distributed systems, networks, computational machines, algorithms for VLSI design, performance evaluation methods and modeling techniques, distributed computing systems, networking algorithms, and web engineering. He is a member of IEEE and ACM. He obtained his MTech and PhD in Computer Science and Engineering from NIT, Rourkela.

Brojo Kishore Mishra, PhD

Professor, Department of CSE, GIET University, Gunupur, Odisha, India, E-mail: brojomishra@gmail.com

Brojo Kishore Mishra, PhD, is a Professor in the Computer Science and Engineering Department at the Gandhi Institute of Engineering and Technology University, Gunupur, Odisha, India. He received his MTech and PhD degrees in computer science from Berhampur University in 2008 and 2012, respectively. He has been selected as a State Student Coordinator (Odisha) and Regional Student Coordinator (CSI Region-IV) of Computer Society of India in 2015–2016 and 2016–2017, respectively. He has been elected as the National Nomination Committee Member (2017–2018) for the Computer Society of India. Similarly, he has been selected as the IEEE Day Ambassador for the Kolkata Section of IEEE Region-10 for 2015 and 2016, respectively. He was the Jury Coordination Committee Member of All IEEE Young Engineers' Humanitarian Challenge (AIYEHUM 2015) project competition organized by IEEE Region 10 (Asia Pacific). His research interests included mining and big data analysis, machine learning, soft computing, and evolutionary computation. He has already published more than 40 research papers in internationally reputed journals and referred conferences, 7 book chapters, edited 1 book, and is acting as a member of the editorial board/associate editor/guest editor for various international journals. He is a life member of ISTE, CSI, and member of IEEE, ACM, IAENG, UACEE, and ACCS.

Contents

Contributors

Sreenivasa Rao Annaluri
Department of Information Technology, VNR Vignana Jyothi Institute of Engineering and Technology, Hyderabad–500090, Telangana, India, E-mail: E-mail: annaluri.rao@gmail.com

Hemant Kumar Apat
Cloud Computing Research Lab, Department of Computer Science and Engineering, National Institute of Technology, Rourkela–769008, Odisha, India, E-mail-hemant.rimt@gmail.com

Ankit Aryan
Department of Computer Science and Engineering, National Institute of Technology, Rourkela–769008, Odisha, India, E-mail: 116cs0163@nitrkl.ac.in

Venkata Ramana Attili
Department of Electronics and Computer Engineering, Sreenidhi Institute of Science and Technology, Telangana, India, E-mail: avrrdg@gmail.com

Shashwati Banerjea
Department of Computer Science and Engineering, Motilal Nehru National Institute of Technology, Allahabad, Uttar Pradesh, India, E-mail: shashwati@mnnit.ac.in

Pranitha Madapathi
Department of Computer Science and Engineering, National Institute of Rourkela, Odisha, India, E-mail: mpranitha18@gmail.com

Prasenjit Maiti
Cloud Computing Research Lab, Department of Computer Science and Engineering, National Institute of Technology, Rourkela–769008, Odisha, India, E-mail: pmaiti1287@gmail.com

A. Manisha
Department of Information Technology, VNR Vignana Jyothi Institute of Engineering and Technology, Hyderabad–500090, Telangana, India, E-mail: nisha661997@gmail.com

Brojo Kishore Mishra
Department of CSE, GIET University, Gunupur, Odisha, India, E-mail: brojomishra@gmail.com

Jangili Narendra
Department of Information Technology, VNR Vignana Jyothi Institute of Engineering and Technology, Hyderabad–500090, Telangana, India, E-mail: jangilinarendra@gmail.com

Abinas Panda
Department of Computer Science and Engineering, National Institute of Technology, Rourkela–769008, Odisha, India, E-mail: abinash.panda1987@gmail.com

Aliva Panda
Department of Computer Science and Engineering, SRM University, Andhra Pradesh–522502, India, E-mail: alivapanda.14@gmail.com

Srinivas V. S. Podili
Department of Computer Science and Engineering, Sreenidhi Institute of Science and Technology,
Telangana, India, E-mail: Pvssrinivas23@gmail.com

G. Suresh Reddy
Department of Information Technology, VNR Vignana Jyothi Institute of Engineering and
Technology, Hyderabad–500090, Telangana, India, E-mail: ithead@vnrvjiet.in

Bibhudatta Sahoo
Cloud Computing Research Lab, Department of Computer Science and Engineering,
National Institute of Technology, Rourkela–769008, Odisha, India,
E-mail: bibhudatta.sahoo@gmail.com

Kshira Sagar Sahoo
Department of Computer Science and Engineering, SRM University, Amaravati, AP, 522502, India
E-mail: kshirasagar12@gmail.com

Tarinee Prasad Sahoo
Department of Computer Science and Engineering, National Institute of Technology,
Rourkela–769008, Odisha, India, E-mail: 116cs0224@nitrkl.ac.in

Moin Sharukh
Department of Information Technology, VNR Vignana Jyothi Institute of Engineering and
Technology, Hyderabad–500090, Telangana, India, E-mail: moinsharukh001@gmail.com

Shashank Srivastava
Department of Computer Science and Engineering, Motilal Nehru National Institute of Technology,
Allahabad, Uttar Pradesh, India, E-mail: shashank12@mnnit.ac.in

Bata Krishna Tripathy
School of Electrical Sciences, Indian Institute of Technology, Bhubaneswar, Argul, Khordha,
Odisha–752050, India, E-mail: bata.krishna.tripathy@gmail.com

Ashok Kumar Turuk
Cloud Computing Research Lab, Department of Computer Science and Engineering,
National Institute of Technology, Rourkela–769008, Odisha, India, E-mail: akturuk@nitrkl.ac.in

Durga Prasad Varma
Department of Information Technology, VNR Vignana Jyothi Institute of Engineering and
Technology, Hyderabad–500090, Telangana, India, E-mail: durgaprasadvarma1994@gmail.com

Koppada Durgaprasad Varma
Department of Information Technology, VNR Vignana Jyothi Institute of Engineering and
Technology, Hyderabad–500090, Telangana, India, E-mail: durgaprasadvarma1994@gmail.com

Abbreviations

AAA	authentication authorization and accounting
ACL	access control list
AP	application plane
APIs	application programming interfaces
ARP	address resolution protocol
ASIC	application-specific integrated circuits
ASP	authentication service providers
BS	base stations
BSSID	basic service set identification
CA	certificate authority
CAB	CAching in Buckets
CC	common criteria
CD	coordinating device
CES	customer edge switching
CH	cluster head
CM	cloud monitor
CMaS	cost-makespan conscious scheduling
CMS	cloud management services
CNF	conjunctive normal form
CNN	convolution neural network
CORA	COnflict RAzor
CP	control plane
CRAFT	cache reduction architecture for flow tables
CRLs	certificate revocation lists
DC	data center
DCS	dynamic controller scheduling
DDMF	DDoS detection and mitigation framework
DDoS	distributed denial of service
DFD	data flow diagrams
DIP	destination IP
DL	deep learning
DMR	deadline miss ratio
DNS	domain name server

DoS	denial of service
DP	data plane
dPaaS	data platform as a service
DPI	deep packet inspection
ECA	event-condition-action
EM	exact match
EMR	electronic medical record
FC	fog controller
FCM	fog control manager
FD	file descriptor
FE	feature extractor
FFTA	fast flow table aggregation
FL-Guard	floodlight guard
FN	fog nodes
FSG	fog smart gateway
GA	genetic algorithms
GNV	global network view
HDFS	Hadoop distributed file system
HEFT	heterogeneous earliest finish time
HFT	hierarchical flow tables
HOIC	high orbit ion cannon
HSS	home subscriber server
HTTP	hypertext transfer protocol
IaaS	infrastructure as a service
ICT	information and communication technologies
IDS	intrusion detection system
IIoT	industrial internet of things
IoC	internet of cloud
IoT	internet of things
iPaaS	integration platform as a service
IPS	intrusion prevention systems
ISPs	internet service providers
ITU	International Telecommunications Union
JVM	Java virtual machines
LOBUS	load balancing over unstructured networks
LOIC	low orbit ion cannon
LPM	layered policy management
LSTM	long-short-term memory

LVAP	light virtual APs
MaaS	machine as a service
Mb	megabits
MFT	multiple flow table
MITM	man-in-the-middle
MME	mobility management entity
MOF	map output files
MU-MIMO	multi-user multiple-input and multiple-output
NAT	network address translators
NBI	northbound interface
NC	network controllers
NFs	network functions
NFV	network function virtualization
NIB	network information base
NP	network provisioner
NRS	network run time state
NV	network virtualization
ODL	OpenDayLight
OF	OpenFlow
ONF	open system establishment
ORTC	optimal routing table constructor
OT	operations technology
OVS	OpenVSwitch
PaaS	platform as a service
PASTA	process for attack and threat analysis
PCH-DGS	path clustering heuristic with distributed gap search
PCRF	policy and charging rules function
PEFT	predict earliest finish time
PKI	public key infrastructure
PM	prefix match
PM	range match
QDR	quad data rate
QoE	quality of experience
QoS	quality of service
RBAC	role-based access control
RBF	radial basis function
RBM	restricted Boltzmann machines
RDF	resource description framework

RDMA	remote direct memory access
RFID	reader in radio frequency identification
RNIC	RDMA network interface card
RNN	random neural network
SaaS	software as a service
SBI	southbound interface
SDIoT	software-defined internet of things
SDMN	software-defined mobile networks
SDN	software-defined networking
SDN-C	SDN controller
SD-WAN	software defined-wide area network
SIP	session initiation protocol
SLAs	service level agreements
SLR	schedule length ratio
SOM	self-organizing Map
SPSL	security policy specification language
SRAM	static random-access memory
SSL	secure socket layer
SSNs	smart sensor nodes
SVM	support vector machine
TC	traffic classifier
TCAM	ternary content addressable memory
TCF	traffic collector and flow installer
TFTP	trivial file transfer protocol
TLS	transport layer security
ToR	top of rack
UI	user interface
UIDs	unique identifiers
VCN	virtual cloud network
VLANs	virtual local area network
VMs	virtual machines
VoIP	voice over internet protocol
VPNs	virtual private network
Wi-Fi	wireless fidelity
WLAN	wireless local area network
WM	wildcard match
XML	extensible markup language

Preface

These days, the usage of the network is growing at a very fast pace; at the same time, a lot of challenges are being faced by the network administrator. The network infrastructure is growing rapidly to meet business needs, but it requires re-policing and reconfiguration of the network. In this regard, software defined network (SDN) is the future generation of Internet technology, which not only solves the ossification of the Internet but also creates innovations and simplifies network management. The key idea behind SDN is the separation of the control plane (CP) from the data plane (DP); as a result, devices in the data plane become the forwarding device. All the decision-making activities have been transferred to a centralized system called a controller. OpenFlow (OF) is the standard and most popular SDN protocol that interacts between the control plane and the data plane. SDN provides many benefits such as reduced costs, ease of deployment and management, better scalability, better availability, better flexibility, fine-grained control of traffic, and security, etc. However, new issues in a different layer of SDN still need to be addressed by future research efforts.

This book contains quantitative research, case studies, conceptual papers, model papers, review papers, theoretical backing, etc. This book will help to investigate areas where SDN could provide help to other emerging technologies for delivering more efficient services such as IoT, industrial IoT, NFV (network function virtualization), big data, blockchain, cloud computing, and edge computing, etc. We believe our readers will be provided with the required knowledge to manage current and future demand for SDN.

This book is organized into ten chapters.

Chapter 1 discusses various security issues in SDN. Different types of design considerations for security requirements are discussed with considerable examples. SDN cloud applications and security challenges are explained with detailed analysis. Finally, big data using Apache Hadoop for processing and analyzing large data has been discussed.

Chapter 2 discusses various DDoS attack possibilities in three different layers of SDN. Additionally, this chapter highlights the different tools used for attack simulation. Finally, it provides state-of-the-art approaches for mitigating DDoS attacks using SDN.

The execution of the network functions (NFs) depends on the implementation of heterogeneous and complex policies in an organization. Chapter 3 provides an introduction to various network policies and the policy management approaches that are widely used in the context of SDN.

Chapter 4 provides various issues related to scalability and its proposed approaches in a software-defined wired network. It discussed the challenges in the flow table and its management. Several solutions and taxonomy have been highlighted in terms of solution approach and problem description, such as dynamic flow table or static flow table management.

Chapter 5 introduces a new four-tier architecture, which includes cloud, SDN-controller, fog-controller, and fog. The authors claim that this could minimize the total make-span of the scheduling algorithms and require less servicing miss ratio compared to the existing architectures.

Chapter 6 talks about a cloud architecture in which the computing resources available nearer to the Industrial IoT network through edge computing. Further, large amounts of data can be accessed securely with minimum latency, with the help of both SDN and blockchain techniques.

The software-defined Internet of Things (SDIoT) framework based on the SDx paradigm consists of a controller pool, SD-IoT switches integrated with an IoT gateway, and IoT devices. In Chapter 7, a broad range of DDoS attacks and detection methods for the IoT environment used in the SDN paradigm have been analyzed. Finally, different future scopes of this evolving field have been discussed.

Chapter 8 proposes an SDN-enabled service architecture model in the fog-computing environment. Fog computing helps to reduce transmission latency because it is available locally to the IoT layer.

Industrial IoT plays a vital role in building smart cities. Chapter 9 discusses the impact of SDN as an innovative approach for smart city development.

There are various reasons for the growth of SDN and NFV. They can drive big data, smart devices, and distributed servers in an extensive manner. Chapter 10 highlighted the major significance and difference between these two emerging technologies.

We hope our readers find this book an excellent guide to future internet technology like SDN, the network revolution in the midst.

There have been several influences from our family and friends who have sacrificed a lot of their time and attention to ensure that we are kept motivated to complete this crucial project. To them, our deep thank you!

We thank Dr. Deepak Puthal, Assistant Professor, School of Computing, Newcastle University, United Kingdom, for his refreshingly unbiased comments on the different chapters of the book.

We are also grateful to Mayank Tiwary, Senior Developer, SAP Labs, Cloud Platform, whose help rendering many of the figures in this book was invaluable.

The editors are also thankful to all the members of Apple Academic Press.

—Editors

CHAPTER 1

Security Issues in SDN

VENKATA RAMANA ATTILI,[1] SREENIVASA RAO ANNALURI,[2] and SRINIVAS V. S. PODILI[3]

[1]*Department of Electronics and Computer Engineering, Sreenidhi Institute of Science and Technology, Telangana, India*

[2]*Department of Information Technology, VNR Vignana Jyothi Institute of Engineering and Technology, Hyderabad–500090, Telangana, India, E-mail: annaluri.rao@gmail.com*

[3]*Department of Computer Science and Engineering, Sreenidhi Institute of Science and Technology, Telangana, India*

ABSTRACT

The exponential rise of data/information and network resources made most of the organizations investing their resources to develop the biggest data centers (DCs) to accommodate. In the process, controlling the workload at the DCs with minimum response time, there is a need for an effective load-balancing system for which routing applications are playing an important role. Some of the routing applications based on software-defined networking (SDN) available in the market handling the traffic loads of these DCs efficiently. Using the centralized routing allows the network engineers to adjust different types of network elements such as switches, links, and ports dynamically based on the traffic loads. The data flow management at these DCs is managed by the routing applications sometimes face a non-conflicting way for the flow of data and towards the instructions for the switches as well. The security of routing applications plays an important role in safeguarding the control of data flow routing or scheduling from the attackers. The possibility of attackers controlling the traffic, servers, and switches at a DC is a serious threat and someone may even shut down the complete system/server. Such attacks may disrupt the routing application and also data flow management. In this chapter, various challenges and security analysis of SDN concerning to routing, cloud, Wi-Fi, and big data will be explored. Different types of design considerations for security requirements are discussed with considerable examples and code analysis. SDN cloud applications and security challenges that are related to the cloud are explained with detailed analysis. Some of the mitigation techniques are proposed for spoofing, data tampering, and repudiation issues. In addition, a detailed discussion on the big data using Apache Hadoop for processing and analyzing the large data sets will be explored.

1.1 INTRODUCTION TO SECURITY ISSUES OF SDN

SDN is one of the best examples of networking standards aiming towards reaching the goals of overcoming the limitations existing with the traditional networks. SDN enables the software to manage the networks dynamically (Sahoo et al., 2019a). Using the software, abstracting of a physical network with the virtual networks is possible using SDN. Apart from that it helps spanning the policies across the physical and virtual networks and allows controlling the data centers (DCs) traffic flow. The performance of SDN lies in the ability of providing consistent policy enforcement, ability to deliver greater scalability and the ability to control entire network from the centralized management systems. Most of the security solutions with SDN are useful for the improvement of policy enforcement, traffic anomaly detection and for the mitigation of serious threats (Hizver, 2015). The possibility of getting under the malicious attacks by a new system using SDN functions is more and some of the attacks are quite common in other existing networks. Some characteristics of SDN are listed below before understanding the security issues:

- They are centrally controlled networks;
- They consists of open programmable interfaces;
- They use switch management protocols;
- Flexible for third party network services;
- They are also known to be the virtualized local networks;
- They consist of centralized monitoring units.

Physically the SDN Controllers (SDN-Cs) are distributed and will be in a cluster form. They will maintain a proper hierarchy and each controller will be having defined number of tasks to control the forwarding domains. However, network security using the SDN helps to improve the control and containment of variety of network security threats. However, found to be very sensitive for Denial-of-Service (DoS) attacks, issues that are related with trust among the networks, and it is proved to be bad due to the lack of better SDN functions and components to deal with network security issues.

1.1.1 SOFTWARE-DEFINED MOBILE NETWORKS (SDMN)

In recent times, most of the mobile operators are facing serious challenges with the rapid growth of mobile (smart) phones and wide range of network services. Most of the network services such as video streaming, television programs on internet, voice over internet protocol (VoIP), electronic transactions, video streaming, cloud services, etc., need a secured data transmission and receiving process, by which the information is not misused at any stage. Therefore, the level of competition among the mobile operators has been raised to a level where they cannot ignore or avoid security-related challenges, especially when they are providing the internet-based applications. There is a need for maintaining the consistency and improvement of the network infrastructure within the limited operational cost with efficient and quality services at attractive price plans. Even the legacy mobile networks are struggling with the limitations of stationary and expensive equipment, complex protocols, and interfacing complexities. In this context, SDN plays a vital role by integrating the mobile networks to design a SDMN with network functions virtualization (NFV) and different types of cloud computing principles. SDN consists of control plane (CP), data plane (DP), and application plane (AP) as shown in Figure 1.1. A centralized SDN-C will control all the three planes with the following three attributes (Liyanage et al., 2016; Cheng et al., 2018; Sahoo et al., 2019b):

- **Centralized Intelligence:** This part of the SDN architecture consists of a controller with a global view which manages complete mobile network.

- **Programmability:** This is the ability of a network to imbibe the advanced software programming techniques that evolve with the modifications in network architectures, behavior, and functionalities.
- **Abstraction:** This explains the ability to hide the important and complex infrastructure and the protocols of the network operating system. Using the SDN, a business application will abstract the underlying network information.

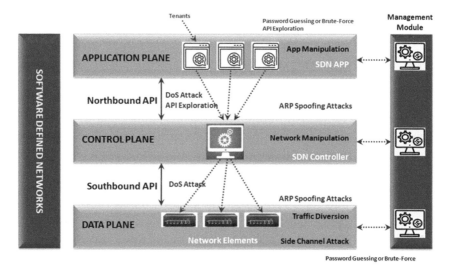

FIGURE 1.1   Security attacks at different levels of a SDN network.

Source: Adapted and modified from Asturias (2018).

Now with the separation of CP and DP from the architecture of SDN, the possibility of improving the security of a mobile network is more and it helps to allow different types of security mechanisms for variety of security challenges threats. The DP considered being more vulnerable for security threats and this is due to availability of gateways, routers, base stations, femtocell stations, etc. In simple, this is also termed as *infrastructure layer.* The CPconsists of a centralized controller (i.e., the brain of a SDN), which helps to control each and every function of a network by using the control protocols. For example, OpenFlow (OF) is used to establish a communication between the DP switches (Liyanage et al., 2015). Finally, the AP consists of communication networks control and different types of business applications (Kolias et al., 2013). Different network control entities of SDMN architecture will run as the software applications in AP layer. The list of such entities includes policy and charging rules function (PCRF), home subscriber server (HSS), mobility management entity (MME) and authentication authorization and accounting (AAA).

1.1.2 SECURITY MECHANISMS OF SDMN

Some of the SDMN based security mechanisms and vulnerable threats involved in mobile networks are discussed here. Perimeter security mechanism is playing a vital role to secure most of the telecommunication networks (Bikos and Sklavos, 2013; Cao et al., 2014). Intrusion prevention systems (IPS), firewalls, customer edge switching (CES), and network address translators (NAT), etc., will help to protect the vulnerable points of mobile networks that are linked with network edge interfacings (Liyanage et al., 2016). However, in case of distributed and diverse set of telecommunication networks, the security mechanism is deployed at different sections. Each mechanism works autonomously with limited knowledge of devices of other networks. Therefore, backward compatibility is needed for establishing synchronization among the old and new technologies to address the diverse set of wireless technologies[1]. Each technology has its own policy and security mechanism to protect from any kind of vulnerable event but such mechanisms create a complex scenario for the resource utilization tasks and therefore reduce overall performance of the mobile networks.

The security policies are also linked with different types of physical resources like switches, ports, interfaces, etc., as well. Most of the telecommunication policies support the voice and text messaging services for variety of transactions using mobile phones such as banking, health applications, etc. For such modern services using the mobile phones with isolated security mechanism with ad hoc polices may not provide sufficient security for the future mobile networks. The reactive mechanisms used for security mechanisms with present networking systems are not consistent to deliver the real-time decisions at a faster rate to meet the security challenges when they are dealing with the diversified networking

---

[1] Today's wireless technologies includes general packet radio services (GPRS); global system for mobile communications (GSM); wideband code division multiple access (WCDMA), long term evolution (LTE); and Wi-Fi.

technologies. Finally, with respect to the mobile networks, it is going to be a challenging task to adjust with the security policies for being quick, dynamic, and detect any kind malicious events. There is a serious clash between tightly coupled networking devices (where the security policies will be static) and the type of mobile network environments (where they demand rapid change of network parameters). Due to the lack of interoperability and vendor varying development process, *mixed*, and *matched* usage of different solutions is highly complex to implement (Cao et al., 2014; Liyanage et al., 2016).

Due to over-provisioned security mechanisms, handling of heavy traffic loads become a challenging task in the complex environment of mobile networking. This in turn create service disruptions and over populating issues so that the network operating companies need to underutilize the security resources for a long time until a solution is evolved. Further, the backward compatibility and interoperability between different technologies need a sophisticated approach to deal in a secured manner.

1.2 TYPES OF SECURITY ISSUES OF SDN

There are so many vulnerable scenarios in SDN that may lead to variety of attacks in the network elements at different DPs. The attacks may impact on the network elements and may redirect to the traffic flows and may even allow the eavesdropping. Some of the potential attacks involved in SDN are listed below with their role towards the security of the networks (Asturias, 2017; Hizver, 2015; Sahoo et al., 2018a):

1. **System Level SDN Security:** It is known for accountability, auditing, inventory of the networking devices and to identify the status of devices at a particular moment.
2. **Malicious/Compromised Applications:** These are poorly designed which exhibits variety of vulnerabilities in a network.
3. **Data Modifications:** These are generally possible due to man-in-the-middle (MITM) due to the transport layer security (TLS) is open flow and it is optional too (D'Orsaneo et al., 2018). In this case, the data can be modified in a controlled way or the hypervisor will try to take over the DPs. These attacks are mostly seen in the CP. By producing the false network data network manipulation/modifications are possible and allows attacks on complete

networking elements. Therefore, strong encryption methods must be adopted for the communication channels to mitigate these types of attacks and the SDN-C need to have redundant entity (Asturias, 2017).

4. **Unauthorized Access to Data or Applications:** It can take place at any level since it is an open architecture. That means the data can be obtained/accessed by the controllers from DPs or applications by the controllers.

5. **Application Manipulations:** It will take place in the AP and any kind of exploitation of the application vulnerability may lead to malfunction, disruptions of the services and/or eavesdrop of the data. Attackers will be able access the SDN application and perform variety of illegal operations (Nakao et al., 2015). To solve this issue the servers needed to be updated with the latest patches and software's regularly.

6. **Application Programming Interface (API) Exploitation:** It is due to the vulnerabilities which allow the hackers to disclose unauthorized information. API exploitation is possible at northbound interface (NBI) and may destruct network flows. To solve these problems the servers needs to be updated with latest patches.

7. **Data Leakage Issues:** These help the attackers to identify the policies and respective packets based on the time delays and relevant information. Based on this information the attackers will create the DoS attacks due to which most of the virtual networks will find the shortage of the storage space (Yan et al., 2015).

8. **DoS Attacks:** These are the threats related to overflow of the controller with lots of messages from a file descriptor (FD). These attacks can overflow most of the memory resources in the network and can be a serious threat to process the actual information at times. Sometimes these attacks are capable of affecting all the elements of SDN and can disrupt partial or complete SDN process. To avoid such attacks most of the network engineers use rate limiting or packet dropping techniques in the controller plane (Dridi and Zhani, 2018).

9. **Configuration Issues:** These are very serious and in SDN they create an opportunity for security options due to poor implementation/misconfiguration (Ageyev et al., 2018). Considerable vulnerabilities can be injected by opening the network components and

interfaces. These issues can be more critical when the networking components are becoming larger in number and heavy to handle.

10. **Traffic Diversion:** These attacks takes place in the DP with the network elements where they are redirect the traffic flow and allow the eavesdropping. Therefore, it is essential to provide a strong encryption system for the network elements and communication channels for improving the security with such attacks.

11. **Traffic Sniffing:** It is one of the popular attacks that help hackers to capture and analyze the network communication information. Eavesdropping and stealing of important information is possible using traffic sniffing with constant traffic on a network. The possibility of misusing the unencrypted communication system of the SDN is very high by intercepting the traffic from a central controller. The data obtained from the traffic sniffing may involve lot of critical information from the flow of traffic on a network. For which it needs a lot of strong encryption method that allows full security for the network elements of SDN.

12. **Side-Channel Attacks:** These are also seen in DP by considering the timing information (i.e., the overall duration spent) on the network. Based on this an attacker make necessary adjustments about the flow rules. These attacks can be avoided by using strong encryption algorithms that operate the network elements.

13. **Password Guessing:** It is also considered as a brute force and it can happen even on a non-SDN element by guessing the password by an unauthorized user. Such type of brute force may allow the complete access to the SDN. To avoid this problem it is always suggested to change the default passwords with some of the strong passwords and update them on a regular basis.

1.2.1 SECURITY THREATS INVOLVED IN SDMN

Most of the mobile networks are IP based:[2] and are seriously vulnerable for different types of security attacks. IP based attacks are mostly experienced on smartphones and tablets using distributed denial of service (DDoS), which is reported to be 90% in 2012 by Liyanage (2014). These devices

---

[2] LTE and LTE-Advanced are most popularly known IP-based mobile networking technologies used widely in the latest mobile phone devices.

are generally unprotected or will be always ON; therefore a botnet will be deployed by the attacker to carryout DDoS attack. Some of the featuring attacks on the mobile networks are given below with possible impacts and disadvantages (Liyanage, 2014):

1. **Distributed Denial of Service (DDoS):** This attack is carried out by sending large amounts of fake traffic to consume the resources of a mobile network. Such attacks will impact the backhaul devices or will be unresponsive for the legitimate traffic on the mobile network (Sahoo et al., 2018b, 2019b).
2. **Replay Attacks:** These are carried out based on the data transmission by intercepting the legitimate signaling traffic. The attackers fraudulently send the repeated messages or delayed messages to make the devices on the network unresponsive for the legitimate signaling traffic.
3. **IP Port Scans:** These are performed by the attackers on the elements of a mobile network to detect and exploit the active ports with their vulnerabilities. The information obtained in this process can be used to plan different strategies for the future attacks.
4. **Overbilling and Billing Evasion:** It is involved with the hijacking IP address of the subscribers and it is used to transfer or download data with the expenses of that particular subscriber, due to which the original customer gets huge bills and losses the revenue.
5. **Domain Name Server (DNS) Hijacking:** It is used to redirect the queries to the rogue DNS servers, so that the quality of service (QoS) is influenced or to terminate the connection with main server.

Apart from these attacks there will be some insider attacks due to some of the unauthorized changes by the employer of networking company. These changes include the size of a buffer, queue lengths, and timer values which influences the network performance.

1.3 ISSUES RELATED WITH SDN ROUTING APPLICATIONS

The DP and CP elements are bounded in one element of a network (i.e., in a switch/router) based on the vendor-to-vendor modifications. This type of closeness allows the vendors to modify network parameters based on the customer demands. Using SDN all these hurdles can be bypassed as it provides a central control point (i.e., a controller) to manage entire networking elements. However, the communications between both the planes are established by using the southbound application programming interface (API) (ex. OF) protocol. The data packets are forwarded by the switches/routers of the DP based on the decisions made by the controller of the CP. The instructions from the controller help the packets to be routed in the network.

The architecture of SDN consists of different interfaces which are also considered as an API between the controllers and switches/routers. They are called to be NBI and southbound interface (SBI) API's. The probability of attackers targeting the controller or cloud to manipulate the messages is more between the network elements and controller. For example, the communication using flooding controller-switches are considered as the main reason for the DoS attacks.

Routing applications obtain the information in SDN based DCs to obtain the complete network topology, server statistics and finally to make decisions for making the dataflow in the network. Routing applications play a crucial role in the DC systems and help to accomplish the complete routing and scheduling management. Therefore, an attacker with control over the routing applications is capable of performing the DoS like attacks, tampering of the information, etc., may crash the complete DC as well. Therefore, in this section security of SDN routing applications are discussed in detail.

1.3.1   *ROUTING APPLICATIONS OF SDN*

Routing applications of SDN help to reduce energy consumption and overall operating cost for the DCs. There are many SDN routing applications such as Plug-n-Serve, Elastic Tree, Aster*x, HyderabadApp, and Hedra (Handigol et al., 2009; Brandon et al., 2010; Al-Fares et al., 2010; Kakinada and Verma, 2012; Rolbin, 2013; Ding et al., 2014; Benson et al., 2011; Norouzi et al., 2018; Sagare and Khondoker, 2018).

1.3.1.1   *PLUG-N-SERVE*

Plug-n-Serve in general considered as an SDN-based routing application with OF SBI API protocol, which is enabled with load balancing applications for most of the DCs (Sagare and Khondoker, 2018). Different types of technologies are used to perform the operations of this applications includes, NOX controller, OpenFlow 0.8, Stanford University Testbed, etc. The performance and overall capacity of the routing applications can be improved by adding extra switches/routers. The major advantage of this application includes the ability to detect any kind of addition or removal of servers; and it also adjusts itself based on the traffic behavior. In technical terminology it is also referred to be as *customized flow routing*.

Load balancing over unstructured networks (LOBUS) algorithm is used in this application for managing the traffic of the network. Based on the server load(s) and path congestion the smart routing process will be taking place by redirecting the traffic, which helps to reduce the overall web services response time in most of the unstructured networks. The architecture of the Plug-n-Serve is shown in Figure 1.2, consists of three functional units: flow manager, net manager and host manager, which helps in managing the traffic flow on any kind of web requests. Flow manager control the flow by using load-balancing algorithm; however, the net manager is responsible for collecting the network topology and linking the switches based on the queries. Finally, host manager keeps an eye on the servers load, their status, and additional servers that are added externally. Major advantage of this routing application is to reduce the overall response time for any kind of external addition or removal of the switches and paths.

1.3.1.2   ELASTIC TREE

Elastic tree efficiently handles the dynamic workloads of the DCs and used NetFlow, SNMP, and OpenFlow 1.0 technologies to operate with low costs and helps in saving the energy by appropriate switching actions when the network elements are not required. A constant monitoring of traffic load will be taking place in this routing application so that to adjust all active elements (i.e., switches, ports, links). The architecture of Elastic tree is shown in Figure 1.3 consists of an optimizer, routing, and power control modules.

Optimizer module helps to obtain topology information from network to decide suitable subset which can fulfill current traffic conditions and sends the same for routing and power controlling modules for processing at further stages.

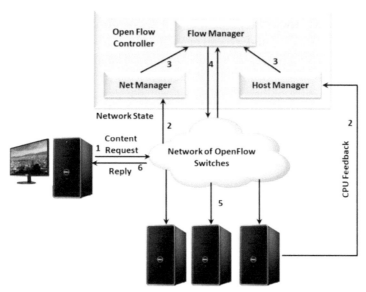

FIGURE 1.2   Architecture of plug-n-serve.

Source: Adapted and modified from Sagare and Khondoker (2018).

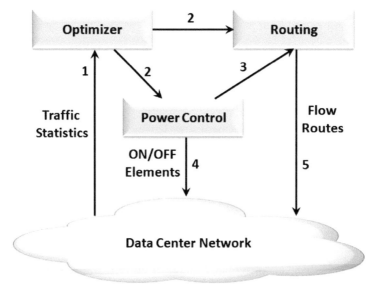

FIGURE 1.3   Architecture of elastic tree.

Source: Adapted and modified from Sagare and Khondoker (2018).

The routing module helps to create flow routes with respect to input data and then forward the same to OF switches. Whereas, the power control module will receives the complete status information from different network elements to ensure the needful elements are functioning and rest of them are in OFF state.

1.3.1.3 ASTER*X

Aster*x depends on Plug-n-Serve and also on the path selection process and uses the NOX controller, and the OpenFlow 1.0 technologies. This routing application also uses the OF architecture for measuring the network state and to control the paths that are taken by requests.

This routing application allows the service providers to select the load-balance based on the application type and performance metric (Handigol et al., 2010). Load balancing decisions are sometimes made pro-actively or reactively based on the request type; sometimes they can be made individually or on aggregated bundles (or even combination of two) as well. However, load-balancing strategy can be static or dynamic as well. The Aster*x control (as shown in Figure 1.4) depends on three functional units, i.e., flow manager, net manager, and host manager, as discussed in Plug-n-Serve routing application.

1.3.1.4 HEDERA

Hedera is considered to be a dynamic flow scheduling system that uses the OF controller, and technologies based on the Portland Testbed. This routing application is scalable and schedules the multi-level switching fabric for using the network elements more efficiently. According to Al-Fares (2010), Hedera can deliver bisection bandwidth with 96% optimal and 113% better as compared with the static load-balancing systems.

1.3.1.5 HYDERABADAPP

HyderabadApp consists of the architecture similar to that of ElasticTree. However, it differs in terms of Power ON/OFF strategy.

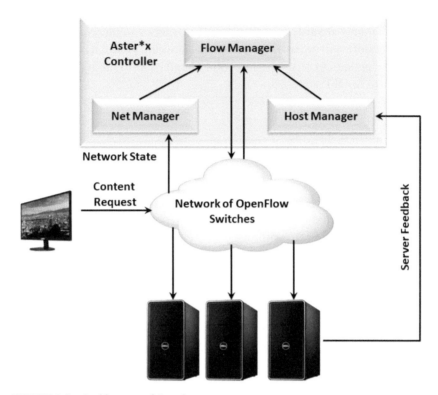

FIGURE 1.4   Architecture of Aster*x.

Source: Adapted and modified from Handigol et al. (2010).

1.3.2 SECURITY ANALYSIS

There are different types of modeling tools for the purpose of security analysis. They include STRIDE, PASTA, Trike, Attack Tree, UMLSec, OCTAVE, DREAD, CORAS, Common Criteria (CC), etc. In these methods, STRIDE is used to focus on application form with respect to the complete system perspective. Process for attack and threat analysis (PASTA) is more suitable for the designers and developers as a methodology for attack simulation. Trike is well suited for design phase since it is one of the requirement centric methods and needs the involvement of stakeholders. AttackTree is an open source modeling method and it is an attack centric method, which is not a good option for complete system analysis. UMLSec is useful for analyzing each component of a system and it is a model-based approach. OCTAVE considers the analysis team to assess the risk and the teams are formed from different departments. CC is the framework to evaluate the security of information technology for the bigger organizations. DREAD is useful for the risk assessment subjective to nature and it is now considered as outdated. CORAS is a risk analysis method requires regular customers for the security analysis.

In general, most of the security analyzes carried out by using the STRIDE and to carry out this process the data flow diagrams (DFD) are used extensively. The components of systems architecture and the different interaction among the components are presented by a DFD. These components help to analyze the system for any kind of threats or different categories of the threat types.

1.3.3   EXAMPLES OF SECURITY ANALYSIS

1.3.3.1   PLUG-N-SERVE DFD AND ANALYSIS

The DFD construction is very important to evaluate the security in Plug-n-Serve applications. The three functional units are located in the controller to make needful decisions for controlling the DC behavior. The Plug-n-Serve DFD consist of three major components representing the interactors include: (a) content requesting PC's for sending the same to the networks; (b) web servers; and (c) OF switches (to establish a communication with the controllers). The modeling of interactors is made to establish the communication among them in the DFD using the data flows. In Figure 1.5 the data flow between different components is shown and the communication to be established between different entities will be located in NOX-based controller are secured as they dwell with the same machine.

The trust boundaries as shown in Figure 1.5 will be considered between different group interactors. In this method, controller, and switches must be independent. However, a trust should be there between other entities (Sagare and Khondoker, 2018).

The security evaluation of this routing application by using STRIDE tool considered and evaluation takes place against spoofing, tampering, redemption, information disclosure, DoS, and evaluation of privilege (Sagare and Khondoker, 2018). The Plug-n-Serve threat matrix with different threat categories which are mitigated by suggested method is shown in Table 1.1.

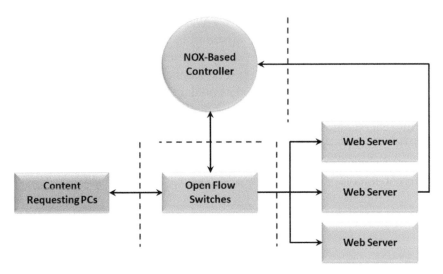

FIGURE 1.5 The DFD of a plug-n-serve routing method.

TABLE 1.1 Summarized Threat Categories Using Plug-n-Serve Threat Matrix

Type	Component	Threat Categories					
		S	**T**	**R**	**I**	**D**	**E**
Process	NOX-based controller	×	×	×	×	×	×
Data flows	Client PC-Switches	–	×	–	×	×	–
	Controller-Switches	–	×	–	×	×	–
	Switches-Wed Servers	–	×	–	×	×	–
	Web Servers-Controller	–	×	–	×	×	–
Interactors	PC-Controller	×	–	×	–	–	–
	Controller-Switches	×	–	×	–	–	–
	Switches-Wed Servers	×	–	×	–	–	–

Note: The symbol × denotes a threat which can be mitigated by using the suggested method.

1. **Process:** Only NOX-based controller component needs protections from the entire STRIDE threat categories.
   • To deal with *spoofing* it needs an appropriate bidirectional authentication or authentic code for mitigation.
   • To deal with tampering, appropriate authorization and then maintaining the access control list (ACL) is required.

- To deal with repudiation, using timestamp is needed and also need to maintain the audit trails are very important.
- To deal with information disclosure, encryption of the information is needed and using privacy-enhanced protocols such as TLS is needed for mitigating this threat.
- To deal with DoS attacks, controller replication techniques can be used along with packet filtering firewalls or authorization can be restricted by using IP restrictions.\
- To deal with evaluation privilege, run the processes with less number of privileges so as to ensure appropriate user rights and resources permissions.

2. **Data Flows:**
   i. **Between PC's and OpenFlow Switches:**
      - To deal with tampering and information disclosure, using TLS might solve the problem of threats related with confidentiality, symmetric data encryption and handshake.
      - To deal with DoS, filtering techniques such as packet filtering firewalls, AVANT-GUARD, and FLOW-GUARD can be used for avoiding the flooding issues.
   ii. **Between Controller and OpenFlow Switches:**
      - To deal with tampering, OF protocol option can be best used for mitigating the threat; and finally appropriate authorization methods or the help of digital signatures can be considered to mitigate the issues.
      - To deal with information disclosure, TLS can be used to maintain the confidentiality. By using the symmetric data encryption and by providing proper authentication using the handshake technique this problem can be efficiently solved.
      - To deal with DoS, packet filtering firewalls and/or the ACL may be more useful. Sometimes the data flow and the bandwidth controlling method are implemented for mitigating the DoS attacks.
   iii. **Between Switches and the Web Servers:**
      - To deal with tampering issues use digital signatures or TLS;
      - To deal with information disclosure TLS can be used;
      - To deal with DoS attacks filtering techniques or IP restrictions can be used.

   iv. Between Web Server and Controllers:
- To deal with tampering and improper load balancing issues, use IPSec protocol as a mitigation technique.
- To deal with information disclosure ACL can be used along with other encryption techniques.
- To deal with DoS attacks filtering technique is more appropriate and/or IP restrictions also can be used.

3. Interactors:
  i. Content Requesting PC's:
- To deal with spoofing, use the bidirectional authentication and/or using the Kerberos is more suitable for the mitigation of spoofing threats.
- To deal with repudiation, proper audit trials and time-stamps will help.

  ii. Web Servers:
- To deal with spoofing, use appropriate authentication mechanism such as Kerberos, firewalls, and apply deep packet inspection (DPI).
- To deal with repudiation, use digital signatures, and timestamps.

  iii. OpenFlow Switches:
- To deal with spoofing, use certification and authentication using IPSec.
- To deal with repudiation, use proper logging methods of data and timestamps.

1.3.3.2 DFD OF ELASTIC TREE AND ANALYSIS

In this method, three modules play an important role, i.e., optimizer, routing, and power control as a part of single system and as a single process as shown in Figure 1.6. The DC network will establish communication by using routing and switch ON/OFF information.

All the units communicated with each other and they considered having trust among them with a trust boundary between DC network and application process.

The security evaluation of this routing application by using STRIDE tool considered and evaluation takes place against *spoofing, tampering, redemption, information disclosure, DoS, and evaluation of privilege.*

The ElasticTree threat matrix with different threat categories, which are mitigated by the suggested method, is shown in Table 1.2.

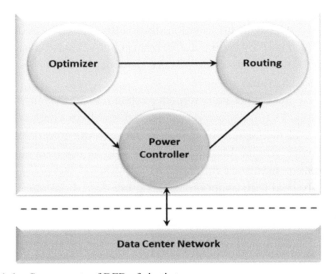

FIGURE 1.6   Components of DFD of elastic tree.

TABLE 1.2   Summarized Threat Categories Using ElasticTree Threat Matrix

Type	Component	Threat Categories					
		S	**T**	**R**	**I**	**D**	**E**
Process	NOX-based controller	×	×	×	×	✓	×
Dataflows	PC-controller	–	×	–	×	×	–
Interactor	Controller-switches	×	–	×	–	–	–

Note: The symbol × denotes a threat which can be mitigated by using the suggested method; and the symbol ✓ denotes a threat which can be mitigated within the architecture which provides the counter measures.

1. **Process:** In this application also, the NOX-based controller is susceptible for all six categories.
   - To deal with spoofing attacks, the routing and the optimizer modules needs be separated based on different servers and the other techniques are also available, such as bidirectional authentication and/or IPSec can be used to mitigate the spoofing threats.

- To deal with tampering threats, use digital signatures or appropriate authorization techniques.
- To deal with repudiation, use timestamp and audit trials as mitigation techniques.
- To deal with information disclosure, use encryption methods, TLS, and by proper authorization by ACL also may be useful.
- To deal with DoS attacks, use deployment design of the applications.
- To deal with the problems related to elevation of privilege attacks run a process with least possible privileges.

2. **Data Flow:** Generally, data flow between the modules and the DC network will be playing a critical role in the data flow and the possible threats are mitigated as follows:
   - To deal with tampering attacks, use digital signatures and/or by using the message authentication techniques as well.
   - To deal with information disclosure, use TLS or OF protocols.
   - To deal with DoS attacks, use appropriate authentication mechanisms.

3. **Interactors:** The possible threats for interactors are due to spoofing and repudiation and the mitigation techniques are as follows:
   - To deal with spoofing of the DC network use appropriate authentication techniques such as IPSec header.
   - To deal with repudiation, use audit trials and timestamps at the time of communication between controller and DC network.

1.4   ISSUES RELATED WITH SDN CLOUD APPLICATIONS

The general expectations from a cloud environment are to obtain flexible, scalable, and secure resources with a huge saving with respect to money, time, and resources. There is a massive mode of modifications in the cloud environments after the introduction of SDN solutions. Most of the cloud networking platforms facilitates great power to configure different types of networks using the cloud, which in term can be more vulnerable in the hands of intruders and hackers. The cloud providers use suitable security standards, but still there is a possibility of risk for most of the cloud applications due to external data storage and important files from the external services. Easy methods of procuring and accessing the cloud allow the intruders to identify and exploit the cloud systems easily.

Introduction of SDN allows decoupling with network controls and functions, and it is directly programmable as well. Unauthorized controller access and controller-switch communication may impact the client application and influences the overall network performance as well (Chikhale and Khondoker, 2018). Control and DPs are highly vulnerable from the security threats in most of the cloud applications and the focus in this section will be on a comparison between SDN cloud applications with Meridian, CloudNaaS, and HPE virtual cloud network (VCN). OF protocol is used in the cloud applications as well for establishing the communication interface among the SDN CP and DPs.

1.4.1 SECURITY ANALYSIS IN CLOUD APPLICATIONS

Different types of modeling tools are used for the purpose of security analysis in cloud applications are similar to that of routing applications such as STRIDE, PASTA, Trike, UMLSec, DREAD, CORAS, CC, Attack Tree, OCTAVE, etc. In the cloud applications also DFD's will play a vital role for analyzing the security of an application. The five DFD components (i.e., data flow, data store, process, interactions, and trust boundaries) are tested against different threat types. Similarly, different types of threat properties such as authentication, integrity, non-repudiation, confidentiality, availability, and authorization are considered for threat analysis.

1.4.2 SDN COULD APPLICATIONS

There are different types of SDN cloud applications with different functionalities are developed and deployed using SaaS, NaaS, IaaS, and PaaS. The popular cloud applications are HP VCN SDN (deploys the dynamic policy of the networks), EOS (is extensible, and event driven OS), OpenStack (an OS that provides storage, computing, and resources), CloudNaaS (is also an extensible networking platform), Microsoft Azure (helps to provide applications and infrastructure), Zimory Cloud Suit (provide distributed, scalable, and decoupled infrastructure), and VMware v Cloud Suit (provides needful infrastructure and management facilities). Most of them are proprietary based and only OpenStack is considered to be an open source application. Similarly, for CloudNaaSthis conditions are not applicable.

1.4.2.1   MERIDIAN

Meridian is considered as an extensible multi-thread platform which is used for variety of cloud networking applications. This will support service-level model with an option of providing multiple options to configure virtual networks of the physical layer.

There are three logical layers in meridian: (i) API; (ii) network orchestration; and (iii) underlying network devices. The abstract API helps to interact with other network components and provides access with the higher layer cloud applications. A graph is used to represent overall network. Logical to the physical translations of the commands are performed by network orchestration at abstraction layer and also helps to convert API calls towards providing proper series of commands for underlying networks. Finally, the OF devices are interfaced by using lowest layer with the logical drivers, creating a virtual network to provide the accompanying services. For this architecture, the configuration rules are facilitated from network control applications and finally it provides the topological views with dynamic set of underlying network resources (Figure 1.7) (Chikhale and Khondoker, 2018).

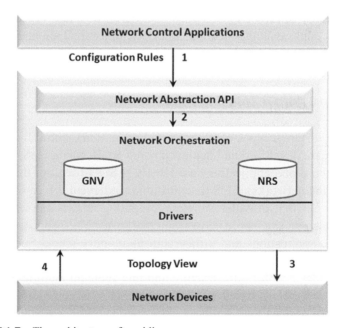

FIGURE 1.7   The architecture of meridian.

1.4.2.2 CLOUD NaaS

Cloud NaaS is mostly used as a SDN based cloud platform for the enterprise applications to provide primitives of a cloud application. It uses NOX controller which is based on the OF protocol, and helps the customers to deploy their applications for an easy access of different virtual functions. This also extends ability to deploy middle box applications for the customers provide intrusion detection, caching, and application acceleration as well.

There are two main components involved in this architecture as cloud controller and network controller as shown in Figure 1.8. The cloud controller needs to manage virtual resources and network controllers (NC); apart from these it supports APIs to set the new network policies. Whereas, the network controller monitors and manages the configuration of all network devices to decide the placement of different virtual machines (VM) in the cloud. The CloudNaaS consist of network controller as an additional component of the cloud management services (CMS) when compared to other clouds and it is implemented over the NOX controller using C++. These cloud controllers accepts the related network policies, specifications, and VM request from different users and forms a communication matrix. This matrix is compiled by the network controller based on the network level rules and then installs the same on the virtual switches and on the physical switches as well using the SDN control channels and also configures the relevant paths too.

The network provisioner (NP) of the NC accumulates the information from the communication matrix of cloud controller (CC). The cloud monitor (CM) will poll status of the switches and the links on a regular basis and both NP and CM acts as data storage elements in the network controller. NC supports VM placement, QoS, diagnosis, real-time monitoring, management, and different security functions as well. The details of placement optimizer and the state optimizer along with their interactions of a NC will be omitted to evaluate the performance. CloudNaaS employs a pre-computation method and alternate paths techniques to catch and minimize the impact of devices or link failures of the underlying networks.

1.4.2.3 HPE VCN SDN

HPE VCN SDN is considered as one of the enhanced networking modules from HPE. It helps to enable enterprises to securely connect with the cloud; and also applies own identity for cloud environment (see Figure 1.9) (Benson et al., 2011a). However, it is already known fact that the VCN is integrated to OpenStack. Most of the public cloud providers try to deliver the self-service solutions for their customers and the enterprise services in a secured way with the public cloud environments.

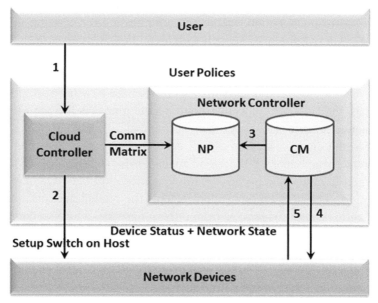

FIGURE 1.8 The architecture of CloudNaaS.

- **HPE Helion OpenStack:** It is one of the open and extensible cloud platforms which are an easier one to build, manage, and deliver to the workloads. This can be moved, integrated, and delivered to different IT environments. It will be secured by offering the secured solutions for hybrid IT Clouds by using the cryptography.
- **HPE VAN SDN Controller:** It is one of the building blocks of the HPEs virtualized DC solutions. This controller manages the policies and forwarding decisions that are communicated with the OF enabled switches of a DC.
- **Networks Devices:** This include HPE FlexFabric 7900 switch series that is compatible with modular DC core switches, which are designed for supporting the virtualized DCs and also for the evolutionary needs of different types of cloud deployments.

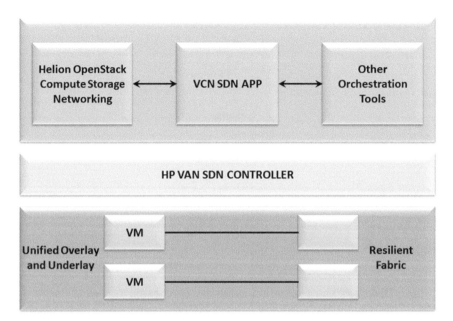

FIGURE 1.9   The architecture of HP VCN SDN.

1.4.3   SECURITY ANALYSIS FOR DIFFERENT CLOUD APPLICATIONS

As discussed earlier in the routing applications, once again a DFD is constructed for evaluating the Meridian with STRIDE, consisting of three layers within a same physical box. The cloud consists of: (a) network control applications; (b) meridian architecture; and (c) network devices. Here it is important to note that the flow between any of the above three components cannot be trusted; hence represented by a trust boundary (see Figure 1.10).

1.4.3.1   EVALUATION OF MERIDIAN

In the meridian architecture, the global network view (GNV) and the network run time state (NRS) are the two data stores in the physical device. DFD of meridian shows the network control applications interacting with the API from CC; and the network devices will interact via API from the available drivers.

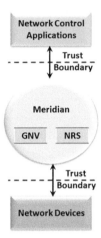

FIGURE 1.10   DFD of meridian.

1. **Process:** The evaluation summary (see Table 1.3) of the security threats for the *meridian* using STRIDE method are given below:
   • To deal with spoofing in a meridian process binary it is recommended to apply authentication mechanism such as Authenticode for validating the code which was signed by the admin.
   • To deal with tampering of data in the meridian process using the access rights list from ACL instead of the digital signature and proper usage of message authentication codes.
   • To deal with repudiation users generally change the binary of meridian with no proof left over and this may be a bit difficult to track at the later stages.
   • To deal with information disclosure, it is better to have a good encryption technique for mitigation. For example, block cipher process the input data blocks to deliver cipher text blocks with small size.
   • To deal with DoS attacks on a meridian process, disk quotas are useful to prevent excess disk usage by the unnecessary data.
   • To deal with elevation of privileges, it is better to have input validation for both users and administrators and allowing the users with low privileges also best suited.
2. **Data Flow:** Now the security measures to be taken for the data flow types are considered for *network control applications* for *Meridian process*.

- To deal with tampering of data, digital signatures are well suited as a mitigation plan and help to test the reliability of data under usage.
- To deal with information disclosure, TLS can be an appropriate solution since it can protect the confidentiality of the network configuration commands with the help of symmetric data encryption and at some scenarios one can use TLS handshake methods to test data authentication.
- To deal with Dos attacks and avoiding the bandwidth bottleneck used data flow control to limit the packets flow in the meridian.

  Now the security measures to be taken for the data flow types are considered for *Meridian process* and *network devices*.

- To deal the tampering of data in this category use Libvert virtualization daemon, with the provision of a remote management system that uses TLS encryption and ×509 certificate for mitigating the possible threats.
- To deal with the information disclosure of the network topology consisting of Libvert provides the Kerberos and also the SASL for the usage of data authentication.
- In case of DoS attacks it may not be possible for the attacker to send network topology packets using meridian process due to existence of Kerberos and SASL in the underlying networks.

3. **Interactors:** In case of interactors only network control applications are having a threat of spoofing.

- To deal with spoofing and avoid policy based connectivity by using proper authentication mechanism like Kerberos, which provides a secured authentication for users by identifying the Meridian process.

  However, due to Kerberos and SASL provided by the Libvert, the possibility of sending a request for getting the overall topological view of the network devices is not possible. These two (Kerberos and SASL) from Libvert provides high-end security with safe authenticated communication for the Meridian process and to the networking devices.

- To deal with repudiation, the in-built TLS in Libvert ensures that there are no issues for communication between the network devices and meridian.

4. **Data Store:** Both GNV and NRS in the data store type have the issues like tampering with data, information disclosure and DoS attacks.

- To deal with tampering of data, and to deal with GNV and NRS alterations or deletions, ACL is used by providing specific access rights for the individual user. Otherwise, role-based access control (RBAC) method also helps to mitigate such conditions.
- To deal with information disclosure, data encryption will be used for the data stored in a database.
- To deal with DoS attacks, message authentication codes are best suitable as compared to the digital signatures because they are not efficient with the problems related with message overheads.

TABLE 1.3　Summarized Threat Categories Using Meridian Components

Type	Component	Threat Categories					
		S	**T**	**R**	**I**	**D**	**E**
Process	Meridian	×	×	×	×	×	×
Data flows	Network control application and meridian	–	×	–	×	×	–
	Meridian and network devices	–	✓	–	✓	✓	–
Interactors	Network and control applications	×	–	–	–	–	–
	Network devices	✓	–	✓	–	–	–
Datastore	Global network view (GNV)	–	×	–	×	×	–
	Network runtime systems (NRS)	–	×	–	✓	×	–

Note: The symbol × denotes a threat which is possibly mitigated by using the suggested methodology; the symbol ✓ denotes a threat which can be mitigated within the architecture which provides the counter measures and symbol-denotes out of scope situation.

1.4.3.2　EVALUATION OF CLOUDNAAS

The DFD built for a CloudNaas (see Figure 1.11) is to evaluate it using the STRIDE method. In the physical box, both the layers (NP and CM) are assumed to be fixed and the trust boundary layers represent the no trust between applications and CloudNaaS. There will not be a No trust between the network devices and CloudNaaS as they are distributed in the cloud. Interaction of the user is established by using the API from CC and the network devices enables the interactions with through the API of NC. In the CloudNaaS architecture, NP, and CM also act as a datastore unit.

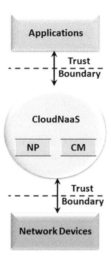

FIGURE 1.11 DFD of a CloudNaaS.

The evaluation summary of security threats for *CloudNaaS* using STRIDE method is shown in Table 1.4.

TABLE 1.4 Summarized Threat Categories Using CloudNaaS

Type	Component	Threat Categories					
		S	T	R	I	D	E
Process	CloudNaaS	×	×	×	×	×	✓
Data flows	User and CloudNaaS	–	×	–	✓	×	–
	CloudNaaS and network devices	–	×	–	×	×	–
Interactors	User	✓	–	–	–	–	–
	Network devices	✓	–	✓	–	–	–
Data store	Cloud monitor	–	×	–	×	×	–
	Network runtime systems	–	×	–	×	✓	–

Note: The symbol × denotes a threat that is mitigated by using the suggested methodology; the symbol ✓ denotes a threat which can be mitigated within the architecture which provides the counter measures and symbol-denotes out of scope situation.

1. **Process:** The security analysis and mitigation methods for the CloudNaas architecture using STRIDE as a single process are given below:

- To deal with spoofing, implementing appropriate security mechanisms is very important to ensure the integrity of binary information (like the message authentication codes).
- To deal with the tampering of data ACL is best suited for mitigating the security issues.
- To deal with repudiation, track the user activity by using time stamps and audit trials.
- Information disclosure issues are solved by implementing appropriate encryption techniques and by restricting the unauthorized entity access from the data.
- DoS attacks may be solved by implementing suitable authentication mechanisms for the administrative entities to shut down the CloudNaaS process and/or by locking most of the resources.
- Finally, the elevation privileges are mitigated by implementing the process with least amount privileges.

2. **Data Flow:** The security measures to be taken for the data flow types are considered for *users* and *CloudNaaS.*
    - The tampering of data can be mitigated by using the digital signatures and also by using different types of authentication codes.
    - Information disclosure issue can be mitigated by incorporating TLS in the OF.
    - Dos attacks and bandwidth bottleneck can be mitigated using data flow control methods.

    Now the security measures to be taken for the data flow types are considered for CloudNaaS and *network devices.*

- The tampering issues can be seen during the transit of the network devices to the network controller and can be mitigated by setting up the virtual switch on host at the time of transit. IPSec authentication header is best suitable for such situations.
- Information disclosure can be seen from the underlying network topology and this can be mitigated by using the proper encryption mechanisms.

3. **Interactors:** The security measures for the interactors are considered here for the *user* and *network devices.*
- The spoofing is possible in CloudNaaS process by receiving NPS and VM requests from authenticated CloudNaaS providers. To mitigate this, proper Kerberos may help in providing appropriate authentication between the users and CloudNaaS.

- In case of network devices, they may get hijacked and topologies can be altered with respect to the network controller. To mitigate these problems usage of Kerberos and IPSec is helpful.
- The repudiation issues occur in CloudNaaS when the status information sent by the networking devices are denied by the network controller when there are no logs to verify. Therefore, to mitigate these issues, appropriate logging mechanism needs to be implemented.

4. **Data Store:** The security measures for the data stores NP and CM is considered here for *tampering, information disclosure,* and *DoS attacks.*

- The tampering of data stored in NP in the form of communication matrix and CM in the form of switches and link status will be modified and sometimes they tend to get deleted. Therefore, to deal with such issues better use ACL as mitigation plan.
- The information disclosure may happen at any time at the NP and CM. This can be mitigated by using appropriate encryption mechanisms for the access of data.
- DoS attacks may influence the data stored in NP and CM by occupying the underlying resources and bandwidth too. To mitigate this digest authentication and using packet-filtering firewalls may be very useful for checking the authentication of the user policy packets and helps to verify the communication matrix.

1.4.3.3 EVALUATION OF HPE VCN SDN

The DFD built for a HPE VCN SDN (see Figure 1.12) is to evaluate it using the STRIDE method. VCN SDN is a key element that comes out of HPE Helion OpenStack distribution and in the DFD both are considered as a part of one part. The remaining actors of the DFD are administrators and network devices that communicate using VCN applications. The communications between all the actors and modules are considered using STRIDE methodology, and the corresponding threats are listed in Table 1.5. The evaluation summary of security threats for *HPE VCN SDN* using the STRIDE method is also shown in Table 1.5.

1. **Process:** The HPE Helion OpenStack cloud model can establish a secured communication with TLS enabled with public API endpoints. TLS protocol helps to mitigate with tampering and the

issues related with information disclosure threats. Usage of encryption mechanism for passwords and sensitive data is suggested. HPE refines the access control with AppArmor provides a unique ability for monitoring, analyzing, and correlating OpenStack logs to the ArcSight Loggers. This helps for a continuous security monitoring of the cloud systems.

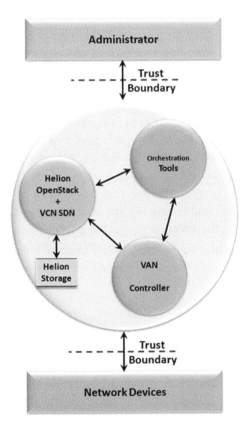

FIGURE 1.12   DFD of a VCN application.

2. **Data Flows:** The traffic from administrators and VAN controllers to the OpenStack services on public endpoints will be secured by using the TLS connections and all the mandatory control system (AppArmor) for mitigating the threats like DoS and information disclosures.

TABLE 1.5 Summarized Threat Categories Using HPE VCN SDN

Type	Component	Threat Categories					
		S	T	R	I	D	E
Process	VCN SDN (V)	✓	✓	✓	✓	✓	×
Data flows	(O) ↔ (V)	–	✓	–	✓	✓	–
	(V) ↔ (N)	–	✓	–	✓	✓	–
Interactors	Administrator (O)	×	–	✓	–	–	–
	Network devices (N)	×	–	×	–	–	–
Data store	OpenStack db	–	✓	–	✓	✓	–

Note: The symbol × denotes a threat that is mitigated by using the suggested methodology; and the symbol ✓ denotes a threat which can be mitigated within the architecture which provides the counter measures.

3. **Interactors:** HPE network devices help to provide high security and they use ACL to filter the traffic for avoiding the unauthorized access. To secure from spoofing and plain text passwords use authentication, encryption, and secure shell (SSHv2).

    The administrators need to use TLS protocols with the MAC system and encryption methods for preventing the issues of spoofing and repudiation issues. Integration of HPE ArcSight helps to reduce the overall response time for most of the security breaches and helps to provide faster analysis logs and events.

4. **Data Stores:** Using TLS and AppArmor helps to maintain the integrity, confidentiality, and availability of the HPE hellion OpenStack since it is having its own database.

1.5   ISSUES RELATED WITH SDN WI-FI APPLICATIONS

Most of the electronic accessories and especially mobile devices are using the wireless fidelity (Wi-Fi) or wireless local area network (WLAN) facilities to connect with the rest of the world using internet. Due to the ability of high-speed connection, the usage of multi-user multiple-input and multiple-output (MU-MIMO) is the most popular and strongly performing hardware networking communication device.

SDN provides centralized controlling capabilities and an API for the networking administrator which helps to initialize the network, to control, and to manage the behavior of a network. SDN decouples data and CPs, and OF is used as communication protocol. The possibility of getting exploited is more between these two layers since the Ethernet switches shares common set of functions. On the other hand, OF allows the interface to program the flow tables in different switches and routers for adding, editing, and removing different entities of the flow dynamically.

The application layer of SDN architecture consists of software's uses the SDN communication services and the interfaces for controlling the layer using the northbound API. Odin Master is one of such frameworks which control the SDN communication services. In this section, a detailed discussion about Odin Master and OpenWiFi technologies are discussed in detail to conduct the security analysis using STRIDE.

1.5.1   EVALUATION OF ODIN

Odin is a hot topic in the area of SDN framework which introduces programmability in WLAN and follows the IEEE 802.11 standard allowing the clients to decide the access points (AP). The AP needs to keep a track of the state information changes regularly due to the dynamic nature of time-varying wireless medium.

Odin provides simplicity for the programmers and entails the light virtual APs (LVAP), which consists of an abstraction layer for separating the association state from physical AP using virtualization. This allows and helps the programmers to connect several numbers of clients to AP. It allows every client to be isolated logically and makes every client feel possessing own AP by facilitating basic service set identification (BSSID) (Huang et al., 2019). Odin architecture to deploy with SDN-C is shown in Figure 1.13.

Odin Master from Figure 1.13 is an OF application over the Floodlight SDN-C used to establish a communication between the switches and APs (Bholebawa and Dalal, 2018). This Master uses the OF protocol and will have a global view of entire clients, APs, and switches. The Master and Agents all together implement a Wi-Fi split MAC that divides all the functionalities of both the parties. Agents also have the logic of LVAP handling and Master will control all the Agents using dedicated channels via TCP. The applications related with Wi-Fi reside in the application layer on top of Odin Master. Odin provides a transparent process to the clients but will not witness the complete process of a network.

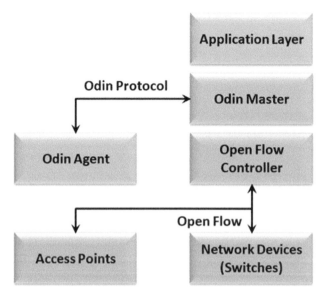

FIGURE 1.13 Odin architecture with SDN controller.

1.5.1.1 THE SECURITY ANALYSIS OF ODIN

A simple DFD representation for the Odin architecture is shown in Figure 1.14 with Odin Master and *n* number of Agents in the model. The trust boundary reflects the suspicious events, where a Master might tamper the Agents and is restricted.

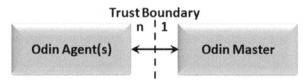

FIGURE 1.14 DFD of an Odin framework.

The security analysis for different types of components using STRIDE is given in Table 1.6.

1. **Interactors:** The security measures for the interactors in an Odin Agent are considered here for spoofing and repudiation.

TABLE 1.6 Summarized Threat Categories Using STRIDE for an Odin Framework

Type	Component	Threat Categories					
		S	**T**	**R**	**I**	**D**	**E**
Interactors	Odin agent	×	–	×	–	–	–
	Odin Master	×	–	×	–	–	–
Data flows	Agent ↔ Master	–	×	–	×	×	–

Note: The symbol × denotes a threat that is mitigated by using suggested methods, techniques, and analysis, outcomes.

- The Odin Agents will not be aware of the Spoofing Master and to deal with such situation usage of mutual authentication is helpful, i.e., by providing the protection like Kerberos.
- The Odin Agent will be lacking with verifiability and possibility of Master sending wrong commands is more. To deal with such digital signatures can be used to sign for the communicated data, so that both the parties are validating their counterparts.

  The security measures for the interactors in an Odin Master are considered here for spoofing and repudiation.

- The Master can be spoofed in a Wi-Fi protected access also by a spoofed Agent. This could be tackled by using an appropriate authentication mechanism like RADIUS (Rigney et al., 2000).
- The repudiation problem comes when a Master is not in a position to get proof about whether an Agent is communicated or not. One can solve this problem by using MAC address but it is also spoofed at times. Therefore, to deal with such repudiation problems will lies in processing each address resolution protocol (ARP) request by permitting only the valid one's. Otherwise Snort also supports to validate the process effectively by monitoring for the ARP spoofing.

2. **Data Flow:** The dataflow between the Agents and Masters are analyzed using STRIDE method for security analysis and mitigating them.

- The attacker may tamper data at the time of transit is more and may change complete payload and execute a malicious code. This type of issues can be mitigated by using the authentication headers of the network layers via TLS on the transport layer to provide integrity checks (Dierks and Rescorla, 2008). The exchange of data between the Agent(s) and Master may need to deal with the traffic and the information disclosure is possible due to the existence of plaintext. This can be sorted out using encrypted data using IPSec and helps in mitigating this risk.

- DoS attacks may even restrict the communication between the Agents and Master. In such attacks, the intruder will focus mostly on Master so that a single point failure can make the complete network inoperative since the Master will control the whole system. To deal with this type of attacks better use rate limiting approach or use load balancing systems.

1.5.2 OPEN Wi-Fi

Common guest Wi-Fi systems are generally implemented with triple-A services and hence unite the access, accounting, and the authentication of a network system. However, OpenWiFi system was introduced as a prototype that separates triple-A services into the single participating components by which the complexity and cost will reduced for the guest Wi-Fi users. This also helps to reduce the burden of remembering overall credentials of different Wi-Fi spots (Yap et al., 2011). The authors also suggest to take the help of third-party service providers for delegation of authentication, so that they can handle it by using OAuth2 or OpenID (Jones and Hardt, 2012; Artmann and Khondoker, 2018). Due to the heavy user amount on this service provider's high guest Wi-Fi user's probability can be realized. Such type of arrangement with more number of APs supports multiple SSIDs. Such an arrangement helps the guest Wi-Fi providers to facilitate distinct Wi-Fi networks to users in parallel connections across all the networks. Finally, a separate accounting service can be made responsible for billing and delegation.

1.5.2.1 THE SECURITY ANALYSIS OF OPENWiFi

A simple DFD representation for the OpenWiFi architecture is shown in Figure 1.15 with an OF Controller, Access Point, and Authentication Service Provider using the STRIDE method. The trust boundary reflects the suspicious events, where a Master might tamper the Agents and is restricted. Summarized threat categories using STRIDE matrix for Open-WiFi are shown in Table 1.7.

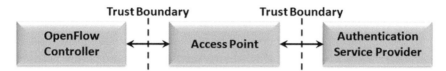

FIGURE 1.15   DFD of an OpenWiFi.

TABLE 1.7   Summarized Threat Categories Using STRIDE Matrix for OpenWiFi

Type	Component	Threat Categories					
		S	T	R	I	D	E
Interactors	OpenFlow controller	×	–	×	–	–	–
	Access points	×	–	×	–	–	–
	ASP	×	–	×	–	–	–
Data flows	OF controller ↔ AP	–	✓	–	✓	×	–
	AP ↔ ASP	–	×	–	×	×	–

Note: The symbol × denotes a threat that is mitigated by using the suggested methods, techniques, and analysis outcomes; and a ✓ represents OpenWiFi mitigating the threats by default standards.

1. **Interactors:** The interactions of an OF controller with other network elements are analyzed using STRIDE method for security analysis and mitigation purposes.
   - The attacker can *spoof* an AP to the controller by providing the fake information about the access control or about the redirections. By defaults this mitigation is not possible by OpenWiFi and therefore, using certificates can solve this problem at the time of communication between APs and OF controller.
   - To avoid issues of *repudiation*, implementation of digital signatures and/or using the timestamps will help to prevent deniability. The possibility of exploiting by using the certificates is also exists by considering them as digital signatures.

     The data flow between the APs is analyzed here using STRIDE matrix for security analysis and mitigation:
     o **Spoofing:** It is possible with APs in two ways, one with the false access controls or by unauthorized decisions at the OF controller; and second by having spoofed authentication services with fake identities. These two cases can

be overcome by using mutual authentication techniques such as Kerberos.

o **Repudiation:** It is possible due to the certificate that is already under usage and also due to the open administrator of an OpenWiFi is not in a position to consider them for their advantage. Therefore, in such scenarios timestamps would be suitable to countermeasure and to mitigate the issues.

The data flow between the authentication service providers (ASP) are analyzed here using STRIDE matrix for security analysis and mitigation.

o **Spoofing:** It does not influence ASP in the OpenWiFi and it need to be protected from spoofed APs only. Since the provider is an external part and may contribute better OpenWiFi. Using common certification authority may help to protect against spoofing.

o **Repudiation:** It may be avoided when the AP and ASP's are already using the certificates.

2. **Data Flow:** between the OF controllers and APs are analyzed here using STRIDE matrix.

- **Tampering:** of data is possible when data is communicated from the OF controller to APs. However, the OF protocol (lies on top of transport layer uses the TLS) provide security any kind of tampering issues.

- **Information Disclosure:** It is not possible due to the involvement of TLS and it is used to encapsulate the traffic. Unauthorized program is restricted from the plain text access due to encrypted traffic.

- **DoS:** It attacks are quite possible in OF controller and APs may create an inoperative network scenario. So by favoring or limiting the traffic only between the entities that are participating for Wi-Fi usage and trolling the remaining users from the traffic.

The data flow between the APs and ASP are analyzed here using STRIDE matrix:

- **Tampering:** of data is possible between AP and ASP and may fake or may use another identity to manipulate the authentication. Using HTTP over TLS can help to mitigate such issues.

Such arrangements use the keyed message authentication codes to verify integrity of the data.

- **Information Disclosure:** It is based on HTTPS between AP and ASP when the data is transported over the channels. However, by having proper TLS configuration with proper cipher suite helps to encrypt the traffic securely.
- **DoS:** It attacks are related with outsourcing of ASP, due to which the OpenWiFi architecture cannot affect the configuration and the protection against DoS is possible. Therefore, an appropriate security mechanism of ASP will not have any kind of influence due to DoS attacks.

In simple, Odin and OpenWiFi are easily extendable by using suitable countermeasures for mitigating the possible threats.

1.6 ISSUES RELATED WITH SDN BIG DATA APPLICATIONS

Big data is involved with large data sets in structured and unstructured forms. Apache Hadoop is well-known framework that is used to store the data, process the data, and finally to analyze the data. Performance aspects of Hadoop are improved with SDN by bandwidth optimization and by taking necessary steps to improve the network management systems (Batista de Almeida et al., 2019). SDN helps to make the network agile by separating conventional DP from the CP. This helps the engineers and administrators to control the traffic on the network from the centralized control point (Kreutz et al., 2013). Using the SDN gives an advantage of connecting multiple switches to an intelligent controller. The separation provides flexibility for the networking engineer but also open the doors for variety of security threats.

Most of the times, the security attacks on SDN-C and switches found to be compromising with complete Hadoop system, which in turn may cause a serious problem. In this section, three advanced approaches are considered: (i) FlowComb; (ii) Pythia; and (iii) Hadoop-Acceleration (Hadoop-A). Hadoop is an open source implementation that provides distributed storage system, which is also called the Hadoop distributed file system (HDFS) and also consists of analysis system, known to be MapReduce.

The functionality of Hadoop is divided into three main phases: (a) map; (b) shuffle/merge; and (c) reduce phase. Hadoop takes input from the HDFS and will be divided into three phases. For each phase, one MapTask runs and produces the list of *<key, values>* pairs (Ahmad et al., 2018). The map output files (MOF) will be written for the local storage and the shuffle phase is to deal with the transferring of the MOFs to nodes so that the reducer can run as per the schedule. MapReduce framework will sort out and groups all the key-value pairs before handing the output for the ReduceTask for process to obtain the final output at HDFS.

1.6.1 IMPORTANCE OF SDN TO HANDLE BIG DATA

Hadoop framework observed to have many loopholes with respect to performance. Serialization barrier creates a big time gap (delay) between the shuffle/merge and reduce phases. ReduceTask needs to wait till all MapTasks are completely executed and MOFs are available. There is a process of smaller data sets merging in Hadoop at the time of ReduceTask, due to the size of total data greater than memory threshold (Wu et al., 2018). Reduce function will takes place only when the merge/shuffle process are completed.

However, there is a second aspect of Hadoop which require multiple disc access due to the demand for repetitive merges. It will be a hectic scenario to keep the data segments at local disks by the ReduceTask once the total size goes over a threshold level. In case of late segment arrival ReduceTask needs additional disk access, leading to the degradation of the performance.

Due to the provision of changing patterns and availability of bandwidth on demand in SDN, many researchers made it as a base for building robust Hadoop systems like FlowComb, Pythia, and Hadoop-A (ElasticTree and NBI, 2018). There is a lot of scope for DoS attacks by injecting the network with huge amounts of packets to exhaust the system resources. Sometimes such attacks may even paralyze complete system and spoofing attacks can possibly obtain the access to the clusters and may allow exploiting the forward plane to manipulate the sensitive data. Possibility of sniffing the data and modifying the code is more to redirect traffic to infiltrate the data.

1.6.2   SDN BIG DATA APPLICATIONS

1.6.2.1   FLOWCOMB

This plays a vital role to improve the job process and to eradicate logging in Hadoop. Predicts the network transfers ahead of scheduling and redirect the traffic to the sources with sufficient bandwidth (Das et al., 2013). FlowComb uses NOX controller and it is considered as a centralized decision making engine to find the alternative paths (Ahmad et al., 2018; Tayyaba and Shah, 2019).

The architecture of a FlowComb consists of three major sections: (a) Hadoop cluster; (b) agents; and (c) FlowComb with its sub-elements predictor, scheduler, and controller as shown in Figure 1.16.

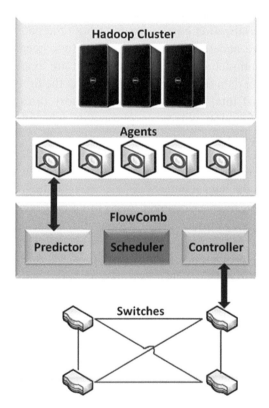

FIGURE 1.16   The FlowComb architecture.

- **Predictors:** It will scan the Hadoop logos to find the MapTasks which have already completed their task and started the transfers to send the same information to flow scheduling module.
- **Scheduler:** It detects the current and pending transfer clogging in the networks on defaults paths, so that it can be scheduled them to new paths.
- **Controller:** It helps the switches by constructing the link to program and maintains network map included with switches and paths and their current flow.

1.6.2.2 PYTHIA

It is a real-time communication intent prediction system in Hadoop and uses this predictive nature to optimize the runtime DC networks to accelerate the MapReduce. The architecture of Pythia (see Figure 1.17) consists of two main components: Hadoop instrumentation middleware and orchestration entity.

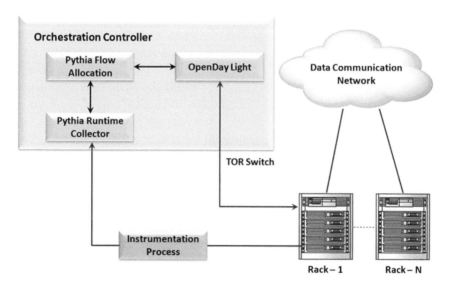

FIGURE 1.17   The Pythia architecture.

During MapReduce runtime the middleware predicts shuffle transfers at a level of mapper/reducer server pair. Orchestration entity further shuffles the communication intent events and in runtime it helps to optimize the network to reduce overall job completion time. The intra-rack data communication is established via the top of rack (ToR) switches and the Hadoop cluster will be deployed these server racks as shown in Figure 1.17. This cluster leverages programmability using OF protocol for achieving the fine-grained, timely, and efficient allocation of the network resources for further shuffle transfers.

At each server hosting TaskTracker the instrumentation process will be initiated and its middleware constantly monitors all the local TaskTrackers to assess the progress activity. Hadoop delays the process of scheduling of Reducers until the complete Mappers finis their tasks. Once the instrumentation process receives notification of generated output, it decodes the file and calculated the size based on *<key, value>* pair of each Reducer. This pair represents the item of data and value of the content.

Within the OpenDayLight (ODL) controller the Pythia network-scheduling module will be implemented and ODL obtains the complete network information to compute an optimized allocation of network path flows to ensure a reduced shuffle transfers (Brooks et al., 2015).

1.6.2.3   HADOOP-A

Two approaches exists in this category of which one is based on remote direct memory access (RDMA) protocol and second one uses FloodLight controllers (Narayan et al., 2012; Pinkerton and Deleganes, 2007; Wang et al., 2011). By using RDMA-capable interconnects over the quad data rate (QDR) InfiniBand, speedup is achieved by Hadoop-A. With the existing Hadoop user interface (UI), it also alternates the data merging algorithms. MOFSupplier and NetMerger are the two plug-in components of Hadoop-A with multi-threaded C++ implementation (as shown in Figure 1.18).

There is a flexibility of using Java also for the RDMA connection mechanism but the biggest disadvantage is with overhead problems with Java virtual machines (JVM). The fetch requests of ReduceTasks are controlled by the RDMA equipped MOFSupplier and it has got a data engine used for indexing and to deal with data files of all MOFs generated by MapTasks.

The event channels are provided between MOFSupplier/NetMerger and Hadoop to synchronize all the Java components in Hadoop-A. They also play a vital role in monitoring progress and coordinating actions of both components. Hadoop log files are used for storing the runtime progress reports and also help to store the execution statistics.

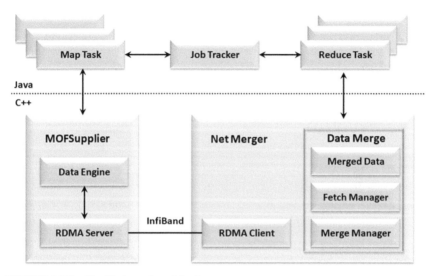

FIGURE 1.18   The Hadoop-A architecture.

Using the InfiBand reliable connected services all the connections between RDMA server and clients are established, to transfer the data via pre-registered memory buffers. The data engine of the MOFSupplier prefetches all the data segments by retrieving the data directly from disk when the memory is not having the same data. This type of data transfer will be taking place by sending a direct request and by using the reply protocol. The RDMA Clients requests with an information of a memory buffer and by which the RDMA server obtain the data and then write the same to the client buffer by using the write operation of zero-copy RDMA.

1.6.3   *SECURITY ANALYSIS OF FlowComb*

A DFD of FlowComb is drawn with parts included in one process and Hadoop instances are modeled as interactors as shown in Figure 1.19. From Hadoop, the logs are read by FC-Agent and then communicate the same with the Flow predictor. Flow controller communicates with the switches and a trust boundary is established between agents and FlowComb process.

The security analysis using STRIDE matrix for FlowComb is shown in Table 1.8 for different types of components.

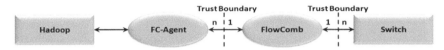

FIGURE 1.19   DFD of FlowComb.

TABLE 1.8   Summarized Threat Categories Using STRIDE Matrix for FlowComb

Type	Component	Threat Categories					
		S	**T**	**R**	**I**	**D**	**E**
Interactors	Hadoop	×	–	×	–	–	–
	Switch	×	–	×	–	–	–
Data flows	Hadoop ↔ FC-agent	–	×	–	×	×	–
	FC-Agent ↔ FlowComb	–	×	–	×	×	–
	FlowComb ↔ Switch	–	×	–	×	×	–
Process	FC-Agent	×	×	×	×	×	×
	FlowComb	×	×	×	×	×	×

- **Spoofing:** It attacks are quite possible in FC-Agent due to the communication with the Flow Predictor. In case of Hadoop, the hackers can access Hadoop logs and HDFS as well. Manipulation of valuable information is possible and they may run malicious programs on cluster. Kerberos authentication is best suitable to tackle the spoofing attacks. In case of switches using SDN-C with the standard Authentication, Authorization, and Accounting (AAA) service may helpful and it can be performed on ODL.
- **Tampering of Data:** It is reported due to centralized NOX controller, on which most of the tampering attacks are made to disrupt the data path and the complete network to make it more compromised. Manipulation of data at nodes is reported after getting control and access to nodes and Master Nodes. Such practices can be preventing by controlling the access tightly. Some of the public key infrastructure (PKI) based authentication protocols are available to mitigate such type of events. Due to involvement of OF with FlowComb data passes via NOX controller. Therefore, security features of TLS may be used to protect from tampering the

data. The issues related with information disclosure can be avoided by encrypting the data carefully.

- **Repudiation:** This issue can be ignored if the network is taking care of spoofing attacks since the Agent lies inside the Hadoop cluster. AAA module helps to provide secured logging mechanism by which this problem of repudiation can be mitigated effectively.

- **Information Disclosure:** It is possible with the network topology and different types of settings at all levels. Using TLS will help to protect the issues of information disclosure issues by prohibiting the unauthorized data access.

- **DoS Attacks:** This influence the performance of Hadoop cluster when the controller or data nodes go offline. These attacks directly impact on the controller, schedules, and generate new paths. The separation of MapReduce process from the Authentication process helps to avoid DoS attacks. Apart from this limiting the number of packets transferred to the controller helps to mitigate the problem.

- **Elevation of Privilege:** It is a problem due to the compromised FC-Agent allowing installing the malicious software's on the host networks. In this way, an attacker identifies different targets, gets the control of network for accessing, attacking, and helps to modify the servers, clusters, and metadata from name nodes.

1.6.4   *SECURITY ANALYSIS OF PYTHIA*

A DFD of Pythia is drawn with orchestration entity and ODL controller is closely connected along with Hadoop machines beyond the trust boundaries as shown in Figure 1.20. TOR switches are used with OF enabled to use its protocol. The summary of threat categories using STRIDE matrix for Pythia is shown in Table 1.9.

- **Spoofing:** In general may not possible with the ODL controller or with switches in Pythia due to the involvement of AAA services in the control platform. AAA is a token-based authentication where the user application needs to gain the access controller resources. For the unauthorized users the access will be denied and each activity logging will be accounted to avoid the malicious attempts.

- **Tampering:** of the data can be dealt by using the TopGuard as a security extension for SDN-Cs to provide the real-time automatic detection of the network topology positioning attacks. With the help of TLS features in OF data between controllers and switches is secured from tampering issues.

- **Repudiation:** It can be mitigated by using the features of AAA module in ODL and the altering of the network paths due to malicious actions can be avoided for Hadoop as these actions are logged in the respective middleware.

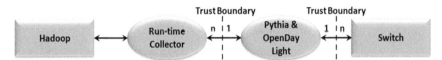

FIGURE 1.20   The data flow diagram of Pythia.

TABLE 1.9   Summarized Threat Categories Using STRIDE Matrix for Pythia

Type	Component	Threat Categories					
		S	**T**	**R**	**I**	**D**	**E**
Interactors	Hadoop	×	–	×	–	–	–
	Switch	✓	–	✓	–	–	–
Data flows	Hadoop ↔ Controller	–	×	–	✓	✓	–
	Controller ↔ Pythia	–	✓	–	✓	✓	–
	Pythia ↔ Switch	–	✓	–	✓	✓	–
Process	Runtime collector	✓	×	✓	×	✓	✓
	Pythia	✓	×	✓	✓	✓	✓

- **Information Disclosure:** These problems occur in runtime collector with sensitive data that is based on the Hadoop computations. Recently the ODL closed the issues related with MD-SAL API and NETCONF protocols. Setting the minimum permissions at the runtime clock will mitigate the information disclosure issues (Triki et al., 2018).
- **DoS:** It attacks in ODL are tackled by using the Defense4All application by detecting some of the attacks against NBI, Process, SBI, and data store (Arbettu, 2016). Usage of AAA module helps to mitigate even the attacks on the highly privileged user access with the help of different network resources.

The elevation of privileges threats also can be sorted out and mitigated using AAA module.

1.6.5 ANALYSIS OF HADOOP-A SECURITY

A DFD of Hadoop-A is drawn with a different type of trust boundaries in this case as compared to the previous case, as shown in Figure 1.21. These trust boundaries are laying between the Hadoop cluster and RDMA clients (i.e., between MOF Supplier and the NetMerger). RDMA protocol helps to accelerate the data transfer rate and helps to improve the data merging. This allows data transfers to be taking place between main memories of all machines of the network by excluding the involvement of caches, processors, and operating systems as well to deliver high-throughput and low-latency. RDMA clients tend to lie outside the trust boundary due to the connection of untrusted users with RDMA components. The summary of different threat categories and security analysis using STRIDE is shown in Table 1.10.

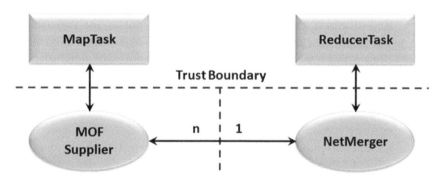

FIGURE 1.21   The data flow diagram of Hadoop-A.

- **Spoofing:** of a valid IP address may impersonate the legal RDMA peer and this may be conducted as a blind attack or in simple words it establishes an RDMA stream with users (Pinkerton and Deleganes, 2007). This will help the attackers to use the memory of victims by executing malicious code. To mitigate such types of attacks use IPSec AH extensions or use ULP authentication.
- **Tampering:** It allows the peers to use the reserved memory locations by using the buffer overflow and sometimes it may be used for

executing the malicious codes as well. RDMA network interface card (RNIC) checks corresponding bounds for preventing such type of attacks. For the data flow between the RMDA clients and the interactors the tampering problems must be solved by the OS of the system only.

TABLE 1.10　　Summarized Threat Categories Using STRIDE Matrix for Hadoop-A

Type	Component	Threat Categories					
		S	T	R	I	D	E
Interactors	MapTask	×	–	×	–	–	–
	ReduceTask	×	–	×	–	–	–
Data flows	Map ↔ MOF	–	✓	–	×	×	–
	MOF ↔ ReduceTask	–	×	–	×	×	–
	NetMerger ↔ ReduceTask	–	✓	–	×	×	–
Process	MOF supplier	×	×	×	×	×	×
	NetMerger	×	×	×	×	×	×

- **Repudiation:** These problems may occur due to the insertion of malicious data in the memory of RDMA peer. These type malicious attacks are mitigated by using an appropriate authentication mechanism.
- **Information Disclosure:** It may be possible from wide range of Hadoop computations and memory areas used for DRMA services must be zeroed ahead of mitigation of the risks. To mitigate these issues encryption must be carried out between RDMA clients using IPSec ESP extensions.
- **DoS:** It attacks are generally susceptible with RDMA protocol like in the case of TCP SYN attacks and these may halt the functioning of Hadoop. To deal with such situations allocation of the resources need to be done by using privileged resources manager, which helps to prevent the peers from access other resources which are not allocated to them.

1.7　SUMMARY

SDN provides a greater advantage for the networking applications, but many security-related issues are discussed in this chapter with respect to routing, cloud, Wi-Fi, and big data applications. The security analysis and mitigation techniques have been discussed using STRIDE method with reasonable examples and mitigation plans. To analyze the system for security issues, DFDs were used to represent the system architectures.

ElasticTree applications proved to have some of the best mitigation techniques for the routing applications. HPE Helion OpeStack has taken care of most of the security issues with the in-built security controls in the cloud applications. They also include defining the rules for firewalls at the edges of HPE deployment. The demand of mobile and telephonic applications with flexible and manageable network approaches evolved the software like Odin and OpenWiFi. The security features are merged with these two systems to ensure a safe platform for the users by providing different types of mitigation platforms for a variety of security issues using the STRIDE method. Finally, the big data applications using SDN are analyzed in this chapter using the FlowComb, Pythia, and Hadoop-A for big data architectures. Whereas, the FlowComb and Hadoop-A do not have security when as compared with Pythia using ODL controller using AAA services.

KEYWORDS

- **address resolution protocol**
- **application programming interface**
- **authentication authorization and accounting**
- **authentication service providers**
- **basic service set identification**
- **cloud controller**
- **cloud management services**

REFERENCES

Ageyev, D., Bondarenko, O., Alfroukh, W., & Radivilova, T., (2018). Provision security in SDN/NFV. In: *2018 14ᵗʰ International Conference on Advanced Trends in Radioelecrtronics, Telecommunications and Computer Engineering (TCSET)* (pp. 506–509). IEEE.

Ahmad, P., Jacob, S., & Khondoker, R., (2018). Security analysis of SDN applications for big data. In: *SDN and NFV Security* (pp. 39–55). Springer, Cham.

Al-Fares, M., Radhakrishnan, S., Raghavan, B., Huang, N., & Vahdat, A., (2010). Hedera: Dynamic flow scheduling for data center networks. In: *NSDI* (Vol. 10, No. 2010).

Arbettu, R. K., (2016). Security analysis of open daylight, ONOS, rosemary and Ryu SDN controllers. In: *2016 17th International Telecommunications Network Strategy and Planning Symposium (Networks)* (pp. 37–44).

Artmann, D., & Khondoker, R., (2018). Security analysis of SDN Wi-Fi applications. In: *SDN and NFV Security* (pp. 57–71). Springer, Cham.

Asturias, D., (2018). *Nine Types of Software Defined Network Attacks and How to Protect from Them.* [Online] Available from URL: https://www.routerfreak.com/9-types-software-defined-network-attacks-protect/ (accessed on 16 December 2020).

Batista, D. A. L., Magoni, D., Perry, P., Cunha, D. A. E., Murphy, J., & Ventresque, A., (2019). Multi-layer-mesh: A novel topology and SDN-based path switching for big data cluster networks. In: *IEEE ICC 2019: IEEE International Conference on Communications.* Shanghai, China. IEEE.

Benson, T., Akella, A., Shaikh, A., & Sahu, S., (2011a). CloudNaaS: A cloud networking platform for enterprise applications. In: *Proceedings of the 2nd ACM Symposium on Cloud Computing* (Vol. 6, No. 2, pp. 1–13).

Benson, T., Anand, A., Akella, A., & Zhang, M., (2011). MicroTE: Fine grained traffic engineering for data centers. In: *Proceedings of the Seventh Conference on Emerging Networking Experiments and Technologies* (p. 8). ACM.

Bholebawa, I. Z., & Dalal, U. D., (2018). Performance analysis of SDN/open flow controllers: Pox versus floodlight. *Wireless Personal Communications, 98*(2), 1679–1699.

Bikos, A. N., & Sklavos, N., (2012). LTE/SAE security issues on 4G wireless networks. *IEEE Security and Privacy, 11*(2), 55–62.

Brooks, M., & Yang, B., (2015). A man-in-the-middle attack against open day light SDN controller. In: *Proceedings of the 4th Annual ACM Conference on Research in Information Technology* (pp. 45–49). ACM.

Cao, J., Ma, M., Li, H., Zhang, Y., & Luo, Z., (2013). A survey on security aspects for LTE and LTE-a networks. *IEEE Communications Surveys and Tutorials, 16*(1), 283–302.

Cheng, R. S., Huang, C. M., & Pan, S. Y., (2018). Wi-Fi offloading using the device-to-device (D2D) communication paradigm based on the software defined network (SDN) architecture. *Journal of Network and Computer Applications, 112,* 18–28.

Chikhale, A., & Khondoker, R., (2018). Security analysis of SDN cloud applications. In: *SDN and NFV Security* (pp. 19–38). Springer, Cham.

D'Orsaneo, J., Tummala, M., McEachen, J., & Martin, B., (2018). Analysis of traffic signals on an SDN for detection and classification of a man-in-the-middle attack. In: *2018 12th International Conference on Signal Processing and Communication Systems (ICSPCS)* (pp. 1–9). IEEE.

Das, A., Lumezanu, C., Zhang, Y., Singh, V., Jiang, G., & Yu, C., (2013). Transparent and flexible network management for bigdata processing in the cloud. In: Da Silva, D., & Porter, G., (eds.), *5th USENIX Workshop on Hot Topics in Cloud Computing, HotCloud'13.* San Jose, CA, USA, USENIX Association.

Dierks, T., & Rescorla, E., (2008). *The Transport Layer Security (TLS) Protocol: Version 1.2.* Network Working Group.

Ding, A. Y., Crowcroft, J., Tarkoma, S., & Flinck, H., (2014). Software defined networking for security enhancement in wireless mobile networks. *Computer Networks, 66,* 94–101.

Dridi, L., & Zhani, M. F., (2018). A holistic approach to mitigating DoS attacks in SDN networks. *International Journal of Network Management, 28*(1), e1996.

ElasticTree, D. F. D., & Nbi, N. B. A., (2018). HPE VCN SDN, 23. *SDN and NFV Security: Security Analysis of Software-Defined Networking and Network Function Virtualization, 30,* 133.

Gude, N., Koponen, T., Pettit, J., Pfaff, B., Casado, M., McKeown, N., & Shenker, S., (2008). NOX: Towards an operating system for networks. *Computer Communications Rev., 38*(3), 105–110.

Handigol, N., Flajslik, M., Seetharaman, S., McKeown, N., & Johari, R., (2010). Aster*x: Load-balancing as a network primitive. In: *9th GENI Engineering Conference (Plenary)* (pp. 1–2).

Handigol, N., Seetharaman, S., Flajslik, M., McKeown, N., & Johari, R., (2009). Plug-n-serve: Load-balancing web traffic using openflow. *ACM Sigcomm. Demo, 4*(5), 6.

Heller, B., Seetharaman, S., Mahadevan, P., Yiakoumis, Y., Sharma, P., Banerjee, S., & McKeown, N., (2010). Elastictree: Saving energy in data center networks. In: *NSDI* (Vol. 10, pp. 249–264).

Hizver, J., (2015). Taxonomic modeling of security threats in software defined networking. In: *Black Hat Conference* (pp. 1–16).

Huang, P. K., Ouzieli, I., Berg, J., Klein, A., Ben-Ari, D., Hitron, A., Cariou, L., & Stacey, R., (2019). *Intra Basic Service set Signaling for Multiple Access Points.* U.S. Patent Application 16/220,950.

Jones, M., & Hardt, D., (2012). *The OAuth 2.0 Authorization Framework: Bearer Token Usage.* In internet engineering task force (IETF), Standard Task.

Kakadia, D., & Varma, V., (2012). Energy efficient data center networks: A SDN based approach. *IBM Collaborative Academia Research Exchange.*

Kolias, C., Ahlawat, S., Ashton, C., Cohn, M., Manning, S., & Nathan, S., (2013). *OpenFlow-Enabled Mobile and Wireless Networks.* White Paper.

Kreutz, D., Ramos, F. M. V., & Veríssimo, P., (2013). Towards secure and dependable software-defined networks. In: Foster, N., & Sherwood, R., (eds.), *Proceedings of the Second ACM SIGCOMM Workshop on Hot Topics in Software Defined Networking, HotSDN* (pp. 55–60). The Chinese University of Hong Kong, Hong Kong, China, ACM, 2013.

Liyanage, M., Abro, A. B., Ylianttila, M., & Gurtov, A., (2016). Opportunities and challenges of software-defined mobile networks in network security. *IEEE Security and Privacy, 14*(4), 34–44.

Liyanage, M., Gurtov, A., & Ylianttila, M., (2015). *Software Defined Mobile Networks (SDMN): Beyond LTE Network Architecture.* John Wiley & Sons.

Liyanage, M., Ylianttila, M., & Gurtov, A., (2014). Securing the control channel of software-defined mobile networks. In: *Proceeding of IEEE International Symposium on a World of Wireless, Mobile and Multimedia Networks* (pp. 1–6). IEEE.

Nakao, A., Du, P., & Iwai, T., (2015). Application specific slicing for MVNO through software-defined data plane enhancing SDN. *IEICE Transactions on Communications, 98*(11), 2111–2120.

Narayan, D., Bailey, S., & Daga, A., (2012). Hadoop acceleration in an openflow-based cluster. In: *2012 SC Companion: High Performance Computing, Networking Storage and Analysis* (pp. 535–538). Salt Lake City, UT, USA.

Neves, M. V., DeRose, C. A. F., Katrinis, K., & Franke, H., (2014). Pythia: Faster big data in motion through predictive software-defined network optimization at runtime. In: *2014 IEEE 28th International Parallel and Distributed Processing Symposium* (pp. 82–90). Phoenix, AZ, USA, IEEE Computer Society.

Norouzi, A., Majidi, B., & Movaghar, A., (2018). Reliable and energy-efficient routing for green software defined networking. In: *2018 9th International Symposium on Telecommunications (IST)* (pp. 221–226). IEEE.

Pinkerton, J., & Deleganes, E., (2007). *Direct Data Placement Protocol (DDP)/Remote Direct Memory Access Protocol (RDMAP) Security*. RFC5042 (Proposed Standard). Internet engineering task force.

Rigney, C., Willens, S., Rubens, A. C., & Simpson, W. A., (2000). *RFC 2865: Remote Authentication Dial in User Service (RADIUS)*. Network Working Group.

Rolbin, M., (2013). *Early Detection of Network Threats Using Software Defined Network (SDN) and Virtualization*. Doctoral dissertation, Master's thesis, Carleton University, Ottawa.

Sagare, A. A., & Khondoker, R., (2018). Security analysis of SDN routing applications. In: *SDN and NFV Security* (pp. 1–17). Springer, Cham.

Sahoo, K. S., et al., (2018a). A learning automata-based DDoS attack defense mechanism in software defined networks. *Proceedings of the 24th Annual International Conference on Mobile Computing and Networking*. ACM.

Sahoo, K. S., et al., (2018b). A machine learning approach for predicting DDoS traffic in software defined networks. In: *2018 International Conference on Information Technology (ICIT)*. IEEE.

Sahoo, K. S., et al., (2019a). ESMLB: Efficient switch migration-based load balancing for multi-controller SDN in IoT. *IEEE Internet of Things Journal*.

Sahoo, K. S., et al., (2019b). Improving end-users utility in software-defined wide area network systems. *IEEE Transactions on Network and Service Management*.

Sahoo, K. S., et al., (2019c). Toward secure software-defined networks against distributed denial of service attack. *The Journal of Supercomputing*, 1–46.

Suresh, L., Schulz-Zander, J., Merz, R., Feldmann, A., & Vazao, T., (2012). Towards programmable enterprise WLANs with Odin. In: *HotSDN'12* (pp. 115–120). Helsinki, Finland.

Tayyaba, S. K., & Shah, M. A., (2019). Resource allocation in SDN based 5G cellular networks. *Peer-to-Peer Networking and Applications*, *12*(2), 514–538.

Triki, A., Betoule, C., Thouenon, G., Henais, O., Pelloquin, N., Lambert, G., Sylla, M., et al., (2018). OpenROADM compliant SDN controller for a full interoperability of the optical transport network. In: *2018 European Conference on Optical Communication (ECOC)* (pp. 1–3). IEEE.

Wang, Y., Que, X., Yu, W., Goldenberg, D., & Sehgal, D., (2011). Hadoop acceleration through network levitated merge. In: Lathrop, S., Costa, J., & Kramer, W., (eds.), *Conference on High Performance Computing Networking, Storage and Analysis* (Vol. 57, pp. 1–57:10). SC 2011, Seattle, WA, USA, ACM, 2011.

Wu, W., Lin, W., Hsu, C. H., & He, L., (2018). Energy-efficient Hadoop for big data analytics and computing: A systematic review and research insights. *Future Generation Computer Systems, 86,* 1351–1367.

Yan, Q., Yu, F. R., Gong, Q., & Li, J., (2015). Software-defined networking (SDN) and distributed denial of service (DDoS) attacks in cloud computing environments: A survey, some research issues, and challenges. *IEEE Communications Surveys and Tutorials, 18*(1), 602–622.

Yap, K. K., Yiakoumis, Y., Kobayashi, M., Katti, S., Parulkar, G., & McKeown, N., (2011). *Separating Authentication, Access, and Accounting: A Case Study with OpenWiFi.* Technical Report, OpenElow 2011-1.

CHAPTER 2

Distributed Denial of Service Attacks in SDN Context

SHASHWATI BANERJEA and SHASHANK SRIVASTAVA

Department of Computer Science and Engineering, Motilal Nehru National Institute of Technology, Allahabad, Uttar Pradesh, India, E-mails: shashwati@mnnit.ac.in (S. Banerjea), shashank12@mnnit.ac.in (S. Srivastava)

ABSTRACT

In recent years, SDN has evolved as a promising alternative to the traditional networking paradigm. This is because the traditional network is decentralized, making it difficult to manage and provide trouble-shooting. SDN is an approach to network management whereby the forwarding process of the data plane (DP) is disassociated from the control plane (CP). The CP is responsible for decision-making. SDN centrally control the network infrastructure and make it programmable. Communication between the two planes (data and control) is carried out by the OpenFlow (OF) protocol. The deployment of SDN was initiated by Mr. Matrin Casado and his research team in 2008. The original projects developed at Stanford University were SANE and ETHANE.

Security reports and web articles suggest that SDN (Software Defined Network) has the caliber to defend DDoS attacks. The year 2017 has been declared as the year of SDN adaption and DDoS mitigation. The initial effort in the direction of compiling the detection and mitigation approaches has been done in (Dayal et al., 2016). Recently a similar effort has been done in (Rochak et al., 2019).

The CP of SDN has a complete visibility of the network which makes traffic monitoring feasible. Moreover, SDN open flow switches contain forwarding logic only; decision-making capability is softwarized at controller. This helps the controller to instruct and configure the switches with new flow rules which the switches follow. This facilitates the network admins to detect and mitigate these attacks easily. SDN have gained momentum among the possible solutions of DDoS attacks due to its decentralized nature of network management, but solutions come with its repercussions. The centralization and open architecture framework makes SDN difficult for widespread adaptation.

The chapter begins with an introduction to DDoS attacks and its classification such as volumetric attack, protocol exploitation attack and application attack. In the next section, we discuss the possible DDoS attacks over SDN framework. We have categorized the vulnerability into three classes: DDoS attack on data, control, and application planes (APs). The DDoS attack on DP can further be classified into TCAM exhaustion, switch DDoS, ICMP flood, TCP flood, TCP_SYN flood, etc. We would discuss Resource depletion, OF bandwidth exhaustion, amplification attacks in DDoS attack over CP. HTTP flooding and Slowloris attack has been discussed in DDoS attack over AP.

The next section highlights the working of attack tools used in performing DDoS attacks. Various DDoS tools have been widely exploited to render DDoS attacks and facilitate attackers to carry out dangerous attack on target; here target may be network resources, server resources, or applications.

The fourth section focuses on the state-of-the-art for detection and mitigation approaches of DDoS attacks. Detection approaches are classified into statistical, policy, and machine learning-based approaches. DDoS mitigation OF switches, including Alcatel Lucent's OmniSwitch, Brocade's MLXe series routers, and applications such as DefensePro by Radware that are available in market; also depend on the statistical threshold to detect the DDoS attack. In addition, this section also incorporates a brief analysis of the previous defense mechanism of the last 10 years and analyzes and compares the products of different security vendors like Cloudflare, Radware, Akamai, Arbor, Nexusguard, etc.

2.1   INTRODUCTION TO DDoS ATTACK

In DDoS, the attacker tries to hamper the services being provided by a machine by flooding it with unnecessary requests with the intention to overload the system and prevent the legitimate requests from getting fulfilled. The attack is carried out by forming a network of bots. Bots are computational devices (such as computers and IoT devices) infected by some malware and controlled remotely. Once a botnet is created, the attacker sends instructions to each bot via remote control. Millions of bots send request to the victim server thereby either creating a huge traffic or overflowing the capacity of the server. The legitimate requests do not get served, resulting in denial-of-service. Since, each bot is a licit machine; it becomes very difficult to separate attack traffic from regular traffic.

2.1.1 CLASSIFICATION OF ATTACKS

Broadly, the DDoS attack is of three types: volumetric, protocol-based, and application-layer attacks. A volumetric attack tries to overwhelm the bandwidth capability of a network by sending a huge amount of request packets. Volumetric attacks are reported to be the largest type of DDoS attack. According to WorldWide Infrastructure Security Report, around 61% of DDoS attack is volumetric. The volumetric attack can either be flooding based or amplification-based. Examples of flooding based volumetric attacks are UDP and ICMP flooding. Examples of amplification-based attacks are Smurf, fragile, NTP amplification, and DNS amplification attack.

Protocol attacks aim to disrupt the service by exhausting the available state table capacity of web application servers. Protocol attacks harness the weak points of algorithms executing in protocol stack layers to keep the target inaccessible. These types of attacks are least, and accounts for only 20% of the total attacks. Examples of protocol attacks include Smurf attack, TCP state exhaustion, and Ping of Death.

Application layer attacks exploit its protocols to disrupt the application or server. Examples of application-layer attacks include Slowloris and hyper text transfer protocol (HTTP) flooding.

2.1.1.1 VOLUMETRIC ATTACKS

The volumetric attacks are of two types: flooding and amplification. In a flooding attack, millions of botnets send request packets to targeted site to overwhelm its network. A valid user trying to access victim website which is under the attack would discover it to be slow or unresponsive.

Amplification attack exploits the difference in the packet size of request message and the corresponding reply message. The general attack scheme is to spoof the source IP address in the request message to the victim's IP address. Thus, all the response messages are directed to the victim IP address. Since, the response message is much larger in size than the request message, the victim gets overflown.

2.1.1.1.1 UDP Flood

This is a connectionless attack where, the attacker need not complete the procedure to establish a connection, and thus, it is easier to launch. The attacker sends a huge number of UDP packets to random ports on the victim server. The target machine gets busy checking for the applications executing on the ports, but does not finds any application executing on those ports. It constantly sends "ICMP destination unreachable" packet to the requesting machines, ultimately making the target machine unreachable. The UDP flooding attack is measured in Mbps and PPS to measure the bandwidth consumed and packets send per second, respectively. Figure 2.1 presents the UDP flooding attack.

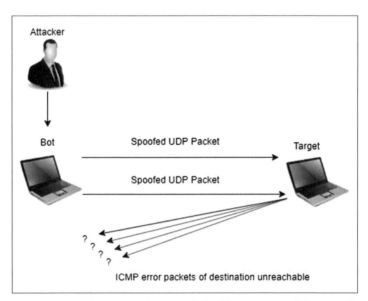

FIGURE 2.1   UDP flooding attack. (Courtesy of Cloudflare, Inc. https://blog.cloudflare.com/)

2.1.1.1.2 Basic Mitigation

In the basic mitigation approach, the operating system keeps a check on the number of ICMP response that can be sent from the machine. However, a major drawback of this approach is legitimate users can also get blocked.

2.1.1.1.3 ICMP Flood

ICMP is connectionless protocol used for connection diagnosis, errors, etc. ICMP is a volumetric attack, whereby millions of botnets send ICMP message to the server. The message can be any simple message such as echo request and echo reply. The server, unable to process the huge number of requests becomes slow or unresponsive leading to state of DoS. Similar to UDP flood attack, the ICMP attack is also measured in Gbps, Mbps, and PPS. Figure 2.2 presents the ICMP flooding attack.

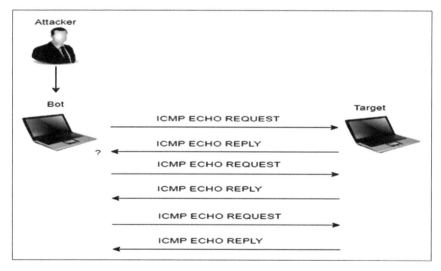

FIGURE 2.2 ICMP flooding attack. (Courtesy of Cloudflare, Inc. https://blog.cloudflare.com/)

2.1.1.1.4 DNS Amplification Attack

This attack takes advantage of the difference in the packet size of request and response message. The response message is much larger in size in comparison to the request message. Millions of bots with a spoofed IP address (IP of victim server) send DNS queries to open DNS resolvers. The targeted victim receives DNS replies from the DNS resolvers. As a consequence, the network of the victim traffic gets clogged, causing DoS. Figure 2.3 presents the DNS amplification attack.

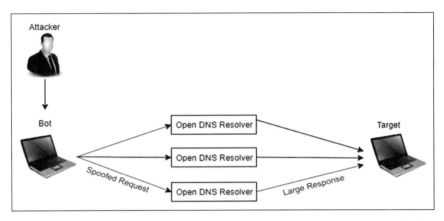

FIGURE 2.3 DNS amplification attack. (Courtesy of Cloudflare, Inc. https://blog. cloudflare.com/)

An analogy to this attack is a group of teenagers calling a restaurant and asking to call them back on a number and read the entire menu for them. The phone number given is that of a targeted victim. The target receives a phone call every few minutes with a lot of information that they have not requested.

> **DNS Amplification Attack Mitigation:**
> - **Proper Configuration of Open DNS Resolvers:** The DNS resolvers who have not been properly configured with security aspects are prone to this attack. A common measure is to configure the DNS resolver in such a fashion that it responds to queries originating only from trusted domain.
> - **Source IP Verification:** The UDP based amplification attacks are generally carried out by spoofing the victim's IP address. The Internet Service Provider (ISP) should keep a check on the packets that are being sent and reject the internal traffic coming from the spoofed IP address.

2.1.1.1.5 Smurf Attack

This attack utilizes the vulnerabilities of IP and ICMP. The malware creates an ICMP ping message and spoofs the IP address to victim IP address. The message is broadcasted in the network. The machines connected to the network responds back to the given source IP, which is actually the IP address of the victim, leading to DoS at the target machine.

➢ **Smurf Attack Mitigation:** The Smurf attack has been mitigated. No cases of Smurf attack has been reported after 1999. The new routers do not forward packets send to their broadcast address by default, making the chance of success of Smurf attacks fairly low.

2.1.1.2 PROTOCOL EXPLOITATION ATTACK

The protocol exploitation attack exploits the vulnerability of the protocols to carry out an attack leading to DoS. The different types of attack are SYN flood attack, RST attack, TCP PSH+ACK Flood, ping of death.

2.1.1.2.1 SYN Flood Attack

To establish a TCP connection with the server, the client sends a SYN packet. The server acknowledges the client by sending the ACK packet containing a sequence number. The server reserves a buffer for each open connection. The attacker uses this characteristic to actualize the attack. Multiple SYN requests are sending to the server which is never acknowledged back. Naturally, after a specific number of open requests, the server is not able to handle legitimate traffic, causing DoS.

Figure 2.4 presents the TCP SYN Flood attack. The possible ways to carry out a SYN flood attack are given below:

1. **Direct Attack:** The IP address need not be spoofed to carry out the attack. The attacker uses the real IP address of the machine and does not respond back to the server's SYN-ACK packets. However, for a single source device, this process of carrying out attack is rarely used as the attacker is highly vulnerable to discovery. On

the contrary, if botnet is used to carryout the attack, then detection becomes difficult.

2. **Spoofed Attack:** The attacker spoofs the IP address on each SYN packet making it looks like it arrived from different sources. Detection of this kind of attack is not difficult provided the ISPs cooperate in detection.

3. **Distributed Attack (DDoS):** The attacker uses bots to execute this attack. Different compromised IoT devices connect to the server by sending SYN packets and do not reply to the ACK sent by the server. This creates half-open connection at the server and ultimately leading to denial-of-service. This type of attack is hard to detect as the packets seem to be legitimate requests.

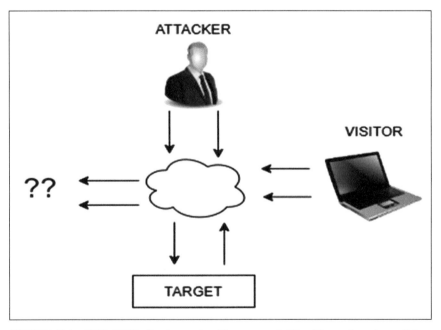

FIGURE 2.4 TCP SYN flood attack. (Courtesy of Cloudflare, Inc. https://blog. cloudflare.com/)

➤ **SYN Flood Attack Mitigation:**

• **Increasing Backlog Queue:** Each operating system allows a specific count of half-open connections. Increasing the number of permissible half-open connections can solve the SYN flood attack to a great extent. In that case, the system would reserve extra memory to handle new requests. The system may suffer performance issues; however, DoS can be prevented.

- **Reusing the Older Half Open TCP Connections:** The second mitigation strategy involves re-using the older half-connection, when the backlog has been filled. However, this technique fails due to small backlog size, or large attack volume.

- **SYN Cookies:** In this technique, the server responds to each packet with an ACK, however, it drops the SYN request and the port is kept open for new request. If the request is a legitimate one, the client would send back a final ACK packet. The server then re-creates the SYN backlog queue entry. Through this technique, some information about TCP connection is lost, however, denial-of-service can be handled using this approach.

2.1.1.2.2 TCP RST Attack

The RST flag of TCP notifies the server to reset the respective TCP connection. In this type of attack, the attacker tries to inactivate an existing TCP connection. The attacker seeks to spoof the IP address of the client by guessing the sequence number of the packet. Upon successfully getting the IP address of the source, it sends the RST packet to server to close the connection.

- ➤ **Mitigation of TCP RST Attack:** To protect the router against TCP RST attack, the TCP ACK-RST-and-SYN can be issued in the Global Configuration mode. If this command is enabled, the router sends an ACK message back to the expected source of the message. There can be two possibilities:

    - In case the source has sent the RST message, it recognizes the ACK message to be spurious and resends another RST message. The router shuts down the connection upon receiving the second RST message.

    - In case the source has not sent the RST message, the source accepts the ACK message and assumes this to be part of an existing connection. The source does not send a second RST message, and the router understands that it was a false attempt by some attacker.

2.1.1.2.3   TCP PSH + ACK Flood

A TCP header with a PUSH flag set to 1 indicates pushing the data imme-diately to the TCP server. The server has to empty the TCP buffer and respond with an acknowledgment back to the sending server. Continuous requests of such kind overwhelm the server. It is unable to process the requests leading to denial-of-service.

2.1.1.2.4   Ping of Death

This type of attack has become obsolete after 1999. The attacker tries to send a packet larger than the maximum size allowed, leading to crashing of the target server. Generally, the ping packets are small in size, however, IPv4 are comparatively bigger in size, and can be as large as 65535 bytes. The TCP/IP systems back in those days were not designed to handle such large packets. A large packet is fragmented into smaller parts to fit in the size of maximum transmission unit. However, when the target server attempts to put the pieces back together, the total size exceeds the allow-able limit, leading to overflow.

2.1.1.3   *APPLICATION LAYER ATTACKS*

These types of attacks deplete the resources of the target server. A single HTTP request is cheap to execute on the client side. However, in order to respond to the request, it could be possible that the server has to load multiple files and run multiple queries. Often, the response is more expensive.

2.2   DDoS ATTACK IN SOFTWARE DEFINED NETWORK

With the proliferation of smartphones, electronic gadgets, handheld devices, the network traffic is growing at an exponential rate. This ever-increasing traffic demands development of new protocols and services for video streaming, improving the quality of service (QoS), handle mobility, etc. However, the current IP networks have a static architecture. The controlling and forwarding rules of data packets are embedded in the packet forwarding devices. This feature of the existing networks make it difficult to incorporate new changes, as any update has to done on every forwarding device separately. In addition to this, in the existing network infrastructure, the time consumed from conceiving a new idea to its design, simulation, testing, and implementation and finally deployment in the actual scenario is very large.

In order to support the dynamic demands of different applications, the network should be easily configurable and adaptable. Software-defined networking (SDN) provides the flexibility to networks. SDN separates the data plane (DP) and control plane (CP). This feature makes SDN different from traditional network where both the decision-making and forwarding capabilities are coupled together in the forwarding device. The CP has a controller which manages the network. The DP comprises of routers and switches. The controller is responsible for taking the forwarding decisions and propagates the same to the routers/switches. The routers/switches are dumb and are left only with the forwarding capability. The detachment makes the network easy to maintain and re-configure. For example, if a new policy has to be introduced, the amendments are required only in the CP. The DP need not be changed for any updates.

2.2.1 SDN ARCHITECTURE: A BRIEF INTRODUCTION

The SDN architecture is categorized into Data forwarding, control, and application layer. The layer wise architecture of SDN is shown in Figure 2.5. Each layer's functionalities are discussed below:

1. **Data Forwarding Layer:** It comprises of packet switches connected to each other. The basic function of packet switch is to forward the arriving packet to the next hop. Each switch contains a flow table to make forwarding decision. The entries in the flow table have a set of header field values, a set of counters and a set of actions. The header consists of eleven fields as shown in figure. Unlike legacy network, where the router is concerned only with the IP header of the datagram, in case of open flow match, selected fields from the three layers are used for matchmaking. That is, in case of legacy network, a link layer frame contains a network layer datagram as its payload which in turn contains transport layer segment as its payload. The intermediate devices

works in the corresponding layer. However, an open-flow enabled device can perform both as a router forwarding datagrams and as a switch forwarding frames, because certain fields from the upper three layers are visible to the open flow switch. In addition, not all the fields in the IP header are required to be matched. For example, OpenFlow (OF) does not allow matching on the basis of TTL filed or datagram length field. If the field values of an incoming packet matches with the entries in the flow table, the packet may be forwarded to a particular physical port, broadcasted to all the ports or multi-casted over a selected set of ports.

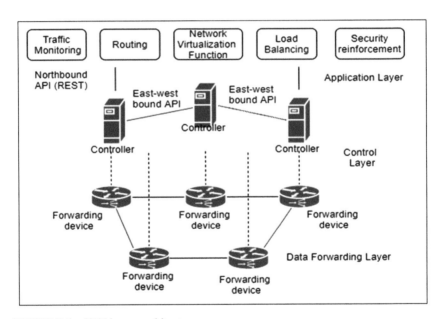

FIGURE 2.5   SDN layers architecture.

If the field value matches with an entry in the flow table, the corresponding action is taken. Otherwise, the packet is sent to the controller. The controller further takes action, for example, send a new flow back to the switch to be followed for this new packet or drop the packet. The counters in the flow table are updated as packets are matched to flow table entries.

2. **Control Layer:** The control layer is called the "brain of SDN." The controller manages the entire network. The software in the

controller decides the route to be followed for every packet and propagates the same to the packet switches. The communication between controller and the packet switches is done through the southbound interface (SBI) of OF protocol. Two controllers communicate via the east-west bound API.

3. **Application Layer:** This abstraction layer defines the set of applications deployed over the SDN controller (SDN-C) that are required for network management. Examples of such applications are security enforcement, traffic monitoring, balancing the load, virtualization of the network, etc. The controller communicates with the application layer through its "northbound" interface.

2.2.1.1   TARGET POINTS OF DDoS ATTACKS IN SDN

An important feature of SDN that makes it different from the legacy network is the decoupling of the data and CP. This feature enables securing the networks with more flexibility and efficient manner. The controller is aware of the entire network. It becomes quite easy to keep track of the anomalous activities taking place in the network. Furthermore, the behavior of the network can be changed if malicious activities are detected. However, the same programmability feature is considered as attractive honeypot by malicious users. Any programer with access to the server that hosts the software would be able to control the network. We highlight the targets that can be used as loophole to carry out DDoS attacks in SDN. Figure 2.6 presents the target points of DDoS attacks on the SDN infrastructure.

1. **SDN Switch:** The open flow switch has limited storage capability. A malicious user may bombard the switch by continuously sending packets. For the malicious packets, the corresponding entry would not be available in the flow table. The switch would continuously send the packet to the controller. However, since the switch has limited memory, it would not be able to process all the packets in a short span of time, leading to overflow. The genuine requests would therefore suffer.

2. **Communication Link between SDN Controller and Switch:** The packets for which the corresponding match is not found in the flow table are forwarded to the SDN-C. The controller sends

back the new flow in a packet through SBI. It is quite possible that the link between the controller and switch is compromised. This can lead to tampering of flow rules and ultimately misdirection of packets.

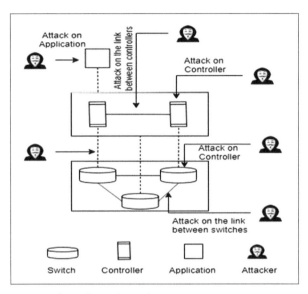

FIGURE 2.6   Target points of DDoS attacks.

3. **Communication Link between Two Controllers:** The east-west interface is used for communication between two controllers. Similar to the vulnerability of the communication link between SDN-C and switch, the link between the controllers is also prone to man-in-the-middle (MITM) attack.

4. **Communication Link between SDN Switches:** The flow packets traverse from one switch to next switch. Generally, the flows are not encrypted and are thus vulnerable to attacks easily.

5. **SDN Controller:** This is by far the biggest threat to the SDN infrastructure. The controller is the brain of SDN that controls the functionality of the entire network. Attack of any kind, such as a DDoS attack or malicious attempt to control the server can paralyze the complete network. This is because the OF switches only execute the commands that are given by the controller. The logic being executed is abstract for the switches.

6. **Applications:** SDN-C implements various applications such as load balancing, traffic monitoring, routing, etc. Generally, these applications are implemented by some third party service providers, which don't take care of the security requirements. When these services are called by the SDN-C via a northbound interface (NBI), there are chances that malicious entries may get injected into the SDN-C.

2.2.2 DEFENSE AGAINST DDoS ATTACK IN SDN

The SDN is prone to several types of DDoS attacks. Separation of routing logic from forwarding makes SDN prone to different threats. There are various approaches to detect and mitigate DDoS attacks over SDN. The solutions can be broadly categorized into DP based, CP based and collaborative approaches.

2.2.2.1 DEFENSE MECHANISMS TO DEAL WITH ATTACK ON DATA PLANE (DP)

DP consists of OF switches which are vulnerable to DDoS attacks, specially flooding based attacks. This is because, SDN switches have limited TCAM. Exploding switches continuously with packets can slow down the processing capability and ultimately stop the service being provided. Research efforts (Xu et al., 2017; Durner et al., 2017) have been proposed in this regard.

The work presented (Xu et al., 2017) is based on the concept that the switch with comparatively less vacancy is selected as the target by the attacker. The switch in the midway is preferred over end points by the attacker. The authors have used three different flow features for detecting attack. Once the attack is detected, a token-bucket based algorithm is implemented in the controller to mitigate the attack. Both detection and mitigation strategies have been discussed in the work. OpenDayLight (ODL) controller and Open vSwitch have been used for simulation of the model.

The work presented (Durner et al., 2017) has also focused on both detection and mitigation of DoS attacks. The detection method is based on header fields' analysis in the flow tables. The controller maintains a list of suspected headers using hashing technique. New rules are generated keeping the list of suspicious headers in account. The detection is simulated using OMNeT++.

2.2.2.2   DEFENSE MECHANISMS TO DEAL WITH ATTACK ON SDN CONTROLLER (SDN-C)

The CP is an important segment of SDN. Any malicious activity on the controller could lead to break down of the entire network. SDN-C is the single point of failure, is the most convenient target of DDoS attacks. Thus, it becomes utmost important to take appropriate measures to detect and mitigate DDoS attacks. Most of the research works (Mousavi and St-Hilaire, 2015; Sahoo, 2018; Wang, 2018) presented attempt to minimize the resource saturation of the controller in case of DDoS attacks.

The research effort presented (Mousavi and St-Hilaire, 2015) is based on using the entropy method for detection of DDoS attacks. Entropy is the function of window size and a threshold value. The threshold is defined by the authors. If the entropy crosses a certain threshold, an alert is generated. The proposed model has been designed for single controller architecture.

Sahoo (2018) also proposed an entropy based approach to identify low rate attacks done at the controller. Statistical features from flow tables are used to detect DDoS attack. The work presented has used entropy and information distance between probability distributions to detect DDoS attack.

The research work presented (Wang, 2018) has proposed a DDoS defense technology called SDN manager, which can update the network according to the flow statistics. The proposed model analyzes the flow statistics, forecast flow bandwidth using these statistics and update network. The proposed model is tested for various types of DDoS attacks. A dynamic controller scheduling (DCS) strategy for multi-controller environment is also proposed that can adapt according to the controller load. The model is capable to prevent failure of both single and multiple controllers.

Mitigating DDoS attacks in multi-controller SDN scenario has also been proposed (Macedo et al., 2016). The authors have proposed an approach called PATMOS that performs three functions: search for bottlenecks, election of controllers and composition. The algorithm first finds the flooded controllers. Among the selected controllers, a leader is chosen. Finally, the controllers are clustered to resolve DDoS attacks collaboratively. Genetic algorithm-based strategy is used to find the highest number of controllers in every controller to handle the overflowing traffic.

Zhang (2016) have used multi-layer fair queuing strategy to protect the saturation of resources at the controller. The controller's resources are shared through the queue. The queues can be adjusted according to the situation. For example, the queue can be expanded and contracted in case of attack and again contracted during normal traffic.

2.2.2.3   *CROSS-PLANE BASED DEFENSE MECHANISM*

In SDN infrastructure the controller is responsible for managing the network. The flow rules are decided by the controller and propagated to the switches. This feature has its own benefits, however, the biggest challenge is that is introduces delay in detecting attacks. Thus, it has been suggested (Han, 2018; Kalkan, Gur, and Alagoz, 2017; Boite et al., 2017) that the responsibility of malicious activity detection should be collaboration between the controller and OF switches.

Han (2018) presented a cross plane based DDoS attack defense strategy called OverWatch. Both attack detection and mitigation have been addressed in the framework. The attack detection system is divided into two sections. In the first part, sensors, and actuators at the DP layer is used to monitor the flow and in the second part, a machine learning based classifier at the CP detects the attack. The experimental results validate that dividing the workload between the DP and CP reduces the communication overhead on the SBI.

Another cross plane based detection approach had been applied (Kalkan, Gur, and Alagoz, 2017). The OF switches are programed to take decisions. A score is calculated from the header attributes. This score is compared with a threshold value to take the decision of forwarding or dropping packets.

Boite et al. (2017) has attempted to embed intelligence into switches using the OpenState specification (Kalkan, Gur, and Alagoz, 2017). The switches are apparently more intelligent than traditional OF switches. The monitoring and detection of DDoS attacks is done at the DP level, while the mitigation is handled by the controller. The authors have used sFlow to analyze the incoming traffic. Entropy-based algorithm has been used to identify anomalies.

2.3   DISTRIBUTED DENIAL-OF-SERVICE (DDoS) ATTACK TOOLS

Although the DDoS attacks can be carried out manually, there are several tools available to carry out the attack. Trinoo and Stacheldraht are the first DDoS tools. There tools were widely used to carry out the attack, however, they were very complex and limited to execution only on the Linux and Solaris operating systems.

In the recent years, plethora of tools have been developed which are more easy to use, can operate on cross platforms, are less complex than the previous ones, and comparatively more dangerous on targets. Many of these tools, such as low orbit ion cannon (LOIC) and Slowloris, were developed as network monitoring and stress testing tools; however, later, these are being used to carry out DDoS attacks. The current section discusses the various tools that are being used to carry out DDoS attacks.

2.3.1   LOW ORBIT ION CANNON (LOIC)

LOIC was developed by Praetox technologies as a network-testing tool. The tool was developed with the intention to subject the servers of the organization to heavy network load for testing purpose. The tool was later released into public domain. The tool was picked up by Anonymous, a group that spawned from the /b/ board of 4chan, to conduct DDoS attack. The tool works by flooding the target server with TCP, UDP, or HTTP packet with the motive to distort the services being provided by the server. Downloading and using LOIC for network testing purpose is legal in the United States, using LOIC for conducting DDoS attack is considered crime and the attacker could be prisoned up to 20 years.

2.3.2   HIGH ORBIT ION CANNON (HOIC)

In the year 2011, Anonymous stepped down from using LOIC as its DDoS tool, as LOIC does not put any effort to hide the IP address of the machines that are used to carry out the DDoS attacks. This resulted in arrest of various users owing those machines for their participation in attacks.

HOIC was the successor of LOIC. This tool came into limelight in 2012, when it was used in Operation Megaupload. It was launched to target the US Department of Justice as retaliation for shutting down the file-sharing website, Megaupload. HOIC is a program for sending HTTP POST and GET requests at the target server. Each request consists of additional text files, also called booster scripts that consist of list of target URLs. The attacker scatters attack traffic and hides their geoloca-tion unlike LOIC, which is unable to hide the IP address of attacker. The HOIC can perform DoS attacks when coordinated by multiple individuals. A successful attack can be carried out with a participation of only 50 users. Unlike LOIC, which is able to launch TCP, UDP, and HTTP GET floods, HOIC attacks are based solely on HTTP GET and POST requests.

2.3.3 *hping*

hping is a famous command-based utility which is used to carry out TCP flooding based attacks. Hping is similar to the ping command; however, unlike ping command which is traditionally used for ICMP requests, the hping command can be used to send large volume of TCP segments to a target server by spoofing the IP address. By spoofing the IP address, it appears to the target that the packet is arriving from some genuine source.

2.3.4 *SLOWLORIS*

Slowloris is a denial of service (DoS) attack tool invented by RSnake. The attack pattern is based on "low and slow" concept. The attacker tries to keep multiple simultaneous connections open at the target server by sending partial request. The HTTP headers are send to the victim in small chunks as slow as possible, that is send a chunk immediately before the server would time out for the request. This enforces the server to keep the connection open for longer duration. Naturally, larger number of half-open connections stops the server from handling the legitimate requests.

2.3.5   R U DEAD YET? (R.U.D.Y)

R.U.D.Y is another DoS tool based on "low and slow" concept. Unlike Slowloris that uses tiny chunks of HTTP headers, R.U.D.Y achieves that objective by directing one byte of information into the POST field at a time. RUDY causes the server threads to wait for the posts that are never going to end. Multiple sessions of this kind overtires the server making it unavailable for the genuine requests. The data is sent in small packs at a very slow rate, generally there is a time lag of ten seconds between each byte, and however, the difference may vary to avoid getting caught.

2.4   DDoS ATTACK DETECTION AND MITIGATION APPROACHES

SDN has gained momentum among the possible solutions of DDoS attacks due to its decentralized nature of network management, but solutions come with its repercussions. DDoS has remained a nightmare for industries and academia since last decade. SDN came with a hope of solving the critical problem of DDoS detection and mitigation. However, due to design issues of OF and centralized point of control, it has been found vulnerable to DDoS Attack. The existing research works for DDoS attack detection are either statistical based or machine learning based. In the current section, we would highlight these two techniques in detail.

2.4.1   STATISTICAL BASED DDoS ATTACK DETECTION

Statistical analysis based detection leverages the properties of network flow based on its statistical pattern to distinguish legitimate flows from malicious ones. It is presumed that the network traffic of a particular network infrastructure follows certain statistical pattern, e.g., in an organization, the network traffic pattern is dependent upon various factors like time, total numbers of network users, geographical location, etc. Therefore, if a network administrator creates a statistical model of normal traffic pattern and fuses this statistical model into the network, then it is somehow possible to distinguish legitimate traffic form maliciously.

Statistical based DDoS detection could be further sub-classified in threshold-based detection based on certain parameters, probabilistic approach of detection and entropy-based detection.

Several researches have been done in current network to detect DDoS attack. Those are mainly entropy-based, probability-based and machine learning-based detection methods. Giseop and Ilkyeun (2009) have introduced two new entropy-based approaches. One is compression entropy and other is fast entropy. However, compression entropy is very sensitive and gives many false negative results. Therefore, they have mainly concentrated on fast entropy method. Fast entropy is a lossless compression that relies not only on packet type but also in volume of traffic. The method is implemented in legacy network. However, we can incorporate the idea in SDN. They have used only source address to calculate entropy. However, data packets come to all the hosts, connected to the network. Attackers attack on single or multiple hosts. Therefore, we can also use destination address to calculate entropy.

Zhang (2010) has described an advanced entropy-based scheme for DDoS detection. It has calculated entropy based on the randomness of destination IP (DIP) and destination Port at router.

Oshima (2010) proposed early DoS and DDoS detection method using short-term statistics. Authors have taken entropy as statistic. Taking entropy in long-term basis means for a large number of packets to detect the DDoS attack is an easy method. Therefore, they took entropy statistic for relatively small amount of packets. Here entropy is calculated based on source IP address. Then they have calculated the threshold value from the acquired statistics. From the variation in result with respect to threshold value, attack is detected.

Oke (2007) has proposed a detection method of DoS attack using Bayesian classifier and neural network. This method mainly based on pattern recognition using probabilistic description. It classify the detection in two part, first normal network condition and second existence of DoS attack. They have used several statistical features to analyze both instantaneous and long-term behavior of traffic. These are Bitrate, Increase in Bitrate, Entropy, Hurst Parameter, Delay, Delay rate. Information has gathered in an off-line mode. Then they have obtained probability density function of attack traffic and normal traffic. After that likelihood ratios has been calculated. Firstly average likelihood values have been calculated, and then likelihood values are used in random neural network (RNN) to distinguish attack traffic and normal traffic.

Vijayasarathy (2011) proposed a DDoS detection method in present network using Naive Bayesian classifier. This chapter used both TCP and

UDP protocol for network modeling. In this chapter, TCP flags distribution has been used to detect the attack traffic. Naive Bayesian classifier has been used to compute probability distribution of TCP flags. DARPA dataset (TCP) has been used to train the system in off-line mode. Whole method is divided into three phases: training phase, deployment phase, and attack detection phase.

Mousavi (2015) proposed an entropy-based DDoS detection approach in SDN environment. In their work, entropy is calculated from destinations IP addresses of consecutive packets samples. Here window size is taken as 50 packets. The detection algorithm relies on threshold-based mechanism where if entropy is less than predefined threshold, attack is detected. However, the method provides great accuracy, but it may be confused in the case of low rate DDoS attack and allows attack traffic.

Sahoo (2018) utilized information distance metric to identify attack traffic at SDN-C. Information distance matric is used to quantify the deviation in network traffic during attack with different probability distribution.

Kalkan (2018) developed a statistical DDoS detection model based on Joint entropy. In this work, authors utilized joint entropy to detect and mitigate DDoS attacks in SDN.

Mao (2018) also used joint entropy-based solution to detect spoofed and non-spoofed DDoS attacks with low false positive. The proposed approach utilized flow duration as a feature for effective detection of malicious flow. Besides flow duration, source IP address, packet payload length and destination port is also utilized to compute joint entropy for DDoS detection in SDN.

Ahmad (2017) proposed a DDoS defense mechanism utilizing sFlow traffic monitoring tool. The proposed mechanism defends DNS amplification attack by utilizing SDN features. SFlow captures the flow packets and processes the header and check whether the packet is originated from DNS server. Controller takes care of suspected flow for attack mitigation purpose. Hong et al. (2018) proposed a SDN-based DDoS defense method for slow HTTP DDoS attack. To detect low rate DDoS attack, the authors proposed a defense module called slow HTTP DDoS defense application (SHDA) and deployed the module on controller. The proposed technique is a threshold-based detection technique where the HTTP request is malicious or legitimate is verified by a threshold value.

Another defense method for slow rate DDoS attack is proposed by Hirakawa (2016). Here the threshold checking parameters are number of

TCP connections from a specific IP address and duration time. If the values of parameters are exceeded above a threshold value, attack is suspected and connections from that IP address are dropped.

Muraleedharan and Janet (2017) proposed a solution for slow rate HTTP based DDoS attack. Here, window size and delta time of the packet were the parameters to analyze traffic patterns. Table 2.1 summarizes the statistical and policy-based approaches.

Radware introduced DefensePro platforms for DDoS detection and mitigation. DefensePro platforms consist of two modules; one is Defense Flow module which keeps the statistics of incoming network traffic and if the traffic behavior deviates from its baseline, then the traffic is diverted to DefensePro module. DefensePro module is having several modules like DoS protection module. Network Behavior Analysis Module and intrusion prevention system module. DoS protection module prevents all types of volumetric attack. Network Behavior Analysis module prevents the malware spreading and protect application resources. Intrusion Prevention System (IPS) modules prevents the network from intrusion especially responsible from Slow rate DDoS. First practical deployment of DefensePro was done in 2014 by HP's Virtual Application network. DefensePro platform comes in different series like DefensePro 200 series is for offering 200 Gbps of DDoS attack mitigation capacity and DefensePro 400 series is for 400 Gbps mitigation capacity.

For finding statistical pattern in network traffic, it is needed to capture and analyze traffic. Dated back to 2002, InMon technologies proposed SFlow, short for "Sampled Flow" for exporting packets at layer 2 of OSI model along with interface counter for network monitoring purpose. Keeping the requirement of network monitoring in SDN based infrastructure, InMon introduced SFlow-Rt for SDN environment in 2015. In order to analyze the traffic in open flow enabled switches, SFlow agents are installed along with sFlow collector. SFlow agents sample the network packets in SFlow datagram and forward these datagram to SFlow collector for analyzing the packets and detecting anomalies if any. In the year 2013, OmniSwitch incorporated the support of SFlow and open flow v 1.3. Here open flow enabled switches analyze the network packets through SFlow agents and report the anomaly to SDN mitigation application. SDN-C communicates with SDN mitigation application and forms the flow rules according to mitigation strategy and installs flow rules to switches.

TABLE 2.1 Statistical and Policy Based Solutions

Attack Types	Detection Approach Types	Simulation Tools	SDN Based/ Traditional	Approach	References
Slow rate DDoS attack	Entropy-based	NS-3	Traditional Network	advanced entropy-based scheme for DDoS detection	Zhang (2010)
DNS amplification	Entropy-based	Two-week dataset s are used	Traditional Network	Authors have taken entropy as statistic. Entropy is calculated based on source IP address.	Oshima (2010)
Volumetric DDoS attack	Probabilistic based	Laboratory Dataset is created	Traditional Network	Detection model is based on a Bayesian classifier and neural network.	Oke (2007)
TCP and UDP Flood	Probabilistic based	DARPA dataset	Traditional Network	Naive Bayesian classifier has been used to compute probability distribution of TCP flags.	Vijayasarathy, Serugudi, and Balaraman (2011)
TCP, UDP, and ICMP flood	Threshold-based entropy	POX Controller and Mininet	SDN	Entropy is calculated from destinations IP addresses. The detection algorithm relies on threshold based mechanism where if entropy is less than predefined threshold, attack is detected.	Mousavi and St-Hilaire (2015)
UDP, TCP, and HTTP flood	Probabilistic based	POX Controller and Mininet	SDN	Information distance metric to identify attack traffic at SDN controller.	Sahoo (2018)
TCP SYN Flood Attack, NTP attack, DNS amplification	Statistical model	RYU controller, Mininet, MAWI Working Group Traffic Archive	SDN	Joint entropy is used to detect DDoS attack	Kalkan, Gur, and Alagoz (2018)
UDP, TCP, and ICMP flood	Entropy-based	RYU controller, OpenVSwitch (OVS)	SDN	Flow duration, source IP address, packet payload length and destination port is also utilized to compute joint entropy for DDoS detection in SDN.	Mao, Deng, and Shen (2018)

In 2014, Brocade communication introduced MLXe series router that also incorporated sFlow agents and open flow protocol. Since sFlow is used to analyze network traffic, so could be used to detect DDoS attack in network.

2.4.2   MACHINE LEARNING-BASED DDoS DETECTION

Generally, DDoS attack detection in SDN is based on statistical analysis. DDoS mitigation OF switches, including Alcatel Lucents OmniSwitch (Alcatel, 2013), Brocades MLXe series routers (Krishnan, 2014) and applications such as DefensePro by Radware (2012) that are available in market; also depend on statistical threshold to counter the DDoS attack. The statistical technique helps in detecting volumetric attacks. For the detection of different class of DDoS attack including volumetric, reflection, and protocol exploitation, traffic analysis is cumbersome. Traffic pattern analysis through machine learning paves a way of effi-cient DDoS detection. For the SDN paradigm, (Braga, 2010) first and foremost suggested the use of self-organizing map (SOM) to classify network flows. They proposed a feature set for the detection of DDoS attack in SDN based infrastructure. Exploiting the proposed feature set, the SOM based classifier classifies the flow as malicious or legitimate. Another machine learning-based model employed support vector machine (SVM) as a classifier for DDoS detection (Kokila, 2014). Kokila (2014) proposed and implemented SVM based model in SDN-C for identifying DDoS attack and obtained less false positive results as compared to other classifier like Random Forest, J48, radial basis function (RBF), and Nave Bayes. Li (2018) also utilized SVM for DDoS attack detection in SDN. They optimized the SVM learning process with genetic algorithms (GA). GA makes SVM training of detection model slow. Gabriel (2014) and Cui (2016) used Neural Network in their proposed DDoS detection model for analyzing network flows to identify malicious behavior. Some research on using machine-learning methods for the detection of attacks has been performed, making use of boosting ensemble strategy. XGBoost is one such algorithm, which makes use of an ensemble of boosted trees. It has been used for the classification of DDoS attacks without compromising network performance (Chen, 2018).

Another research on using deep learning (DL) in OF based SDN for detection of DDoS attack has been done (Li, 2018). They discuss the vulnerability of SDN network to DDoS attacks and how machine learning can help tackle the problem. Table 2.2 summarizes the machine learning-based solutions.

According to Acamai quality report (2016), India maintains its ranking among the top ten origin countries for the origination of the DDoS attacks and is responsible for about 2% malicious attack traffic. In the year 2016, Indian bitcoin exchange came under DDoS attack. Because of this on December 19 (2016), Indian bitcoin exchange Coinsecure became a witness of sudden high spike in traffic.

According to Acamai report (Trak, 2015), along with the source countries of DDoS attack, India has emerged as the fourth largest victim of DDoS attack. India faces 7.43% of DDoS attack as a victim whereas China is the top most victims.

On 25th July 2016, internet service providers (ISPs) in Mumbai became the victim of DDoS attack which is listed as the largest ever cyber-attack in India (of size 200GBPS) (Tech, 2016). Due to this attack, Internet users around Mumbai experienced a slowdown in Internet-based services.

In India, very few researches have been done for DDoS attack in SDN. In the year 2014, a team of researchers from Anna University (Kokila, Selvi, and Govindarajan, 2014) proposed a solution for DDoS detection in SDN-based environment. The solution is based on SVM classifier.

Quamar, Weiqing, and Ahmad (2016) proposed a stacked autoencoder based detection system. The detection module is deployed on controller. The detection module consists of three modules, i.e., traffic collector and flow installer (TCF), feature extractor (FE), and traffic classifier (TC). The approach relies on each packet rather than flow for attack detection thus minimizing false positives. The proposed SAE model provides accuracy up to 99.65% but simultaneously suffers from processing overhead.

Li et al. (2018) proposed a DDoS defense model based on convolution neural network (CNN), recurrent neural network (RNN) and long-short-term memory (LSTM). The proposed detection model is deployed on open flow switches.

Ahmed, Kim, and Park (2017) proposed a DDoS attack mitigation module utilizing SDN features. The proposed model protects the servers from DNS query-based DDoS attacks. The model is deployed on controller, consists of three modules. The first module is a traffic statistics manager that captures the incoming flow from switches and extracts the features from the flows. The second module, the Learner component is used to

TABLE 2.2 Machine Learning-Based Solutions

Attack Types	Target Resources	Simulation Tools	Controller	Approach	References
Volumetric attacks (ICMP, UDP, TCP flooding)	Network Bandwidth, System memory	POX, Mininet	Single controller is used (POX)	Approach is based on stacked autoencoder-based deep learning.	Quamar, Weiqing, and Ahmad (2016)
Volumetric attacks (Ping flood, Smurf attack, SYN Flood	Network Bandwidth, System memory	—	Single controller is used	Defense model based on CNN, RNN, and LSTM.	Li et al. (2018)
DNS amplification, DNS flooding	Processing power, DNS servers	—	Single controller is used	Work on preexisting dataset	Ahmed, Kim, and Park (2017)
Volumetric attacks (TCP SYN Flood, ICMP Flood, UDP Flood)	Network Bandwidth, System memory	RYU, Mininet	Single controller is used	Neural network is used	Cui et al. (2016)
UDP Flooding	Network Bandwidth	Real Time Attack and detection	Single controller is used	Game Theory is used to protect SDN Controller	Assis (2017)
DNS Amplification attack	System memory and processor	ONOS controller and real time	Single controller is used, but could be multiple controller	The detection model used SVM to classify the traffic behavior and detects the DNS attack.	Chen et al. (2017)
ICMP Flooding attack	Network Bandwidth	Real Time Attack and detection	Single controller is used	Apache spark is used to analyze network traffic.	Yan (2017)
ICMP Flooding attack	Network Bandwidth	Floodlight Controller, Mininet emulator	Single controller is used	DDoS attack detection module used SVM to classify normal and malicious flows.	Liu (2017)
TCP SYN Flood, ICMP Flood, UDP Flood	Network Bandwidth and System memory	NOX Controller, OpenFlow switches	Single controller is used	Self-Organizing Maps (SOM) is used to classify network flows.	Braga, Mota, and Passito (2010)

detect the malicious flow and the third module, network resource manager is responsible for maintaining records of device resource utilization.

Assis (2017) proposed a defense model based on Game Theory (Holt-winters and Digital Signature GT-HWDS) against DDoS attacks. The proposed defense model protects the SDN-C from DDoS attack.

Chen et al. (2017) designed DDoS defense solutions to counter DDoS reflection attack. The proposed detection model is deployed on SDN CP, consists of two modules; one is traffic monitoring tool and the other one is machine learning classifier. The detection model used SVM to classify the traffic behavior and detects the DNS attack.

Yan (2017) utilizes SDN and Apache spark and developed a DDoS detection and mitigation framework (DDMF). Apache spark is used to analyze network traffic. The proposed framework consists of capture server, detection server, and SDN solution application. SDN router application sets up the flow rules of the packets. It detects and blocks the malicious flow. Capture server is responsible for maintaining the log file of captured traffic. Detection module notifies the router application about the malicious flow.

Liu (2017) proposed a module floodlight guard (FL-Guard) to detect and mitigate DDoS attack in SDN. In this approach, authors deployed and anti IP spoofing module in Floodlight controller. Attack detection and attack blocking modules are deployed on application plane (AP) of SDN. DDoS attack detection module used SVM to classify normal and malicious flows. Attack blocking module utilizes the SDN features to set up flow rules for blocking attack flows.

2.5 CONCLUSION

In the current work, we have presented a brief overview of the various DDoS attacks and the different attack tools that can be used to carry out the attacks. It has been observed that changing the legacy network to programmable network can handle the DDoS attacks to a great extent. However, this requires replacing the existing network with SDN based infrastructure. This entire replacement would not be economically feasible across the globe. Furthermore, the easy-to-change and centralized behavior makes SDN prone to DDoS attacks. For example, SDN switches can store a limited number of flow rules. Flooding attacks on SDN switches exhaust the processing capability of switches, disrupting the functioning of network. In addition, since SDN switches cannot take any routing decisions, the packets for which flow rule does not exist have to be forwarded to the SDN-C. This creates a huge volume of traffic at the controller. The controller is the weakest point in the SDN infrastructure. Any kind of DDoS attack on the controller can lead to the complete destruction of the network.

We have highlighted the loopholes in the SDN infrastructure that could serve as a potential target to DDoS attack. Furthermore, a comprehensive literature survey of the detection and mitigation approaches on the control and DP has been discussed.

ACKNOWLEDGMENT

The research work is funded by Department of Science Technology, Interdisciplinary Cyber Physical System Division (ICPS), New Delhi, INDIA/2018/490(G).

KEYWORDS

- **convolution neural network**
- **DDoS detection and mitigation framework**
- **distributed denial-of-service**
- **dynamic controller scheduling**
- **feature extractor**
- **floodlight guard**
- **genetic algorithms**

REFERENCES

Ahmad, A. A., Mohd, A., Megat, N., Megat, M. N., Shadil, A., & Zainal, A., (2017). DNS amplification attack detection and mitigation via sFlow with security-centric SDN. In: *Proceedings of the 11th International Conference on Ubiquitous Information Management and Communication (IMCOM'17)* (p. 7, Article: 3). ACM, New York, NY. doi: http://dx.doi.org/10.1145/3022227.3022230.

Ahmed, M. E., Kim, H., & Park, M., (2017). Mitigating DNS query-based DDoS attacks with machine learning on software-defined networking. In: *Proceedings of the 2017 IEEE Military Communications Conference (MILCOM'17)* (pp. 11–16).

Alcatel Lucent Enterprise, (2013). *SDN Analytics for DDoS Mitigation-Solving Real World Enterprise Problem Today.* Technical Report.

Biao, H., Xiangrui, Y., Zhigang, S., Jinfeng, H., & Jinshu, S., (2018). OverWatch: A cross-plane DDoS attack defense framework with collaborative intelligence in SDN. *Security and Communication Networks, 2018.*

Boite, J., Nardin, P. A., Rebecchi, F., Bouet, M., & Conan, V., (2017). Statesec: Stateful monitoring for DDoS protection in software defined networks. In: *Proceedings of the 2017 IEEE Conference on Network Softwarization (NetSoft'17),* (pp. 1–9).

Braga, R., Mota, E., & Passito, A., (2010). Lightweight DDoS flooding attack detection using NOX/OpenFlow. In: *IEEE 35th Conference on Local Computer Networks (LCN)* (pp. 408–415). IEEE.

Chen, C. C., Chen, Y. R., Lu, W. C., Tsai, S. C., & Yang, M. C., (2017). Detecting amplification attacks with software defined networking. In: *Proceedings of the 2017 IEEE Conference on Dependable and Secure Computing* (pp. 195–201).

Cui, Y., Yan, L., Li, S., Xing, H., Pan, W., Zhu, J., & Zheng, X., (2016). SDAnti- DDoS: Fast and efficient DDoS defense in software-defined networks. *Journal of Network and Computer Applications, 68,* 65–79.

Dayal, N., Maity, P., Srivastava, S., & Khondoker, R., (2016). Research trends in security and DDoS in SDN. *Security Comm. Networks, 9,* 6386–6411. doi: 10.1002/sec.1759.

De, A. M. V. O., Hamamoto, A. H., Abrão, T., & Proença, M. L., (2017). A game theoretical based system using holt-winters and genetic algorithm with fuzzy logic for DoS/DDoS mitigation on SDN networks. *IEEE Access, 5,* 9485–9496. doi: http://dx.doi.org/10.1109/ACCESS.2017.2702341.

Durner, R., Lorenz, C., Wiedemann, M., & Kellerer, W., (2017). Detecting and mitigating denial of service attacks against the data plane in software defined networks. In: *Proceedings of the 2017 IEEE Conference on Network Softwarization (NetSoft'17)* (pp. 1–6). doi: http://dx.doi.org/10.1109/NETSOFT.2017.8004229.

Giseop, N., & Ilkyeun, R., (2009). An efficient and reliable DDoS attack detection using a fast entropy computation method. In: *Communications and Information Technology, 2009 ISCIT 2009 9th International Symposium* (pp. 1223–1228). IEEE.

Giuseppe, B., Marco, B., Antonio, C., & Carmelo, C., (2014). OpenState: Programming platform independent stateful OpenFlow applications inside the switch. *ACM SIGCOMM Comput. Commun. Rev., 44*(2), 44–51.

Gulay, O., George, L., & Erol, G., (2007). Detecting denial of service attacks with Bayesian classifiers and the random neural network. In: *Fuzzy Systems Conference, 2007 FUZZ-IEEE 2007 IEEE International* (pp. 1–6). IEEE.

Hong, K., Kim, Y., Choi, H., & Park, J., (2018). SDN-assisted slow HTTP DDoS attack defense method. *IEEE Communication Letter, 22*(4), 688–691. doi: http://dx.doi.org/10.1109/LCOMM.2017.2766636.

Jie, Z., Zheng, Q., Lu, O., Pei, J., Jian, R. L., & Alex, X. L., (2010). An advanced entropy-based DDOS detection scheme. In: *Information Networking and Automation (ICINA), 2010 International Conference* (Vol. 2, pp. V2–67). IEEE.

Jing, L., Yingxu, L., & Shixuan, Z., (2017). FL-GUARD: A detection and defense system for DDoS attack in SDN. In: *Proceedings of the 2017 International Conference on Cryptography, Security and Privacy (ICCSP'17)* (pp. 107–111). ACM, New York, NY. doi: http://dx.doi.org/10.1145/3058060.3058074.

Kalkan, K., Altay, L., Gür, G., & Alagöz, F., (2018). JESS: Joint entropy-based DDoS defense scheme in SDN. In: *IEEE Journal on Selected Areas in Communications* (Vol. 36, No. 10, pp. 2358–2372). doi: 10.1109/JSAC.2018.2869997.

Kalkan, K., Gur, G., & Alagoz, F., (2017). SDNScore: A statistical defense mechanism against DDoS attacks in SDN environment. In: *Proceedings of the 2017 IEEE Symposium on Computers and Communications (ISCC'17)* (pp. 669–675).

Kokila, R. T., Selvi, S. T., & Govindarajan, K., (2014). DDoS detection and analysis in SDN-based environment using support vector machine classifier, In: *Sixth International Conference on Advanced Computing (ICoAC)* (pp. 205–210). IEEE.

Krishnan, R., Durrani, M., & Pal, P., (2014). *Real-Time SDN Analytics for DDoS Mitigation, Brocade Communications*. Technical report.

Kshira, S. S., Deepak, P., Mayank, T., Joel, J. P. C. R., Bibhudatta, S., & Ratnakar, D., (2018). An early detection of low-rate DDoS attack to SDN based data center networks using information distance metrics. *Future. Generation. Computer. Syst., 89*, 685–697.

Li, C., Wu, Y., Yuan, X., Sun, Z., Wang, W., Li, X., & Gong, L., (2018). Detection and defense of DDoS attack based on deep learning in open-flow based SDN. *International Journal of Communication Systems.*

Macedo, R., De Castro, R., Santos, A., Ghamri-Doudane, Y., & Nogueira, M., (2016). Self-organized SDN controller cluster conformations against DDoS attacks effects. In: *Proceedings of the 2016 IEEE Global Communications Conference (GLOBECOM'16)*, (pp. 1–6).

Mao, J., Deng, W., & Shen, F., (2018). DDoS flooding attack detection based on joint-entropy with multiple traffic features. In: *2018 17th IEEE International Conference on Trust, Security and Privacy in Computing and Communications/ 12th IEEE International Conference on Big Data Science and Engineering (TrustCom/BigDataSE)* (pp. 237–243). New York, NY.

Mihai-Gabriel, I., & Victor-Valeriu, P., (2014). Achieving DDoS resiliency in software defined network by intelligent risk assessment based on neural networks and danger theory. In: *15th International Symposium on Computational Intelligence and Informatics (CINTI)* (pp. 319–324). IEEE.

Mousavi, S. M., & St-Hilaire, M., (2015). Early detection of DDoS attacks against SDN controllers. In: *Proceedings of the 2015 International Conference on Computing, Networking and Communications (ICNC'15)* (pp. 77–81). doi: http://dx.doi. org/10.1109/ICCNC.2015.7069319.

Muraleedharan, N., & Janet, B., (2017). Behavior analysis of HTTP based slow denial of service attack. In: *Proceedings of the 2017 International Conference on Wireless Communications, Signal Processing and Networking (WiSPNET'17)* (pp. 1851–1856). IEEE.

Peng, Z., Huanzhao, W., Chengchen, H., & Chuang, L., (2016). On denial of service attacks in software defined networks. *IEEE Netw., 30*(6), 28–33.

Qiao, Y., & Wenyao, H., (2017). A DDoS detection and mitigation system framework based on spark and SDN. In: Meikang, Q., (ed.), *Smart Computing and Communication* (pp. 350–358). Springer International Publishing, Cham.

Quamar, Weiqing, S., & Ahmad, Y. J., (2016). *A Deep Learning-Based DDoS Detection System in Software-Defined Networking (SDN)*. CoRR abs/1611.07400. http://arxiv.org/abs/1611.07400 (accessed on 16 December 2020).

Radware, and NEC Corporation, (2012). *Denial-of-Service (DoS) Secured Virtual Tenant Networks (VTN)*. Technical Report.

Rochak, S., Mayank, D., & Virender, R., (2019). Software-defined networking-based DDoS defense mechanisms. *ACM Computation. Survey, 52*(2), 36, Article: 28. doi: https://doi.org/10.1145/3301614.

Shunsuke, O., Takuo, N., & Toshinori, S., (2010). Early DoS/DDOS detection method using short-term statistics. In: *Complex, Intelligent and Software Intensive Systems (CISIS), 2010 International Conference* (pp. 168–173). IEEE.

Tao, W., Hongchang, C., Guozhen, C., & Yulin, L., (2018). SDNManager: A safeguard architecture for SDN DoS attacks based on bandwidth prediction. *Security and Communication Networks, 2018.*

Tech, (2016). http://tech.firstpost.com/news-analysis/internet-service-providers-in-mumbai-targeted-in-ddos-attack-326708.html (accessed on 16 December 2020).

Tetsuya, H., Kanayo, O., Bhed, B. B., & Toyoo, T., (2016). A defense method against distributed slow HTTP DoS attack. In: *Proceedings of the 2016 19th International Conference on Network-Based Information Systems (NBiS'16)* (pp. 152–158). IEEE.

Trak, (2015). http://trak.in/tags/business/2015/08/21/india-ddos-attack-growth-web-app-gaming-target/ (accessed on 16 December 2020).

Vijayasarathy, R., Serugudi, V. R., & Balaraman, R., (2011). A system approach to network modeling for DDoS detection using a naive Bayesian classifier. *Communication Systems and Networks (COMSNETS), 2011 Third International Conference.* IEEE.

Xu, T., Gao, D., Dong, P., Foh, C. H., & Zhang, H., (2017). Mitigating the table-overflow attack in software-defined networking. *IEEE Trans. Network. Serv. Manage., 14*(4), 1086–1097. doi: http://dx.doi.org/10.1109/TNSM.2017. 2758796.

Zhang, P., et al., (2016). On denial-of-service attacks in software defined networks. *IEEE Network, 30*(6), 28–33.

Zhuo, C., Fu, J., Yijun, C., Xin, G., Weirong, L., et al., (2018). XGBoost classifier for DDoS attack detection and analysis in SDN-based cloud. *IEEE International Conference on Big Data and Smart Computing.*

CHAPTER 3

Policy Management in Software-Defined Networks

BATA KRISHNA TRIPATHY[1] and KSHIRA SAGAR SAHOO[2]

[1]*School of Electrical Sciences, Indian Institute of Technology, Bhubaneswar, Argul, Khordha, Odisha–752050, India, E-mail: bata.krishna.tripathy@gmail.com*

[2]*Department of Computer Science and Engineering, SRM University, Amaravati, AP, 522502, India*

ABSTRACT

Software-defined network (SDN) platform is an emerging networking technology that offers efficient and seamless processing of traffic flows in the network. This is achieved by executing different network-control functions in a centralized controller. The execution of these network functions (NFs) depends on the implementation of heterogeneous and complex policies in an organization. The network administrators in the organization enforce a wide range of policies that are defined based on various factors. These factors range from different service providers' requirements in terms of service level agreements (SLAs) to varying application context and network dynamics. The controller generates appropriate flow rules and pushes to the data plane (DP) switches based on these policies enforced by application layer servers. Managing these complex and heterogeneous network policies in SDN is important, but a challenging problem. In this chapter, we discuss various network policies and the policy management approaches that are widely used in the context of SDN. Then, we present an efficient policy management framework in SDN to ensure secure and efficient implementation of these heterogeneous policies, which in turn drive the generation of flow rules in forwarding switches.

3.1   INTRODUCTION

Software-defined networking (SDN) has emerged as an efficient network architecture for network traffic processing by decoupling the network control functions (NFs) or simply network functions (NFs) from the network devices (Nishtha et al., 2014; Sahoo et al., 2019a). The various network devices include access points, routers, hubs, bridges, gateways, switches, etc. SDN executes different NFs meant for processing traffic requests in the network devices in a logically centralized controller. The controller is the core of SDN that offers seamless control to the users adapting to the on-demand requirements and dynamic configuration of the network resources (Kreutz et al., 2015).

SDN architecture comprises of three layers or planes, i.e., application, control, and infrastructure (data) layers as shown in Figure 3.1. The managers and leaders of an organization prepare different service providers and application requirements (in terms of service level agreements (SLAs)) for desired service provisioning (Sahoo et al., 2019b). The network administrators implement the network-wide policies to configure the underlying networking devices with respect to these requirements. It is the task of the controller to appropriately translate these policies enforced by different levels of administrators into flow rules for traffic request processing. These flow rules are then pushed to the flow tables of corresponding SDN data plane (DP) switches. Hence, the process of flow rules generation by the SDN controller (SDN-C) heavily relies on the heterogeneous network policies enforced by geographically distributed application layer servers. In a large-scale enterprise network, the complexity of these policies significantly increases due to large number of application servers in the network. This in turn affects the functionality, performance, and security perimeter of the underlying network. Hence, the policy management in SDN has attained the attention of the research communities.

In organizations, the different policies may vary from the resource configuration to various spatio-temporal access control rules. The policy rules may also include rules for protection against emerging cyber threats. However, the accurate implementations of different network policies have always remained complicated because of the complexity level of various requirements and the evolution of ubiquitous computing and cyber resources. In addition, the distributed nature of policy implementations, network dynamics, and the inter-dependencies between resource configurations complicate the policy management in SDN. On the other hand, network service level inter-dependencies may open the door for hidden access channel attacks which in turn may expose the organization's critical resources to the outside world. As per the recent reports, 50–80% of security vulnerabilities arise because of the misconfiguration of the network policies in an organization (formal methods for Safe configuration of cyber infrastructure, [online] Available at: https:// www.sigsac.org/ ccs/ CCS2010/ tutorial4.shtml). Moreover, the manual implementation of large-scale network-wide policies in an organization is overwhelming and potentially imprecise because of the high possibilities of human errors.

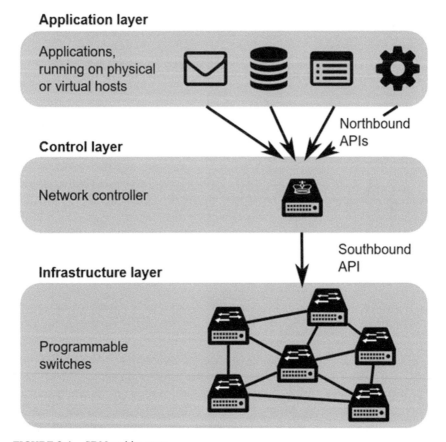

FIGURE 3.1 SDN architecture.

Source: An introduction to SDN [online], Available at: https://qmonnet.github.io/whirl-offload/2016/07/08/introduction-to-sdn/. https://creativecommons.org/licenses/by/4.0/

The challenges in policy enforcement in SDN are summarized as follows:

- Malicious configuration of network policies by potentially compromised application servers may lead to malfunctioning of the network flow control.
- The misconfiguration of heterogeneous policy rules from different application servers may lead to improper flow entries in underlying SDN switches and thereby affecting the routing function.
- The potential inconsistencies in the flow tables due to policy updates may lead to insecure routing of traffic.

In this chapter, we present an efficient and secure policy management solution for SDN platform.

3.2   RELATED WORKS

A significant number of researches have contributed to effective policy management in the SDN platform. The majority of the state-of-art works emphasize on implementing the role-based access control policies in organizations.

Bera et al. (2011) proposed a role-based access control policy management approach for enterprise network. This scheme dynamically implements the policies in geographically distributed zones. The authors use different security servers such as CARS and GPS. CARS are used for authentication and role assignment to each network entity in a zone whereas GPS computes and configures the role-based access control policies in the entities in each zone.

In another work, Ferguson et al. (2012) developed a hierarchical policy management framework in SDN which uses HFT (hierarchical flow tables) in the switches. In order to optimize the policy implementation in this scheme, the researchers used a dynamic network information base (NIB) to abstract the high-level network policies from the underlying topology. Another abstract traffic request processing mechanism for SDN was proposed by Monsanto et al. (2013) that use virtual fields for relating packets with the high-level network policies. SIMPLE (Qazi et al., 2013) is a middlebox that control policy enforcement in SDN switches and works within the constraints of the traditional middlebox and the present SDN platform in organizations. Another approach namely layered policy management (LPM) (Han et al., 2014) specifies and implements the policies in individual SDN layers considering both intra-module and inter-module dependencies in the NFs.

On the other hand, EnforSDN (Itzhak et al., 2015) is a different policy management approach in SDN that uses network function virtualization (NFV) to reduce the complexity of policy implementation. This is achieved by creating a strong isolation between the policy resolution layer and enforcement layer in the SDN devices. Another group of researchers (Machado et al., 2015) proposed a framework for specifying the high-level requirements as SLAs that are automatically transformed into the flow rules in SDN switches. In his work, Nicolae (2015) presented a secure policy management model for authentication of policy servers and implementation of high-level network policies in SDN. These policies may be defined by different service operators, network applications and, the logical controller module in SDN.

The following are the observations inferred from the state-of-art policy management solutions in SDN:

- The present policy management schemes in SDN do not highlight the potential threats from application servers as there is a possibility of these servers being compromised leading to incorrect and insecure traffic propagation in the network.
- The state-of-art approaches do not incorporate heterogeneous policies in an organization. There can be different classes of policies in an organization (Chadha et al., 2008) such as spatio-temporal role-based access control policies, configuration policies, event-condition-action (ECA) policies, etc. The conflicts between all heterogeneous policy rules must be identified and resolved accurately to ensure flaw-less traffic flow in the underlying network.
- The current policy management works in SDN do not address the potential inconsistency between the changes in policy rules and the existing SDN flow table entries to adapt to the dynamic application requirements and context.

3.3   BACKGROUND

The field of policy management in enterprise networks has been in existence for over a decade irrespective of the networking implementation platform (Sahoo et al., 2019b). Hence, the concept of policy management in SDN platform does not differ in any sense from the traditional network. The "policy" terminology has different meanings in different fields of application and is defined based on its use in a specific field. The application fields vary in a wide range of domains varying from government legal system to the field of networking environment. The term "policy" has no common definition that is standardized for all application fields. This is due to the heterogeneity of the application fields and the variety of policy rules in a specific application domain. In the enterprise-networking context, the administrators perceive the term "policy" in different ways. The term "policy" can be defined in the following ways for the purpose of explaining policy management in networks.

3.3.1 DEFINITION OF POLICIES

1. **Policies as "Rules Defining Behavior":** The standard convention of policies in enterprise networks is creating rules for configuration and management of network resources in the organizations. The policy rules are authoritative those define the types of actions to be performed on network resources by the managers or administrators or the systems under specific conditions. Here, the policy rules are procedurally defined for performing the management actions that include configuration parameters of the network entities and services. The policy rules for defining behavior are illustrated with the following examples:

   - r_1: Perform an action A, if automatic reconfiguration is set on receiving a failure F.
   - r_2: Update virus signatures on the servers at 9 pm daily.

   The policy rule r_1 signifies that if a specific event (i.e., a failure F) occurs, then a condition is checked (i.e., whether automatic reconfiguration is set?). Then, the prescribed action (i.e., action A) is performed, if the condition is true. On the other hand, the policy rule r_2 says that an action (i.e., update virus signatures) is performed at a certain time instant (i.e., 9 pm) on a daily basis. These policies define specific type of management actions to be performed as per the given rule.

2. **Policies as "Rules Defining Permission":** Another convention of policies in enterprise networks is creating rules for describing whether the network resources are permitted to be accessed by a specific user or a class of users. Here, the policy rules are declarative in nature. The permission can be "grant" or "deny" indicating the type of access to a network entity such as a file or a network service such as a management application. The rules for defining permission are illustrated with the following examples:

    * r_3: The managers are authorized for video conferencing with 1 Mbps bandwidth limit.
    * r_4: Only accountants are allowed to access the financial records of the organization.

    Here, the policies r_3 and r_4 specify rules for accessing a specific network resource. However, they do not describe how to perform a specific action.

3. **Policies as "Rules Defining Constraints":** In some context, the policies define certain constraints to control the functionality of the enterprise network resources. The constraints are defined declaratively specifying certain conditions that must be satisfied in a network. In some cases, these policy rules can be defined as invariants representing an expression of users' requirements in a network such as commander's mission (in battlefields), administrative rules, etc. Here, the policy rules are defined to be directly used by the network entities or translated into a readable format by the network administrators. The constraints are usually the parameters for the management of network entities. The policies for defining the constraints are illustrated with the following examples:

    * r_5: Network activities must be monitored periodically in every 5 minutes.
    * r_6: Video-conferencing can be allowed a maximum of 1 Mbps bandwidth.

    In the above examples, the rule r_5 defines a parameter value (i.e., periodically every 5 minutes) for the network monitoring module. On the other hand, the policy r_6 is a constraint on the network bandwidth that can be allocated for video-conferencing application.

4. **Policies as "Rules Defining Configurations":** Another usage of policy rules in networks is creating rules to define various configuration parameters of the network entities and services. This terminology is generally used in organizations for a wide range of configuration parameters for services such as routing, congestion, QoS, or for entities such as switches, gateways, firewalls, etc. Configuration policies are implemented by communicating the configuration instructions to the network entities at the DP. The examples of a few configuration policies are listed below:

   - r_7: 10% of the network bandwidth is always allocated to traffic monitoring.
   - r_8: The incoming packets from subnet 10.0.1.0/8 to 10.0.4.0/8 must be encrypted with AES.

Here, the rule r_7 defines the configuration of network bandwidth in the routers and switches to keep a certain portion of network bandwidth for a specific activity. On the other hand, the rule r_8 defines the configuration of the switch or router between the subnets 10.0.1.0/8 and 10.0.4.0/8 as the source and destination subnets to encrypt data packets with AES.

3.3.2 TYPES OF POLICIES

The different policies in enterprise networks are categorized into three types which are presented below:

1. **Event-Condition-Action (ECA) Policies:** These policies represent the rules defining behavior of a management system in enterprise networks. The different management actions with respect to specific events occurring inside and outside of the network in certain conditions are defined as ECA policies. The ECA policies are illustrated with the following example:

   - r_9: <Event: e_1, Condition: c_1, Actions: a_1>
   - e_1: Switch S_3 receives malicious packets through port I_2.
   - c_1: Denial of Service (DoS) attack is detected on port I_2 of switch S_3.
   - a_1: ClosePort I_2 of switch S_3.
   - r_{10}: <Event: e_2, Condition: c_2, Actions: a_2>.
   - e_2: A VPN connection is requested on port I_3 of switch S_1.

- **c_2:** None.
- **a_2:** OpenPort I_3 of switch S_1 and establish a connection instance of VPN.

    In the above examples, the policy r_9 defines the rule for an event e_1 (i.e., receipt of malicious packets on port I_2 of switch S_3) under a certain condition c_1 (i.e., DoS attack is detected on the same port of the switch). Then, it performs an action a_1 (i.e., closing the port that is under attack). On the other hand, the policy rule r_{10} dictates if an event e_2 (i.e., request for a VPN connection is received on port I_3 of switch S_1) occurs, then perform an action a_2 (i.e., establishing the VPN connection). It is to be noted that, in policy r_{10}, there is no such condition for the action to be performed. Hence, the condition c_2 is denoted as "none."

2. **Access Control Policies:** The administrators of an organization define policies to control the access of network resources by different classes or levels of users. These types of policies are defined as access control policies. These policies represent the rules that dictate type of permission (i.e., allow or deny) to different users for accessing specific network resources. A few examples of the access control policies are as follows:

    - **r_{11}:** <employee, ftp, any zone, any time, allow>
    - **r_{12}:** <student, http, academic zone, 9 am–5 pm, deny>

    In the above example, the policy r_{11} states that the employees are allowed to access ftp service from any zone at any point of time. On the other hand, the policy rule r_{12} dictates that the students are not permitted to access http service in the academic zone from 9 am to 5 pm.

3. **Configuration Policies:** The configurations of the cyber and computing resources in enterprise networks are usually guided by the configuration policies defined by the administrators. The network resources include different security appliances, servers, protocols, services, and software components in the network. Few examples of configuration policies are as follows:

    - **r_{13}:** Employees of finance department accounting related transactions through some secure channel.
    - **r_{14}:** The traffic rate between the subnets 10.0.1.0/8 and 10.0.4.0/8 should be limited to maximum of 1 Mbps. If the

traffic rate exceeds the limit then the rest part of the traffic should be dropped.

In the above example, the policy rule r_{13} defines the configuration rule for a security appliance, i.e., the accounting related transactions performed by the employees must be done through some security appliance such as stateful firewall, intrusion detection system (IDS) or Intrusion Prevention System (IPS). Whereas, the policy rule r_{14} dictates the configuration parameter for network bandwidth, i.e., limiting the traffic rate between the subnets 10.0.1.0/8 and 10.0.4.0/8 to maximum of 1 Mbps.

3.3.3   POLICY SPECIFICATION LANGUAGE

For effective network policy management in SDN, it is important to define the policies clearly in a format that is simple, precise, and understandable to the policy-makers and decision-makers in the organization. In addition, the policy specification language must be easy and flexible for implementation by the network administrators. Moreover, the policy specification language should represent the characteristics of the cyber and computing resources in a standard format that is independent of the vendor-specific information of the network resources. The policy specification language must be in an effective format for resolving potential conflicts among the heterogeneous policies within the resource constraints of the underlying network. Among several state-of-the-art policy specification languages, we focus on the following languages because of their widespread use:

1. **Ponder:** It is a standard policy specification language using which the role-based access control rules for different security policies can be specified for the cyber and computing resources in the network. The resources include IPS, IDS, firewalls, proxy servers, software components, services, protocols, etc. Ponder supports the following types of managerial policies:

    i.   **Authorizations:** i.e., the actions that can be performed by a user or entity on specific resources in a target network domain.
    ii. **Obligations:** i.e., the actions that must be performed by a manager or agent on target network resources.

    iii. **Refrains:** i.e., the actions that should not be performed by a user or entities on target resources.

    iv. **Delegation:** i.e., transferring the rights to the target users to perform the managerial actions with specific privilege levels.

In addition, Ponder can be used by the administrators to create complex policies including structures like roles, classes, zones, time, dependency, hierarchy, privilege levels, etc., in an organization. Ponder is an object-oriented and strongly typed language. It is flexible, versatile, declarative, and extensible in nature. It is to be noted that the policies can be used as a formal arguments or parameters to other methods during implementation.

2. **OWL:** It is a formal language for authoring ontologies characterized by formal semantics. It is Web Ontology Language for the Semantic Web and represents authoring ontologies in the network. OWL ontologies include the classes, properties, and parameters of the network resources and are stored as Semantic Web documents. The semantic web data in OWL is presented in the following two ways:

    i. **Extensible Markup Language (XML):** that is a resource description framework (RDF) model and uses tags to identify, store, and organize the data by appropriate encoding.

    ii. **Notation3 (N3):** That is a non-XML RDF model and uses triplets to represent the data and their relationship between entities with first order logic.

OWL facilitates better representation of the data and the semantics as compared to simple XML. Hence, OWL is capable of representing that data in human readable as well as machine interpretable format on the web.

3. **Security Policy Specification Language (SPSL):** It is used for defining different security policies in the network. It is a platform as well as vendor-independent policy specification language. The security policies include the rules defined for controlling communication of traffic through the use of IPsec and IKE protocols. In addition, the flexible and extensible syntax of SPSL enables easy expression of stateless and stateful packet filtering rules through different firewalls. SPSL supports the specification of the following attributes:

    i.   IPsec/IKE and other traditional security policies;
    ii.   Node-based as well as domain-based policy models;
    iii. Multiple distributed policy enforcement points;
    iv. Authentication and authorization policies;

3.4　PROPOSED POLICY MANAGEMENT FRAMEWORK FOR SDN

The rapid growth of ubiquitous computing and communication technologies, SDN's inherent characteristics, extensive high-level requirements, and emerging cyber threats demand an effective policy management framework in SDN. However, as discussed in Section 3.2, the state-of-art approaches do not ensure an efficient and secure policy implementation in the organizations. In this chapter, we present an effective policy management framework for SDN that ensures optimal and secure implementation of complex and heterogeneous policies in the underlying network. The proposed policy management framework for SDN comprises of the following policy control layers:

    i.   **Trust_Verify:** That verifies the trustworthiness of the application servers which are meant for enforcing different policies.
    ii. **Policy_Conflict_Resolve:** That identifies and resolves potential conflicts among heterogeneous policies.
    iii. **Policy_Consistency_Check:** That ensures consistency between the updated policy sets and existing flow table entries.

Figure 3.2 illustrates the architecture of proposed policy control functions with secure flow of traffic through these functional modules. The proposed policy control functions are presented in the following subsections.

3.4.1　TRUST_VERIFY: VERIFYING APPLICATION SERVERS' TRUSTWORTHINESS

The distributed application servers in the enterprise networks are responsible for the generation of heterogeneous policy rules with respect to different high-level requirements. These policies guide the functionality of different network applications by appropriately configuring and managing the network resources. There is a potential possibility of these

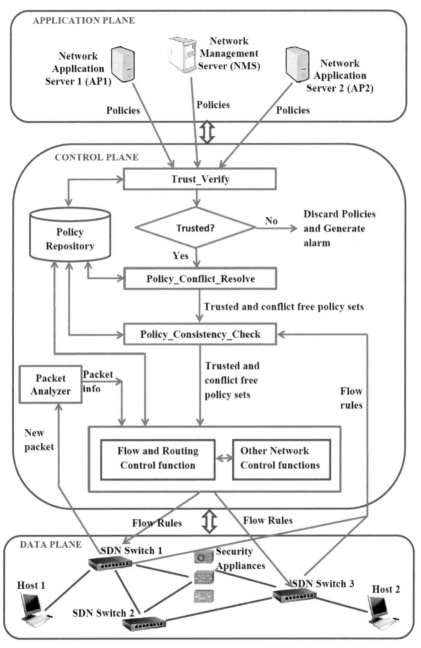

FIGURE 3.2 Architecture of proposed policy management solution for SDN.

Source: Reprinted with permission from Tripathy, et al., (2016). © IEEE.

servers being attacked and compromised intentionally or unintentionally as they are exposed to the outside world via the internet. This, in turn, leads to modifying the policy rules maliciously and/or incorrectly for the underlying NFs in the controller. Subsequently, the NFs might misguide the traffic propagation in the network by creating inaccurate and insecure flow table entries in the SDN data layer switches. The attacks can extend to emerging ransomware attacks, hidden tunnel attacks, SQL code injection, Distributed Denial-of-Service (DDoS) attacks, Sybil attacks, etc. This, in turn, may have a huge impact on an organization's critical resources.

The Trust_Verify function in the controller plays a key role in ensuring the secure influx of policy rules to the controller. This is achieved by certifying the policy rules through SSL (secure socket layer) certificate verification of the respective policy enforcing servers. This process is automatically triggered whenever new policies arrive at the control layer from the application layer. The proposed Trust_Verify function certifies the policy servers by checking whether the following properties are satisfied:

i.   The certificate of the server has been issued by a valid certificate authority (CA).
ii.   The certificate of the server has not been expired (or been revoked).
iii. The names mentioned in the certificate match the domain names.

In addition, it performs verification of PKI (public key infrastructure) certificate and trust of the links (interfaces/ports).

Algorithm 3.1 demonstrates the functionality of the proposed Trust_ Verify function. The parameters and the predefined functions used in Algorithm 3.1 are illustrated in Tables 3.1 and 3.2, respectively. Algorithm 3.1 verifies the chain-of-certificates for the policy-enforcing server using SSL standard libraries. Each SSL connection maintains an SSL_CTX object and SSL_CTX is associated with an SSL_STORE object. The SSL_STORE object holds the server's certificate details which include the IP address, port no, hash functions, etc. The SSL_CTX object for the policy server is created by the built-in function create_SSL_CTX() at the time of connection establishment request from the server to the controller. In the next step, the function SSL_CTX_set_verify() accepts a bitmask of flags using the SSL_STORE object that is a member of the SSL_CTX object. Then, the SSL_CTX_set_verify() function guides the SSL to verify the certificates of the server. After successful execution, the verification function returns the valid SSL_CTX object. Then, the connection from the server to the controller is established by ensuring the certificate of the server is trusted. Otherwise, the connection is denied, if the return value is 0 and an alarm is generated reporting that the connection from the server to the controller is compromised. The certified policy rules are saved in a data structure called Policy repository for further processing.

Algorithm 3.1: Trust_Verify

Procedure Trust_Verify(SPC_STORE)

    Import SSL Libraries

    Set verify_flags=0, SSL_CTX_handler=0, and SSL_STORE_handler=0

    Call verify_callback()

    If (SSL_CTX_new()==NULL)

        Print error

        Call SSL_STORE_free()

        Call SSL_CTX_free()

        Return 0

    End If

    If (SPC_create_STORE()==NULL)

        Print error

        Call SSL_STORE_free()

        Call SSL_CTX_free()

        Return 0

    End If

    Call SSL_CTX_set_cert_store()

    Call SSL_CTX_set_options()

    Call SSL_CTX_set_cipher_list()

    Set verify_flags=SSL_ALL_MASK

    Call SSL_CTX_set_verify()

    Call SSL_CTX_use_certificate_chain_file()

    Call SSL_CTX_use_PrivateKey_file()

    Return SSL_CTX_handler

    EndProcedure

TABLE 3.1   Parameters Used in Algorithm 3.1

Parameters	SSL syntax
Verification flags	verify_flags
SSL connection object	SSL_CTX
SSL_CTX object handler	SSL_CTX_handler
SSL container object for connection	SSL_STORE
SSL_STORE object handler	SSL_STORE_handler
SSL certificate Pre-verification status	Preverify_ok = 0 or 1
Structure for SSL library methods/functions (implements SSL/TLS protocol versions)	SSL_METHOD
Structure for Software Publisher Certificate (SPC) store that is digitally signed by the publishers. It contains flags, use_certfiles, use_keyfiles, etc., to be used for verification of SSL certificate	SPC_STORE
SSL bitmask options	SSL_OPTIONS
List of SSL ciphers	SSL_CIPHER
Combination of all SSL verification flags	SSL_ALL_MASK
Flag for loading a private key and certificates to SSL_CTX object	SPC_STORE_USE_CERTIFICATE

Source: Reprinted with permission from Tripathy, et al., (2016). © IEEE.

The functionality of the Trust_Verify function in Algorithm 3.1 is illustrated with the following example of OpenSSL (OpenSSL Cryptography and SSL/TLS Toolkit [Online], Available at: https://www.openssl.org/). The OpenSSL creates an X509_CTX object having X509_STORE as a member object. The X509_STORE object consists of the server's certificates and certificate revocation lists (CRLs). Then, OpenSSL calls the function X509_verify_cert() to verify the certificate of the server using the X509_STORE object. After successful verification, the connection from the policy server is accepted by the controller. The certified policy rules are further passed to the Policy_Conflict_Resolve function for the detection and resolution of potential conflict among the policy rules. The Policy_Conflict_Resolve function is discussed in the following subsection.

3.4.2   *POLICY_CONFLICT_RESOLVE FUNCTION: RESOLVING POLICY CONFLICTS*

As discussed in the previous subsection, the Trust_verify function protects against potential security breaches that may be originated from

TABLE 3.2 Predefined Functions Used in Algorithm 3.1

Function	Input Parameters	Task	Return Value
verify_callback()	Preverify_ok, SSL_CTX_handler	verifies the SSL certificate	1 for success, 0 for failure
SSL_CTX_new()	SSL_METHOD	creates a new SSL_CTX object to establish TLS/SSL enabled connections	SSL_CTX object for success, NULL for failure
SPC_create_STORE()	SPC_STORE	creates a new SSL_STORE object from the information contained in the SPC_STORE object	SSL_STORE object for success, NULL for failure
SSL_CTX_set_cert_store()	SSL_CTX_handler, SSL_STORE_handler	sets the certificate verification storage of SSL_CTX to SSL_STORE object	No Return value
SSL_CTX_set_options()	SSL_CTX_handler, SSL_OPTIONS	adds the options set via bitmask in options to SSL_CTX object	the new options bitmask after adding options
SSL_CTX_set_cipher_list()	SSL_CTX_handler, SSL_CIPHER	sets the list of available ciphers for SSL_CTX object	1 if any cipher is selected and 0 on failure.
SSL_CTX_set_verify()	SSL_CTX_handler, verify_flags, verify_callback()	sets the verification flags for SSL_CTX to be verify_flags and specifies the verify_callback() function to be used	No return value
SSL_CTX_use_certificate_chain_file()	SSL_CTX_handler; SPC_STORE → use_certfile	loads a certificate chain from SPC_STORE → use_certfile file into SSL_CTX object to allow the use of complete certificate chains	1 on success and any other value for error
SSL_CTX_use_PrivateKey_file()	SSL_CTX_handler; SPC_STORE → use_keyfile	adds the first private key found in SPC_STORE →use_keyfile file to SSL_CTX object	1 on success and any other value for error
SSL_STORE_free()	SSL_STORE_handler	frees the SSL_STORE object	No return value
SSL_CTX_free()	SSL_CTX_handler	frees the SSL_CTX object	No return value

Source: Reprinted with permission from Tripathy, et al.. (2016). © IEEE.

any compromised application server during policy enforcement. After certificate verification, the policy rules from different application servers are used by flow and routing control functions to generate flow rules for the SDN switches. The policy rules generated by distributed application servers are usually heterogeneous in nature. The reason is the policy rules are generally created by administrators of different levels with respect to the high-level business requirements in an enterprise network. In such a communication environment, there is a potential possibility of conflicts among this large volume of policy rules incorporated by the geographically distributed servers. The conflicts among the policy rules may, in turn, lead to violations of functional, performance, and security requirements of the underlying network.

The proposed Policy_Conflict_Resolve function plays a major role in identifying potential conflicts among the heterogeneous policy rules using appropriate pattern matching. Then, the conflicts are resolved using the overriding function. The overriding function uses rule ordering, prioritizing application servers, or type of rules, and network domain knowledge to resolve the potential conflicts among the policies. The proposed Policy_Conflict_Resolve function is presented in Algorithm 3.2.

The algorithm resolves the conflicts between homogeneous policy rules (i.e., rules from the same application servers) using subsuming relation on the rule components. On the other hand, it resolves the conflicts between heterogeneous policy rules having matched network application service rule components using the priority or order of the application servers. For subsuming checking, we have used source IP (SIP) and destination IP (DIP) associated with different flow parameters. There is various flow parameters used for conflict resolution such as bandwidth, congestion control, etc. For heterogeneous rules, we use network application or service for finding the matching between a pair of rules and accordingly higher priority rule overrides the low priority rule.

Algorithm 3.2: Policy_Conflict_Resolve

Input: Policy rule set, $P = \{S_1 <r_1, r_2, ..., r_m>, S_2 <r_1, r_2, ..., r_n>., S_t <r_1, r_2, ..., r_k>\}$, where S_i represents ith application server or administrator role.

Output: Conflict-free policy rule set P'

Procedure Policy_Conflict_Resolve

Create a topological order P' of Policy rule set P on priorities of S_i's

$P' = \{S'_1 < r'_1, r'_2, \ldots, r'_q >, S'_2 < r'_1, r'_2, \ldots, r'_u >., S'_v < r'_1, r'_2, \ldots, r'_w >\}$

Parse P'

For $(r'_i \in P'$ and $r'_j \in P')$

    If $(\text{index}(\text{Server}(r'_i)) == \text{index}(\text{Server}(r'_j)))$

        Resolve_conflict(r'_i, r'_j):: Check_subsume(r'_i, r'_j)

    Else

        Resolve_conflict(r'_i, r'_j):: Priority_order(r'_i, r'_j)

    End If

End For

End Procedure

Procedure Check_subsume(r_x, r_y) /*A pair of homogeneous rules (r_x, r_y)*/

If $(\text{index}(r_x) > \text{index}(r_y))$ /* r_x overrides r_y */

    If $(\text{action}.r_x != \text{action}.r_y)$

        If $(\text{SIP}(r_x) \subseteq \text{SIP}(r_y))$

            Modify SIP(r_y) as r'_y: $<\text{SIP}(r_y)-\text{SIP}(r_x).>$

            Output: (r_x, r'_y)

        Else

            Delete r_y

            Output: r_x

        End If

    Else

        Delete r_y

        Output: r_x

    End If

Else   /*r_y overrides r_x*/

    If $(\text{action}.r_y != \text{action}.r_x)$

        If $(\text{SIP}(r_y) \subseteq \text{SIP}(r_x))$

            Modify SIP(r_x) as r'_x: $<\text{SIP}(r_x)-\text{SIP}(r_y).>$

            Output: (r'_x, r_y)

```
Else
        Delete r_x
        Output: r_y
    End If
Else
    Delete r_x
    Output: r_y
End If
End If
End Procedure
```

```
Procedure Priority_order(r_x,r_y)      /*A pair of heterogeneous rules (r_x,r_y)*/
If (r_x.service == r_y.service)         /* service=<protocol, port number>*/
    If (index(Server(r_x)) > index(Server(r_y)))
            Modify r_y as r'_y : Add conditions of r_x to r_y
            Output: (r_x, r'_y)
    Else
            Output: (r_x, r_y)
    End If
End If
End Procedure
```

The proposed conflict resolution process is illustrated with the example of a military network as follows by considering the heterogeneous rules of a military application:

- r_{15}: A soldier can telnet a battalion control server from on-field subnet.
- r_{16}: Telnet to a battalion control server must be done through an encrypted tunnel.

    Here, as r_{16} overrides r_{15} based on Priority order procedure, so, conditions of r_{16} is added to r_{15} and thereby r_{15} is modified as:

- r'_{15}: A soldier can telnet a battalion control server from on-field subnet through an encrypted tunnel.

Now, let us consider the following homogeneous rules.

- **r₁₇**: A commander can access the internet from any subnet.
- **r₁₈**: Employees cannot access internet from command center.

Here, as r_{18} overrides r_{17} based on Check subsume procedure, so, r_{17} is modified in terms of source IP (SIP) as follows:

- **r'₁₇**: A commander can access the internet from any subnet except command center.

Now, let us consider the following heterogeneous rules:

- **r₁₉**: Squadron leaders can run instant messaging through VPN with no limit on bandwidth.
- **r₂₀**: Soldiers can communicate via instant messaging from designated devices with bandwidth limited to 500 Mbps.

Here, if server of r_{20} has higher priority than server of r_{19}, then r_{19} is modified as follows:

- **r'₁₉**: Squadron leaders can run instant messaging through VPN with 500 Mbps bandwidth.

Our proposed Policy_Conflict_Resolve algorithm resolves conflicts between all policy rules from different servers. The policy repository is updated with this conflict-free policy rule set.

The following subsection presents the Policy_Consistency_Check function to control asynchronous update of policy repository due to changes in requirements.

3.4.3   POLICY_CONSISTENCY_CHECK: ENSURING CONSISTENCY BETWEEN POLICY REPOSITORY AND FLOW TABLES

SDN platform facilitates dynamic changes in high-level requirements in the application layer. The various types of changes are due to modification of existing policies, removal of policies, addition of new policies, installation, or removal of applications, update, or upgradation of software components, etc. The changes in the application layer must be reflected in the DP switches in the form of flow rules to ensure the correct flow of traffic across the network segments.

Our proposed Policy_Consistency_Check function checks the inconsistency between the application layer and the data layer. This problem is reduced to checking satisfiability between the existing flow rules in the SDN switch and the updated conflict-free policy rule set in the policy repository. It is triggered by any change in policy repository or/and the arrival of successive packets in SDN switches. The procedure of the proposed Policy_Consistency_Checkfunction is presented in Algorithm 3.3.

It is to be noted that the structure of the flow rules in the switches is: <Source IP, DIP, Next-hop, action, flow parameters>. For satisfiability checking, we model the policies and flow rules as Boolean clauses in conjunctive normal form (CNF). Then, we check the satisfiability of the following query:

$$F \Rightarrow P' \equiv (F \vee P') \wedge (F \vee P')$$

For the implementation of satisfiability checking, we used Zchaff SAT solver (Zchaff official documentation. [Online] Available at: https://www.princeton.edu/ ~chaff/ zchaff.html).

Algorithm 3.3: Policy_Consistency_Check

ProcedurePolicy_Consistency_Check

    If (changes in policy rules || arrival of packet)

        Run Policy_Conflict_Resolve(P): generate conflict-free policy rule set P'

        Extract flow rule set F from the respective switch

        Check Satisfiability F ⇒ P'

        If (SAT)

            return F   /*no change in flow rule set*/

        Else   /* UNSAT*/

            Run flow and routing function with P' to generate new flow rule set F'

        EndIf

    EndIf

EndProcedure

The proposed NFs: Trust_Verify, Policy_Conflict_Resolve, and Policy_Consistency_Check together enable secure and dynamic configuration of policies in DP switches, effectively achieving the functionality of the network.

3.5 SUMMARY

Software-Defined Network (SDN) has emerged as a common communication backbone for desired service provisioning on heterogeneous application domains. SDN facilitates efficient and seamless processing of traffic flows in the network by executing different network-control functions in a centralized controller. The execution of the NFs relies on the implementation of heterogeneous and complex policies by the network administrators in the organization. The controller generates appropriate flow rules for the DP switches based on these policies. Managing these complex and heterogeneous network policies in SDN is an important, but a challenging problem. In this chapter, we discussed various network policies and the policy management approaches that are widely used in the context of SDN. Then, we presented an effective policy management solution for SDN that ensures secure and efficient implementation of heterogeneous policy rules. These policy rules, in turn, drive the generation of flow rules in forwarding switches which guide the flow of traffic effectively in a secure channel across the network segments.

KEYWORDS

- **certificate authority**
- **certificate revocation lists**
- **conjunctive normal form**
- **denial of service**
- **distributed denial-of-service**
- **event-condition-action**
- **extensible markup language**
- **hierarchical flow tables**

REFERENCES

Bera, et al., (2011). A WLAN security management framework based on formal spatio-temporal RBAC model. *Journal of Security and Communication Networks, 4*(9), 981–993. Wiley.

Chadha, R., & Kant, L., (2008). *Policy-Driven Mobile Ad Hoc Network Management*. John Wiley & Sons, New Jersey.

Ferguson, et al., (2012). Hierarchical policies for software defined networks. In: *Proceedings of the first Workshop on Hot Topics in Software Defined Networks (HotSDN '12)* (pp. 37–42) ACM.

Han, W., Hu, H., & Ahn, G. J., (2014). LPM: Layered policy management for software-defined networks. *Data and Applications Security and Privacy XXVIII* (Vol. 8566, pp. 356–363). Lecture Notes in Computer Science, Springer Berlin Heidelberg.

Itzhak, et al., (2015). EnforSDN: Network policies enforcement with SDN. In: *2015 IFIP/IEEE International Symposium on Integrated Network Management (IM)* (pp. 80–88).

Kreutz, et al., (2015). Software-defined networking: A comprehensive survey. In: *Proceedings of the IEEE, 103*(1), 14–76.

Machado, et al., (2015). Policy authoring for software-defined networking management. In: *2015 IFIP/IEEE International Symposium on Integrated Network Management (IM)* (pp. 216–224).

Monsanto, et al., (2013). Composing software-defined networks. In: *Proceedings of the 10th USENIX Conference on Networked Systems Design and Implementation* (pp. 1–14). ACM.

Nicolae, P., (2015). Towards secure SDN policy management. In: *1st International Workshop on Cloud Security and Data Privacy by Design, Limassol, Cyprus* (pp. 1–5).

Nishtha, & Sood, M., (2014). Software defined network: Architectures. In: *Proceedings of 2014 International Conference on Parallel, Distributed and Grid Computing (PDGC)* (pp. 451–456).

OpenSSL Cryptography and SSL/TLS Toolkit, (2020). [Online], Available at: https://www.openssl.org/ (accessed on 16 December 2020).

Qazi, et al., (2013). SIMPLE-fying middlebox policy enforcement using SDN. In: *Proceedings of the ACM SIGCOMM 2013 Conference on SIGCOMM* (pp. 27–38). ACM.

Quentin, M., (2016). *An Introduction to SDN* [online]. Available at: https://qmonnet.github.io/whirl-offload/2016/07/08/introduction-to-sdn/ (accessed on 16 December 2020).

Sahoo, K. S., et al., (2019a). ESMLB: Efficient switch migration-based load balancing for multi-controller SDN in IoT. *IEEE Internet of Things Journal*.

Sahoo, K. S., et al., (2019b). Improving end-users utility in software-defined wide area network systems. *IEEE Transactions on Network and Service Management*.

Sahoo, K. S., et al., (2019c). Toward secure software-defined networks against distributed denial of service attack. *The Journal of Supercomputing*, 1–46.

Sanjai, N., & Ehab, A. S., (2010). *Formal Methods for Safe Configuration of Cyber Infrastructure* [online]. Available at: https:// www.sigsac.org/ccs/CCS2010/tutorial4.shtml (accessed on 16 December 2020).

Tripathy, et al., (2016). A novel secure and efficient policy management framework for software defined network. In: *Proceedings of 40th IEEE COMPSAC* (pp. 423–430).

Zchaff Official Documentation, (2004). [Online]. Available at: https://www.princeton.edu/~chaff/zchaff.html (accessed on 16 December 2020).

CHAPTER 4

Flow Table Scalability in Software-Defined Networking: A Brief Overview

ABINAS PANDA[1], ASHOK KUMAR TURUK[2], ALIVA PANDA[3],
TARINEE PRASAD SAHOO[1], ANKIT ARYAN[1], and
KSHIRA SAGAR SAHOO[3]

[1]*Department of Computer Science and Engineering,
National Institute of Technology, Rourkela–769008, Odisha, India,
E-mail: abinash.panda1987@gmail.com*

[2]*Cloud Computing Research Lab, Department of Computer Science
and Engineering, National Institute of Technology, Rourkela–769008,
Odisha, India, E-mail: akturuk@nitrkl.ac.in*

[3]*Department of Computer Science and Engineering, SRM University,
Amaravati, AP, 522502, India
E-mail: kshirasagar12@gmail.com (K. S. Sahoo)*

ABSTRACT

Software-defined networking is a new networking architecture that gives the idea for separation of the control plane (CP) from the data plane (DP) with respect to break the vendor lock-in and simplifies the network management. In order to communicate between the data link layer and controller, a southbound protocol which is popularly known as OpenFlow (OF), which forwards the packets based on flow as compared to traditional destinations based forwarding. With the increase in demand for the number of hosts and devices and ports, it becomes critical to accommodate all flows to provide scalability, as the flow is based on the fine-grain granularity of OF protocol.

This chapter provides all the issues related to scalability and its proposed approaches in a software-defined wired network. It discussed the challenges in the flow table and its management. Various solutions and taxonomy or classification in terms of solution approach and problem description such as dynamic flow table or static flow table management are discussed in this chapter. This chapter also provides useful insights and guidelines for designing scalable SDN-based data centers (DCs) for any sort of campus network.

4.1 INTRODUCTION

Software-defined networking (SDN) (Astuto et al., 2014) is a new form of network architecture, which is independent of the vendor-specific network hardware. In traditional networks, all the decisions of routing and packet forwarding is taken in switches itself, which results in relatively slow processing, and in doing so, they are not able to utilize the actual bandwidth of the network, not efficiently to be accurate. Apart from all that, the network admin needs to set up switches and routers individually. The primary feature of SDN is separating control components from other network devices. Therefore, it divides the network into two planes, namely, control plane (CP) and data plane (DP). The CP gives instructions regarding how a packet is to be moved around the network while the DP moves the packet through the network. As the controller manages and controls the network decisions and operates the network from a global view, the DP can utilize the bandwidth efficiently.

SDN requires a standard method for the CP to communicate with the DP. OpenFlow (OF) (Mckeown et al., 2008) is one of them. OF lets the controller or the network administrator remotely control the routing table. The routing table is called a Flow table. Every switch in the network has its Flow table. The flow table contains a set of rules to route the packets through the corresponding switch. The controller in the flow tables installs the rules. Each rule consists of three major fields; Match field, Action, and Counter. The match fields determine which packets are going to follow what rule, and once a match occurs, the action field comes into play. The OF device will apply the action in the Action field to the packet. If none of the rules match, then the controller is interrupted, and the controller determines the routing path for the recent packet and installs a rule in the flow table for the packet to follow accordingly. If the controller interruption time is much higher than the packet is being dropped. In the de-facto industry standard, the flow table is being maintained by ternary content addressable memory (TCAM) (Agrawal and Sherwood, 2008). TCAM is a high-speed memory that can match packet headers against stored entries in constant time. Although TCAM is highly efficient regarding the speed of searching and yet the network devices are equipped with as minimal TCAM size as humanly possible due to its costly hardware and power requirements.

To achieve scalability, various works have been proposed, which are combined to basically three types. Type I designs new hardware that will offer ample space in terms of memory with lower cost and less power consumption. Type II reduces the storage requirement by the process of composition and aggregation wild card rules, and Type III optimizes the flow table and makes efficient re-use of storage space so that the same flow table can support the maximum number of flow tables. Different ways to handle floatable scalability, but in general, we are going to discuss three different ways that are an aggregation of wildcard or traffic rule, caching of essential rules, and timeout based eviction of non-important rules.

With the growing need for fine-grain current traffic management, implementing the policies, and to the DP places, much pressure on the commodities switch memory. By reducing the rules, on-demand resources of the flow table can be used optimized. With the increasing versions of OF, the number of fields supported is increasing, which in turn makes the size of the matching fields higher. Due to the difficulty in predicting the arrival pattern of flow in advance leads to decrease the network throughput and makes it difficult for proactive Rule placement. So in order to reduce the number of flows in the network employing aggregation of the same set of rules.

In the rule caching system, the higher the cache hit ratio better is the system. Rules are overlapped with one another, which lead to a problem of rule dependency leading to the overflow of flow table by the same set of rules in order to maximize the utilization; we have to minimize the rule dependency problem employing catching the best rule which has a better-hit ratio. There are various ways to catch the rules, such as cover set and partition-based method. The number of methods has been proposed by this approaches to deal with rule dependency problem to catch all the dependent rules directly or indirectly various authors have proposed to convert the wildcard rules to a new set of non-overlapping rules in other cases author proposes decision tree to make the partition of full matting tree into non-overlapping bucket. It always checks the matrices as a catch hit ratio and catches the miss ratio. Uncover said the rule dependency is handled by creating a new rule of which will cover all the rules that have the same match field and priority with the descendant rules which connection has rule partition is under the rule dependency by partitioning a real significant rule into a subset of descendant rules both it got its advantages, but it is always time-consuming to catch the rules at a curtain call the catching module repeatedly one hour in new rule is being placed.

In order to who developed the close, which is completed open flow controller supported by timeout searches, ideal time out, and hard time out. Due to the uncertain behavior of the arrival rate of flows and duration of stay is pretty tricky. Thereby it is challenging to assign a strategic timeout to decide the removal of a table, which leads to the wastage of resources of the flow table. In order to use the flow table efficiently, we have to manage the timeout in such a way that it will lead to maximum utilization of the flow table along with minimization of the miss rate of flows.

4.1.1   PROPOSED CHAPTER

In this chapter, we are going to present brief details of how to handle the flow table in SDN and what are the various issues associated with handling of the flow table that leads to the scalability of the network:

- First of all, we are going to discuss what scalability is SDN in the data link layer;
- Different methods and solutions have proposed to achieve the scalability flow table;
- Finally, the future research direction is given for different aspects of flow table scalability.

4.1.2   CHAPTER ORGANIZATION

The rest of the chapter is organized as follows in Section 4.2, and we give the details of SDN, OF, and how OF table works. In Section 4.3, we describe the different flow table scalability issues related to open flow enabled SDN environment in Section 4.4 identification key research area for further exploration are, and Section 4.6 concludes this chapter.

4.2   BACKGROUND OF SDN

The possibility of a programmable system has been proposed as an approach to streamlining organizes assessments. Particularly, SDN is another systems administration model in which the CP is isolated from the information plane to empower increasingly mechanized provisioning and strategy based administration of system assets. Its focus on encouraging system, the board a long time before this engineering started to be utilized in information systems. Its enable secure stockpiling to programming designer and furthermore deal with the PC assets. Presently in SDN, the system gadgets are basic bundle sending gadgets (DP), which are customized by the open interface, e.g., OF, and the system knowledge is intelligently brought together in programming based (CP). SDN gives various advantages to both industry and foundation. It gives the focal administration, open and standard interface, and dynamic setup. The specialist organizations and the gathering of system administrators, merchants, have as of late assembled the open system establishment (ONF). SDN advanced by the business association and OF convention gives the interface between CP and the SDN switches (DP) (Figure 4.1).

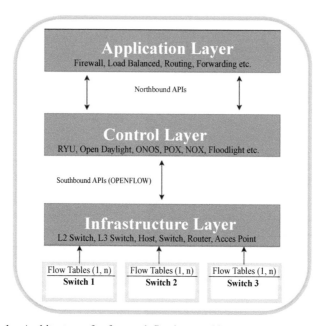

FIGURE 4.1   Architecture of software-defined networking.

4.2.1 LAYERS OF SDN

SDN layers are of three types namely:

1. Data link layer;
2. Control layer; and
3. Application layer.

4.2.1.1 DATA LINK LAYER

In SDN, the switches and the routers are connected by physically wired or wireless devices. Switch forwards the network packet in the network field by merely through the Flow table in a wired or wireless media, consisting of thousands of rules that have to be formulated. Rules of flow table have three fields: the action, the counter, and the patterns. The pattern field has the set of the header field values of the packets received. The switches have to be the search of its flow table. Counter will be increased by one if the switch finds a matching rule and the packet follows. In all other cases, the controller will be interrupted. The forwarding rules are generated by the controller and are placed in switches to minimize the interruption count.

4.2.1.2 CONTROL LAYER

SDN has to manage the control layer and the entire network layer through these network node implementations for the functionality of the SDN controller (SDN-C), and it is stressful for the physical network devices with some specific software. The SDN-C has to communicate through the switches from standard southbound API interfaces, e.g., OpenFlow and have to have a complete overview of the full network topology at the data-forwarding layer, i.e., links, hubs, and switches. The data forwarding that takes place in the data layer depends on the instructions of the controller. Open flow has to be designed, so a replacement has to be done if a potential failure takes place. Floodlight and Open Daylight have to improve the scalability and availability of the resources in the layered architecture of SDN. The single controller has to be responsible for controlling all the switches in the network and the router in packet forwarding. East-west bound APIs can be used by the controller to communicate with other controllers if required in any way.

4.2.1.3 APPLICATION LAYER

Through the Application layer the network operators have to utilize the rapid packet utilization. Network virtualization (NV), topologies monitoring traffic discovery security and load balancing have to be a different part of SDN. Northbound APIs such as REST API are used to achieve the communication between the application and control layers. The network's physical resources such as routers, switches have to provide the abstraction from application layers, which means the data paths have to be changed centrally in the SDN-C so that it does not have to be configured by the switches individually.

4.2.1.4 ADVANTAGES AND LIMITATION OF SDN

4.2.1.4.1 Benefits of SDN

- SDN are traffic programmability and it offers the agility, flexibility, and creates a policy-driven network supervision implementing network automation.
- SDN can control the data traffic and it has a ability to direct and automate the data traffic.
- SDN permit to access all the component of network via the visibility plane and it also supports the management of physical and virtual switches from a single centralized controller.
- SDN gives a centralized view of the entire network which makes it easier to streamline.
- Enterprise management and provisioning.

4.2.1.4.2 Limitation of SDN

- Staff should be trained;
- SDN is also a vulnerable;
- The New tools should to be procured and all have to be trained to use it;
- Single point failure in case of centralized management of the controller.

4.2.1.5   OPENFLOW (OF) PROTOCOL

OF convention gives a correspondence between an SDN-C (CP) and an SDN switch (information plane). The SDN-C gathers the data by OF burrow which additionally gives the order guidelines to the switch. OF is a standard multivendor convention that is characterized by the Open Networking Foundation (ONF) to empower SDN in systems administration gear. The OF convention gives a correspondence between an OF controller and an OF switch. OF empowers the switches to handle where to send the information parcel, and it likewise recognizes and examines bundles from an entrance port dependent on various parcel header fields (Pfaff et al., 2012). Two kinds of OF switch stores the sending rule. The first is the equipment based business switch, which usually utilizes TCAMs and a restrictive working framework to actualize the stream table and the OF convention. The subsequent one is the product based switch that utilizations UNIX/Linux frameworks to actualize the OF switch capacities. Two stream tables are overseen in the product based OF switch.

4.2.1.6   FLOW TABLE AND ITS OPERATIONS

4.2.1.6.1   Flow Table and Its Components

An OF switch contains several flow tables of fixed size. To store the forwarding rules in the flow table, which consists of flow entries, as shown in Table 4.1.

TABLE 4.1   Different Attributes of a Flow Table

Match Fields	Priority	Counter	Instruction	Timeout	Cookie

- **Match Fields:** To match against packets. These consist of ingress port, packet headers and optionally other pipeline fields such as metadata specified by a previous table.
- **Priority:** Matching precedence of the flow entry.
- **Counters:** Updated when packets are matched.

The priority and match fields are to identify the flow table entry: here, both priority and match fields are used for identifying the different flow table entries in a specific flow table. If all the fields of flow entry are wildcards and has the priority is equally to 0 that means this is the table-miss flow entry. The instruction of a flow entry may consider an action to be implemented on the packet in the pipeline. To rewrite some header field by specifying the action field. The different flow tables of the same switch cannot support the same subset and each flow table entry cannot support every set-field or action defined by this specification.

The rule is a basic entity of a flow table under which is any packet enters into a flow table should match rule and forward the packet as per the instructions. Therefore, rules can be stored in a table according to the OF versions and corresponding fields where different methods fields are supporting different types of matching. There are four types of matching of flow field attributes:

- Exact match (EM);
- Prefix match (PM);
- Range match (PM); and
- Wildcard match (WM).

All the matching is supported by the hardware, whereas software-based matching supports all the matching by converting WM and RM to PM. TCAM is also not able to support RM, but it can convert RM to PM. In Table 4.2, it is showing off an example of all types of matches that are supported by TCAM and corresponding rule, which is present. In general, the network consists of several switches connected. It is a particular port. Which operates by taking the packet, observing the packets header field that is source IP address, destination IP (DIP) address, source ports, destination port, and type of preliminary protocol match those fields against a pattern stored in the switch flow table setting in the ticket. According to the predicate, excel has been performed like for the packet drop the packet forwarded to some other port, etc. Generally, the rule is being formed by taking the predicate of the match field and action together. In Exact rule is each rule is in the form of {0,1}, whereas range rule in the form of [100, 110] to cover [4, 6]. However in case of prefix rule {01*} indicate a match of 010 and 011 and in wildcard match {0*1} indicate {001,010}.

In Table 4.2, it is showing an example of a flow table with different types of match fields with different support of match field corresponds to different actions. Various rules have a dependency on one of the other rules by a combination of matching priority and action. Therefore, to reduce this size of the flow table, we have to have a better mechanism on

TABLE 4.2 Example of Different Rules in a Flow Table with the Corresponding Action

RID	Ingr.	Meta-data	Eth_source	Eth_destination	Eth_type	VID	Vprty	MPLS_lbl	MPLS_tfc	SA	DA	Ptrl	ToS	SP	DP	Action
R0	5	*	0:13	0:06	0 × 0800	*	5	0	*	001*	*	TCP	0	*	*	Action 0
R1	*	*	0:07	00:FF	*	100	7	16000	0	00*	1011*	UDP	*	*	*	Action 1
R2	*	*	*	0:00	0 × 8100	4095	7	*	*	1*	1011*	*	*	100–005	5000–5005	Action 0
R3	1	*	00:FF	*	*	4095	*	*	*	1*	1*	*	0	123–1024	5010–5600	Action 2

* *indicates wildcard.*

how to detect the dependency e r conflict in the flow table and manage them. There are various types of dependencies that correspond to rule as a direct dependency and indirect dependency.

4.2.1.6.2   Matching Fields and Their Matching Type

Here we have presented different matching fields, size of the matching fields, description of the magic fields and matching it supports in TCAM in hardware in OF version 1.3 (Table 4.3).

TABLE 4.3   Description of Different Matching Fields and Their Matching Type Correspond to Openflow v1.3

Field_name	Matching Type
ingress_port	Exact match
ingress_phy_port	Prefix Match
metadata	Range match
ethernet_destination	Wildcard match
ethernet_source	Exact match
ethernet_type	Range match
vlan_vid	Prefix
vlan_pcp	Wildcard match
ip_dscp	Exact match
ip_ecn	Exact match
ip_protocol	Exact match
ipv4_source	Prefix Match
ipv4_dest	Prefix Match
tcp_source	Range match
tcp_destination	Range match
udp_source	Range match
udp_destination	Range match
sctp_source	Range match
sctp_destination	Range match
icmpv4_type	Range match
icmpv4_code	Wildcard match
arp_op	Wildcard match

TABLE 4.3   *(Continued)*

Field_name	Matching Type
arp_spa	Prefix match
arp_tpa	Prefix match
arp_sha	Exact match
arp_tha	Exact match
ipv6_source	Prefix match
ipv6_destination	Prefix match
ipv6_flabel	Prefix match
icmpv6_type	Wildcard match
icmpv6_code	Wildcard match
ipv6_nd_target	Exact match
ipv6_nd_sll	Wildcard match
ipv6_nd_tll	Wildcard match
mpls_label	Wildcard match
mpls_tc	Wildcard match at
mpls_bos	Wildcard match
pbb_isid	Wildcard match
tunnel_id	–
ipv6_exthdr	Wildcard match
pbb_uca	Wildcard match
tcp_flags	Wildcard match
actset_output	Wildcard match

4.2.1.6.3   *Storage of Flow Table*

- OpenFlow switch faces two main design challenges as it stores different no of the rule due to the increase in the number of match fields in a different version as the volume of flows recognizable by the switch explodes. Theoretically, 2^{356} flows are possible at any instance of time (356 bits are required in OpenFlow 1.3). Network parameters such as action, host, and flows have a major role to play in the determination of actual number of flow entries. The rational number is around 1 M, which seems to be quite high compared to the conventional switch (Agrawal and Sherwood, 2008).

- The operations taking place in OF switches are of quite different nature. The number of flows in conventional switches is lesser and majority of them are just lookups. The number of flows is much higher in OF as a result of which larger number of entries is required to be stored. Therefore, operations such as writes, invalidation, and update will definitely become prominent apart from just lookups (Curtis et al., 2011).
- Flow table can be stored in hardware such as TCAM, static random-access memory (SRAM), Software switches. Nevertheless, due to its nature is best suitable in TCAM due to its wildcard support, whereas, in software, switches can Store flow tables, to do that it has to change the data structure which can handle wildcard support, but it cannot provide the lookup and matching speed compare two in can build hardware (McGeer and Yalagandula, 2009).
- **TCAM (Hardware):** TCAM represents TCAM, which can suit the third express that is any cost. It makes TCAM an essential issue of Cisco Layer three switches and current switches has given that they can spare their directing table inside the TCAMs, allowing for quick queries, which is remarkably higher than steering tables put away in normal RAM. TCAM is a specific CAM intended for quick work area queries. TCAM manages three outcomes: zero, 1, and "do now not give it a second thought." TCAM is the most crucial use for building tables for taking a gander at the most extended fits, which incorporate IP directing tables composed by utilizing IP prefixes. The TCAM table shops ACL, QoS, and various insights typically identified with upper-layer handling. Because of utilizing TCAM, utilizing ACLs does not influence the exhibition of the switch. Most extreme switches have more than one TCAMs so both inbound and outbound insurance, notwithstanding QoS ACLs, might be assessed simultaneously or absolutely in parallel with a Layer 2 or Layer 3 sending choice. Problems associated with TCAM based flow table.
- First, TCAM chips have restricted limit. The broadest accessible TCAM chip has a limit of 72 megabits (Mb), while 2 Mb and 1 Mb chips are the most mainstream, and all out no of the standard can be put away arranged by 4 K as in Table 4.4.
- Second, TCAM chips use a great deal of force due to their parallel looking. The power ate up by a TCAM chip is about 1.85 Watts per

TABLE 4.4 Problems Associated with TCAM Based Flow Table

OpenFlow Version	Match Fields (no)	Size (bits)	TCAM Size(1 Mbit/2 Mbit)	No of Flow		Round up a Number of Flows	
1	10	248	1048576	2097152	4228.129032	8456.258065	4228	8456
1	12	264	1048576	2097152	3971.878788	7943.757576	3972	7944
1.1	15	320	1048576	2097152	3276.8	6553.6	3277	6554
1.2	36	603	1048576	2097152	1738.932007	3477.864013	1739	3478
1.3	40	701	1048576	2097152	1495.828816	2991.657632	1496	2992
1.4	41	709	1048576	2097152	1478.950635	2957.901269	1479	2958
1.5	44	773	1048576	2097152	1356.50194	2713.003881	1357	2713

megabit (Mb) (Agrawal and Sherwood, 2008), which is roughly on various occasions greater than an also estimated SRAM chip.

- Third, the speed and power adequacy of each memory get to reduces out and out as TCAM chip limit augments considering the way that the whole and significance of equipment expected to perform both the parallel chase and the need encoding addition basically as TCAM chip limit increases. For example, considering the point-by-point TCAM control model in, a lone request on a 72-megabit (Mb) TCAM chip, the greatest open, takes 1047.9 Nano joules (nj) and 17 nanoseconds (ns), however a comparative interest on a 1 Mb TCAM chip takes 34.5 nj and 1.8 ns. Finally, upgrading the TCAM-based stream table likewise has financial motivating forces. Huge TCAM chips are expensive, frequently costing more than organize processors. In spite of the fact that the restricted market size may add to TCAMs significant expense, the fundamental explanation is that TCAM chips have a monstrous bite the dust territory. A TCAM chip involves multiple times load up space than an identical limit SRAM chip.

4.3   FLOW TABLE SCALABILITY ISSUES AND DIFFERENT SOLUTION APPROACHES

As in Figure 4.2, it is given taxonomy of floatable scalability in terms of hardware flow table and software flow table. In hardware and software tables, there are mainly three ways to handle it. First, catching the type of rule from the flow table depends on rule dependency, second effectively aggregate wildcard rules to minimize the number of rules in the flow table, and finally, fiction of non-important rule based on timeout value of that rule.

4.3.1   FLOW TABLE AGGREGATION

Table 4.5 showing a example of rule aggregation of having 7 rule and 7 matching rule M1 {0111}, M2 {1111}, M3 {*101}, M4 {*011}, M5 {1*0*}, M6 {1*1*}, M7 {****} with 4 actions which will aggregate to form 3 match rules (Table 4.6).

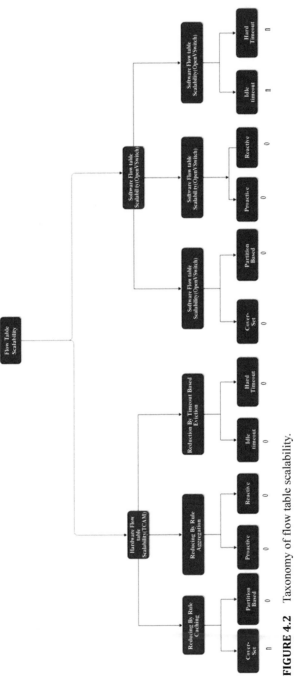

FIGURE 4.2 Taxonomy of flow table scalability.

TABLE 4.5 Example of Rule Table Before Aggregation

Rule-ID	Match	Action
R1	M1	Forward 1
R2	M2	Forward 1
R3	M3	Forward 2
R4	M4	Forward 1
R5	M5	Forward 3
R6	M6	Forward 3
R7	M7	Drop

TABLE 4.6 Example of Rule Table After Aggregation

Rule-ID	Match	Action
R1	M3	Forward 1
R2	M8(M2 + M6)	Forward 2
R3	M9(M5 + M2 + M6)	Forward 3
R4	M7	Drop

Wang and Youn (2019) deal with the problem of Flow Table optimization. The chapter is focused on reducing the number of flow entries. The author first explains how the introduction of multiple flow table (MFT) with OF version 1.3 brought a change in the working of TCAM. Nevertheless, at the same time brings the drawbacks of working with MFT. They say that the pipeline mechanism, which is followed to deal with MFT, causes time overhead, and keeping MFT caused memory overhead. To deal with all this, he proposes a method of entry based rule reduction and aggregation and a method to select popular entries. He uses the technique of pruning to get rid of redundant entries and uses the Quine McCuskey algorithm to aggregate the entries obtained after removing redundant entries. This sequence of reduction technique is applied periodically. After this aggregation of entries is done the author proposes to use Hidden Markovnikov Model from ML to select popular entries from all those entries present so as to improve the flow table entries further. The final flow entries which are obtained after doing this entire are stored in a different table, which the author calls Agg-ExTable. The author shows the results depicting a 45% saving of space of MFT and an efficient decrease in the flow processing time compared to the existing scheme.

Iot, Saha, Misra, and Bera (2018) proposed a key-based technique to solve the flow table overflow problem, minimizing the impact on the quality of service (QoS) internet of things (IoT) traffic simultaneously. Presents stick method which will take the best possible path in order to minimize the number of policy in the network find satisfying the curious constants and it produces a gain of 33% in average delay and 12% packet drop where is throughput is being improved by 20% compared to all other existing schemes — using the aggregation of rules in terms of flow path which satisfies equality of service parameter concerning a particular path having a more significant impact on the reduction of rules compared to normal reaction due to overflowing rules.

Zhang et al. (2017) proposed a method that considers the local route while there is a value in the link congestion and all the flows are being dynamically aggregated to reduce the number of operations between switch and controller. It will solve the flow table overflow problem by minimizing the number of rules required to communicate between devices. Here to the installation and whenever a link got congested or fails to switch off automatically invokes that path without invoking the controller. It will address link your problem between libraries notes after which flows are being aggregated to make a big flow without increasing the number of flow entries.

Kosugiyama et al. (2017) addresses the problem of unlimited flow table entries and proposes day fuel level routing, which executes the routing mechanism with lower number of control messages. Using mixed Int programming method solve to assign a standard two different floors having aggregated at different intermediate switches by considering the network utilization and throughput as it is tough to computer using static programming, so it also provides a heuristic approach to solve this problem in an efficient method to achieve reduction in number of rules in OF enabled SDN network and link congestion. However, how to aggregate some dependent rules in the entire network, which is still a challenging task.

Luo, Yu, and Li (2015) propose both online, and offline approaches to aggregate flow table in SDN by aggregation o non-prefix rule to solve the problem occur due to inconsistency in data and CP reachability failures loops and leakage. It consists of two steps by splitting or partition the rules and then apply the optimal method to aggregate search rules it uses public data set and real network scenario experiments which performs better in terms of both efficiency and effectiveness compared to the previous approaches and produces a better compression ratio with less time in computing. It doesn't require any modification in hardware or OF protocol to implement and it is compared with all the state of art techniques and provide an improvement of 48% in terms of average aggregation ratio and 200 times faster and in terms of efficiency (Table 4.7).

4.3.1.1 FLOW RULE CACHING

Li and Wang (2019) implemented both cover-set and rule-partition approaches to solve the problem of TCAM memory shortage. They proposed two different algorithms one is called online and the other one offline. In the Offline algorithm, they used a proactive approach for rule installation in TCAM while in an online algorithm, they used a reactive approach. The rule-partition method is implemented in an online algorithm, and the cover-set approach is implemented in an offline algorithm. They almost implemented everything, but it cost them a lot of computational and design complexity in doing so.

Li et al. (2018) proposed COnflict RAzor (CORA) for solving conflicts among rules in the flow table. The basic idea is to migrate the different rules between switches in the network. Note that, the rules can only be moved around if the semantics correctness holds. This migrating policy technique does reduce the number of overlaps among rules, but it does not resolve the conflicts between routing policies.

Yan, Xu, Xing, Xi, and Chao (2014) proposed a novel approach for rule caching called CAching in Buckets (CAB). The basic idea of CAB is to cache all the related rules together (just like a bucket). Note that a rule can belong to one or more buckets. A bucket is an atomic unit in this algorithm. All the rules in a bucket are cached together to ensure semantic correctness. There are several problems with this approach, but the main problem is that it takes a lot of TCAM entries to cache buckets and moreover, in this algorithm, a reactive approach is used, so for an enormous rule set even after dividing the rules into buckets it takes a lot of time searching for the appropriate bucket in RAM.

Li and Xie (2017) proposed a cache reduction architecture for flow tables (CRAFT). CRAFT is implemented as a two-stage rule caching structure as two tables (just saying). The first stage is called the Rule table and the second stage is called the child. The Rule table is used for caching

TABLE 4.7 Summary of Flow Aggregation Related to the Scalability of the Flow Table

Year	Technique Used	Objectives	Type of Aggregation	Limitation	References
2019	QM algorithm, HMM	To achieve better utilization of flow tables.	Entry Aggregation and Early Match	Only popular entries are taken into consideration. The priority of entry has no role here.	Wang and Youn (2019)
2018	The key-based mechanism, Best-fit heuristic	To address the problems related to the flow table in SDN.	QoS-aware adaptive flow-rule aggregation	A low rate of IoT traffic is considered. Traditional internet traffic will affect the QoS.	Iot et al. (2018)
2017	Heuristic algorithm and MIP	To reduce the number of flow entries without modifying forwarding semantics	Flow aggregation.	Aggregately flows are prepared in advance. No method to examine how to determine aggregately flow sets.	Yoshioka, Hirata, and Yamamoto (2018)
2017	Local Fast Reroute	To deal with a situation of a link failure in the SDN network.	Flow aggregation	This method is not very useful in a network such as a tree model where the route of flows can be uniquely determined.	Zhang et al. (2017)
2017	Heuristic algorithm	—	Flow aggregation	The aggregation results in a coarser traffic statistics	Kosugiyama et al. (2017)
2015	Optimal routing table constructor (ORTC), BST, Bit merging	—	FFTA (fast flow table aggregation) and iFFTA (improved-FFTA)	The design of an orchestrated system where the controller is able to infer the detailed statistics of original rules from the aggregated statistics, is	Luo et al. (2015)
2014	Optimal routing table constructor (ORTC), BST, Bit merging	—	FFTA (fast flow table aggregation) and iFFTA (improved-FFTA)	The aggregation results in a coarser traffic statistics.	Luo, Yu, and Li (2014)

a subset of rules, and the children table is used for caching the rules that overlap with the rules in the rules table to keep the semantic correctness of the packets. This is a perfectly reasonable approach; the only thing is that it fails while handling longer dependency chains.

Katta, Alipourfard, Rexford, and Walker (2016) proposed a CacheFlow technique for rule caching. The basic idea is the same as CRAFT (Li and Xie, 2017); only they proposed a way to avoid the long chain of dependencies by splicing technique. In splicing, they replace a large number of unpopular rules by a few new rules, which save a lot of TCAM space even while caching long dependencies. Nevertheless, the problem is that it causes pseudo-hitting (Table 4.8).

From the above table, we concluded that there are several techniques to deal with rule dependencies, and they can be broadly divided into two categories namely rule-partition and cover-set. Rule-partition deals with dependencies in the reactive approach of rule installation, and cover-set deals with a proactive approach. Seeing the results claimed by the authors, a new approach with taking cover-set and rule partition both into consideration and setting rules timeout along with reducing the conflicts across the network would produce a considerably high hit-rate sparing some computational overhead.

4.3.1.2   FLOW RULE EVICTION

4.3.1.2.1   Timeout Based Eviction

In order to explore explain the distribution of low duration and flow packet interatrial time have plotted a graph of flow duration with relative distribution function and packet inter-arrival time with cumulative distribution function and explain why you hear favoring dynamic timeout instead of static timeout where we have taken three real traffic traces UNIV1 (Kannan and Banerjee, n.d.), UNIV2 and MAWI (Challa, Lee, and Choo, 2016) UNIV1 and UNIV2 two data sets are from the campus data center (DC) running a variety of applications and protocol whereas MAWI is a transitional link between Japan and the USA and the data set is publicly available in working group of WIDE Project (Li et al., 2019):

1. **Flow Duration:** Zhang, Wang, Xu, Lin, and Yu (2015) shows that the distribution of lower duration differs among different traces in

TABLE 4.8 Summary of Flow Caching Related to the Scalability of the Flow Table

Name	Technique	Objective	Shortcomings	References
CuCa	Both Rule-partition and Cover-set	Maximizing hit rate of the network	High Computational and design complexity	Li and Wang (2019)
CORA	Migrating Policies	Minimization of the number of conflicts across the network	The conflict between two routing policies are not resolvable	Li et al. (2018)
CRAFT	Two table architecture to cache dependent rules	Reducing the chances of installing multiple overlapped rules into the flow table	Poor performance at resolving long dependency chains	Li and Xie (2017)
CacheFlow	Splicing technique to break long-chain dependencies	Installing the simplified rules in the flow table and removing as many unpopular rules as possible	Cover-set rules cause pseudo hitting	Katta et al. (2016)
CAB	Caching all associated rules together as in a bucket	Maximizing the hit rate of the network	Costs lots of TCAM entries to cache buckets	Yan et al. (2014)

univ1 most flows are short-lived whereas in Univ2 most flows are long live in Univ1 60% of the flows are taking less than a hundred milliseconds, and more than 80% of the floors are taking less than 1 second to complete the floor and there are more than 50% of bust transmission which carries fewer than 10 packets however in unit 2 there are more than 20 flows 20% of flows lasted for more than 10 seconds, and more than 10% of the floors lasted for 35 seconds(Benson, Akella, and Maltz, n.d.) Packet Inter-arrival time.

Zarek (n.d.) shows the distribution of packet inter-arrival time over some time, and it shows that most of the short flow duration, just like 90% of the flows are taking less than 1 seconds, and more than 80% of the time packets are taking less than. It shows the most packet of a Floor tends to arrive for a short period.

From the above observation, we can draw a conclusion that is static Timeout values will harm flow management due to timeout very easy and of low duration and packet, inter-arrival time in order to determine an optimal Timeout value in advance is challenging.

Allocating last time what value will influence limited fluid table size where is small timeout will impact the flow table heat rate instead of that if you can predict whether a flow is a busty or extended leave We will allocate different Timeout values allowing to the flows and discover the limit of flow table capacity to achieve a balance between the table hit rate and overflowed number. It seems the matches with earlier timeouts are likely coincidental (Zarek, n.d.). DevoFlow (Curtis et al., 2011) used a 10-second timeout and was designed for high-performance DC networks. However, UNIV, a DC network, has a timeout of 5 seconds, instead of DevoFlow's 10 seconds. Cumulative UNIV's timeout from 5 to 10 seconds mark would cut the miss rate by 0.24% but would add the overhead of collective table size by 34% (Table 4.9).

In this chapter, PoTia (Wang, Zhou, and Chen, 2018) author proposed popularity and timeout based flow table management to protect the controller from the harm of flooding attack. When the arrival of the packet to the controller exceeds the marked threshold, then a proactive policy is going to be applied in the switches to provide the popular destination addresses service. Here, miti-gate the low priority by sending timeout value while the packet intercourse has been made, and it takes into account to determine the flow type such as malicious or normal based on timeout value it considered only hard time what value here it achieves the detection rate of 99.9% false alarm rate off 0.04%.

TABLE 4.9	Description of Different Default Timeout for Different Controller

Controller	Idle Timeout (s) (0 Through 65,535)	Hard Timeout (s) (0 Through 65,535)
OpenDaylight (Ambient, 2005)	0	0
Floodlight	5	0
POX (Software-defined network (SDN) experiment using Mininet and POX Controller, n.d.)	10	30
Ryu (Zhang et al., 2015)	0	0
Beacon (Erickson, 2013)	5	0

In HQ-timer (Li et al., 2019) highlights the rule dependency problem due to wildcard behavior of including rules and improper timeout mechanisms for safe and adaptable SDM. Hear proposes a hybrid Timeout mechanism under Q learning-based adaptation logic, which solves this problem effectively and provides flexibility to the network, and the result shows that it provides better plane efficiency and stability compared to other approaches. It uses two type of datasets such as class bench and syn dataset (Li et al., 2019).

In the chapter, the solution is based on a two-step first (Shirali-Shahreza and Ganjali, 2018). It faster the eviction of the present rule as soon as possible and the second is delaying the installation of non-TCP rules. By doing this, it has accomplished much production in flow table Occupancy by considering the TCP-FIN in RST header to predict a TCP flow. Objectives to minimize the flow table Occupancy to deal with the flu table size limitations for that we need to decide how to minimize the average median and maximum floatable Occupancy and from the observation author find it out that average table Occupancy is the objective write function to optimize because it provides a better experimental result on different Real-world data sets behave in other cases. It reduces floatable Occupancy between 16 to 62% in various networks with less than 1.5 in hit ratio.

Wang, Li, Wang, Sinnott, and Jiang (2017) show how a larger Timeout is going to West the switch memory while assorted Timeout leading causes multiple packet in request to the controller, which will eventually leads to the controller overhead in software-defined network to overcome this particular challenges author proposes a hybrid mechanism to handle rule dependency flexibility and assign it idle Timeout value to the table MS flows and no time out to the dependent rule which will eventually e evict proactively. Moreover, the result shows that it significantly reduces the number of table misses when the heart timeout reaches above 4 seconds. Number of table misses will be optimal in the case of 123 2nd; however, when the hard timeout increases from 3 to 4 seconds, the table misses increases significantly.

The TF-idle timeout considers the packet arrival on the ideal time out of the flow (Lu, Deng, and Shi, 2017). Here in order to increase the utilization of the flow table and thus enhance the scalability of SDN, it proposes dynamically idle timeout based on the slow entry of the real-time network traffic in the software-defined DC network. No Entry missing number and dropping number for all types of the network consists of small to a large number of the host are presented and scenario the number of the host are small it performs better compare two large number of the host. However, it does not consider in real-world other factors such as flow rate and rate to type may affect the other idle timeout conditions.

In this chapter, Zhang et al. (2015) suggest how to maximize the flow table by setting adaptive Timeout value using combining the traffic characteristic of flue types and floatable utilization ratio to decide the time out of each entry. It shows how static timeout works poorly on the floor table size is very small in terms of table MissNumber and block packet number. It gives it is not flexible and efficient to set the dynamic timeout for a flow equals its duration when the size is small, when the size is sufficient high idle timeout and 60-second hard timeout still causes large table miss and block packets compared to 10 seconds of ideal time out and heart time out of 5 seconds. It performs better compared to other approaches where statically taken idle-timeout from 52nd to 60 seconds and hard timeout starting from 5 seconds to 60 seconds. It significantly reduced the table miss number and blocked packet number by a percentage of 18%.

Zhu, Fan, Luo, and Jin (2015) proposes an intelligent timeout minister which will assign a proper time out according to the flow characteristics and conduct a feedback control fix the maximum timeout according to the floatable utilization to avoid overflow of the flow table it utilizes floatable loads as a feedback control to maximize the Timeout value cash is used to record the afflicted flow to predict the real timeout values which will event feedback to the system to decide the maximum Timeout value along with the flow table occupation to prevent flow table overflow this method is suitable for handling lighter traffic where it performs better compared to a more substantial traffic where it frequently occurring slow table overflow.

Zhang, Lin, Xu, and Wang (2014) proposes adaptive hard Timeout management to improve the flow table utilization by optimizing the hard time out of the flow entries in the flow table scalability in this model will act as a Queen system and derive a closed-form formulas for packet arrival and eviction of the flow table performs better in both the scenarios where trafficker light that leads 20 blocking power probability with a truncated x of 20 seconds of Ideal hard timeout which will make a blocking probability of 21. Person, in case of massive traffic scenario probability, is higher, so we have fusion small Timeout value to decrease the load of the controller.

Xiao et al. (2017) proposed the mechanism to controller proactively deletes the rule which is going to be deleted with the shorter interval of time. In this method, author applied machine learning techniques to determine which flows to be removed based on flow characteristics searches inter-arrival of the packet the duration of the packet and the lifetime of the packet. Based on the historical data, weedicides and assign a proper time out for this entry to be evicted, which will lead to a better flow table availability e that makes the higher utilization of flow table by making 23% lesser capacity MS compared to random and FIFO deletion process policy.

2. **Why Idle Timeout:** Distribution of packet inter-arrival time is non-uniform which leads to a proper idle timeout rather than the hard timeout. As the packet arrives at a random interval, a smaller timeout value can be good. However, a setting of a small idle timeout can lead to more frequent usage of controller overhead whereas significant value can lead to more wastage of space due to longer waiting time for eviction or deletion. In case of a hard

timeout, the rule will evict or delete irrespective of packet matching or not. Accordingly, the controller will suffer from frequent control messages. Our objective is to keep the rule active during the lifetime of the flow and so, idle timeout is a better choice for randomization instead of hard timeout (Table 4.10).

4.4 A SOFTWARE APPROACH TO SEE AND EXPERIMENT ON FLOW TABLE SCALABILITY

4.4.1 CONTROLLER USED

Open source controller and proprietary controller present in the software-defined network to simulate the network environment search POX (Shalimov, Zuikov, Zimarina, Pashkov, and Smeliansky, 2013), RYU (Asadollahi, Goswami, and Sameer, 2018), Beacon (Erickson, 2013), floodlight (Medved, Varga, Tkacik, and Gray, 2014), OpenDaylight (ODL). Different proposed and simulated their work okay in different controller, however open source controller most widely used compared to preparatory controller.

4.4.2 SIMULATOR USED

Various researchers have used different simulators and emulators, such as Mininet (2014), Estinet (Wang, Chou, and Yang, 2013), NS-3 (ns-3 Consortium, 2014), and Omnet++ (Varga, 2010). However, maximum people have used mininet due to testing ability in simulated as well as hardware environment. It provides flexibility to write your code and deploy it in a real-world environment.

4.4.3 OPENFLOW (OF) VERSION AND ITS IMPORTANCE

Due to an increase in the requirement to support all the network functionality, OF is making excellent grain policy with many changes in support of various researches. Due to this changing pattern, it is challenging to focus on a particular version and its deployment in specific hardware. Therefore, they are always much scope for improvement in OF protocol regarding the scalable flow table.

TABLE 4.10 Summary Table of Timeout Based Flow Table Eviction Based

Objective	Method Used	Limitation	References
To improve the hit ratio and decrease the flow overflow number	idle-timeout + Q learning	Unable to handle vast scale network due to a minor increase in hit ratio	Li et al. (2019)
reducing the number of packet-in events	flow-based timeout management	Not support idle and hard timeout	Zhu et al. (2015)
To reduce the long-term control plane overhead introduced between the controller and the switches	reinforcement learning (RL) algorithms and Bloom Filter	Challenging in a real-world scenario	Mu (2017)
Assign the timeout for the new coming flows to change their survival probability	Idle timeout	due to Less sampling period scalability is not supported	Liu, Tang, Yuan, Ran, and Hu (2017)
Improve the Flow Table utilization ratio to design an adaptive timeout method.	idle timeout	Does not consider in a real-world scenario	Zhang et al. (2015)
reduces average flow table occupancy	expedite the eviction of installed rules using an idle timeout and to delay rule installation for non-TCP flow	Difficult in handling different types of the packet other than TCP	Shirali-Shahreza and Ganjali (2018)
To improve the Flow Table utilization.	hard timeout	Does Not consider idle timeout which leads to wastage of resource	Zhang et al. (2014)
reduces the number of table misses and the flow table occupation	hard timeout	Increases the controller to switch overhead	Wang et al. (2017)
low table management to protect the controller from a flooding attack	popular flow table and hard timeout	Difficult in real-world scenario	Wang et al. (2018)
To reduce flow entry missing number and flow dropping number	idle timeout	Does not consider the rate of flow and flow type	Lu et al. (2017)

4.5   RESEARCH TRENDS IN FLOW TABLES SCALABILITY IN SDN

4.5.1   *RESEARCH SCOPE TOWARDS RULE CACHE MANAGEMENT*

There are several techniques to deal with rule dependencies, and they can be basically divided into two categories namely rule-partition and cover-set. Rule-partition deals with dependencies in the Reactive approach of rule installation, and cover-set deals with a proactive approach. Seeing the results claimed by the authors, a new approach with taking cover-set and rule partition both into consideration and setting rules timeout and reducing the conflicts across the network as possible would produce a considerably high hit-rate with the cost of some computational overhead. In the future, research can be done on achieving similar results with minimal computational and design overhead.

4.5.2   *RESEARCH SCOPE TOWARDS RULE AGGREGATION MANAGEMENT*

Rule aggregation has gained much attention from industry and academia in terms of providing the solution for a scalable flow table. However, there is much scope for improvement in aggregating or minimizing the number of prefix rules in both reactive as well as a proactive approach. There are various ways to improve searches aggregating the rules in different flow table having a common dependency, aggregating the wildcard rules before it comes to the flu table by analyzing the flow pattern, efficiently detect the malicious flow to make it wildcard, and robust system to handle real-time manner rule aggregation.

4.5.3   *RESEARCH SCOPE TOWARDS TIMEOUT MANAGEMENT*

The timeout can be set proactively or reactively weather controller to decide the lifetime of a flow. Well, it is always a problem to decide the optimal time out (hard timeout, ideal time out). Problem with static timeout can leverage the chance of setting a dynamic timeout by the controller if you know it in advanced the flow pattern flow execution time and flow completion time. However, it is complicated to predict the flow pattern by a heuristic approach to their behavior in real-time. It is better to set up reactive timeout value, and it depends on some of the behavior patterns of close after a specific interval of time by sampling outflow behavioral patterns. The various areas where you can set the optimal Timeout values by using machine-learning algorithms to set the timeout values for accurately classified the sensitive and non-sensitive flow switch into the network. Different deep reinforcement learning methods to be applied to decide the different types of flows in advance and predict the network behavior in real-time so that we can set the optimal timeout. In the future, to decide different parameters such as flow type flow rate to decide the timeout.

4.6   CONCLUSION

SDN and OF simplify the work of a network administrator to manage the network and reduce the capital expenditure for deployment. In this chapter, we have given a detailed overview of the flow table scalability issue and its limitation in the current network scenario. We have identified what are the different causes of flow table overflow and possible solution by means of caching of rule, aggregation of dependent rules, and eviction of non-important rule by means of a suitable timeout value. We then discuss the different possible approaches to handle this problem by the different authors having different techniques. Finally, we have pointed out various researches areas in which improvement can be made and other evolving related researches to achieve a scalable flow table.

KEYWORDS

- **cache reduction architecture for flow tables**
- **caching in buckets**
- **conflict razor**
- **fast flow table aggregation**
- **megabits**
- **multiple flow table**
- **open system establishment**
- **optimal routing table constructor**

REFERENCES

Adam, Z., Ganjali, Y., & Lie, D., (2012). *OpenFlow Timeouts Demystified*. Univ. of Toronto, Toronto, Ontario, Canada, Citeseer.

Agrawal, B., & Sherwood, T., (2008). Ternary CAM power and delay model: Extensions and uses. *IEEE Transactions on Very Large Scale Integration (VLSI) Systems, 16*(5), 554–564. https://doi.org/10.1109/TVLSI.2008.917538.

Ambiental, T. D. P., (2005). *Open Daylight*, 0–16.

Asadollahi, S., Goswami, B., & Sameer, M., (2018). Ryu controller's scalability experiment on software defined networks. In: *2018 IEEE International Conference on Current Trends in Advanced Computing, ICCTAC*. https://doi.org/10.1109/ICCTAC.2018.8370397.

Astuto, B. N., Mendon, M., Nguyen, X. N., Obraczka, K., Astuto, B. N., & Mendon, M., (2014). A survey of software-defined networking: Past, present, and future of programmable networks to cite this version. *IEEE Communications Surveys and Tutorials, 16*(3), 1617–1634. IEEE.

Benson, T., Akella, A., & Maltz, D. A., (2010). Network traffic characteristics of data centers in the wild. *Proceedings of the 10ᵗʰ ACM SIGCOMM Conference on Internet Measurement,* pp. 267–280.

Challa, R., Lee, Y., & Choo, H., (2016). Intelligent eviction strategy for efficient flow table management in OpenFlow Switches. *IEEE NETSOFT-2016 IEEE NetSoft Conference and Workshops: Software-Defined Infrastructure for Networks, Clouds, IoT and Services* (pp. 312–318). https://doi.org/10.1109/NETSOFT.2016.7502427.

Chih-Heng, K. *Software Defined Network (SDN) Experiment Using Mininet and POX Controller*. http://csie.nqu.edu.tw/smallko/sdn/mySDN.pdf (accessed on 25 February 2021).

Curtis, A. A. R., Mogul, J. C. J. J. C., Tourrilhes, J., Yalagandula, P., Sharma, P., & Banerjee, S., (2011). DevoFlow: Scaling flow management for high-performance networks. *Proceedings of the {ACM} {SIGCOMM} 2011 Conference on Applications, Technologies, Architectures, and Protocols for Computer Communications* (pp. 254–265). Toronto, {ON}, Canada. https://doi.org/10.1145/2043164.2018466.

Erickson, D., (2013). *The Beacon Openflow Controller* (p. 13). https://doi.org/10.1145/2491185.2491189.

Goransson, Paul, B., Chuck, C., & Timothy, (2016). *Software Defined Networks: A Comprehensive Approach*. Morgan Kaufmann.

Iot, S., Saha, N., Misra, S., & Bera, S., (2018). *QoS-Aware Adaptive Flow-Rule Aggregation* (pp. 1–6).

Kannan, K., & Banerjee, S., (n.d.). *Compact TCAM : Flow Entry Compaction in TCAM for Power Aware SDN* (pp. 1–18).

Katta, N., Alipourfard, O., Rexford, J., & Walker, D., (2016). CacheFlow : Dependency-aware rule-caching for software-defined networks categories and subject descriptors. *Proceedings of the Symposium on SDN Research,* pp. 1–12.

Kosugiyama, T., Tanabe, K., Nakayama, H., Hayashi, T., & Yamaoka, K., (2017). A flow aggregation method based on end-to-end delay in SDN. *IEEE International Conference on Communications* (pp. 1–6). https://doi.org/10.1109/ICC.2017.7996341.

Li, H., Chen, K., Pan, T., Zhou, Y., Qian, K., Zheng, K., & Hu, C., (2018). CORA: Conflict razor for policies in SDN. *Proceedings-IEEE INFOCOM* (pp. 423–431). https://doi.org/10.1109/INFOCOM.2018.8485983.

Li, Q., Huang, N., Wang, D., Li, X., Jiang, Y., & Song, Z., (2019). HQTimer: A hybrid q-learning based timeout mechanism in software-defined networks. *IEEE Transactions on Network and Service Management, PP*(0010) (pp. 153–166). https://doi.org/10.1109/TNSM.2018.2890754.

Li, R., & Wang, X., (2019). *A Tale of Two (Flow) Tables : Demystifying Rule Caching in OpenFlow Switches.*

Li, X., & Xie, W., (2017). CRAFT: A cache reduction architecture for flow tables in software-defined networks. *Proceedings-IEEE Symposium on Computers and Communications* (pp. 967–972). https://doi.org/10.1109/ISCC.2017.8024651.

Liu, Y., Tang, B., Yuan, D., Ran, J., & Hu, H., (2017). A dynamic adaptive timeout approach for SDN switch. In: *2016 2nd IEEE International Conference on Computer and Communications, ICCC 2016-Proceedings* (pp. 2577–2582). https://doi.org/10.1109/CompComm.2016.7925164.

Lu, M., Deng, W., & Shi, Y., (2017). TF-Idle timeout: Improving efficiency of TCAM in SDN by dynamically adjusting flow entry lifecycle. In: *2016 IEEE International Conference on Systems, Man, and Cybernetics, SMC 2016-Conference Proceedings* (61471060), (pp. 2681–2686). https://doi.org/10.1109/SMC.2016.7844645.

Luo, S., Yu, H., & Li, L. M., (2014). Fast incremental flow table aggregation in SDN. *Proceedings-International Conference on Computer Communications and Networks, ICCCN, (2013)* (pp. 1–8). https://doi.org/10.1109/ICCCN.2014.6911781.

Luo, S., Yu, H., & Li, L., (2015). Practical flow table aggregation in SDN. *Computer Networks, 92,* 72–88. https://doi.org/10.1016/j.comnet.2015.09.016.

McGeer, R., & Yalagandula, P., (2009). Minimizing rulesets for TCAM implementation. *Proceedings-IEEE INFOCOM* (pp. 1314–1322). https://doi.org/10.1109/INFCOM.2009.5062046.

Mckeown, N., Anderson, T., Peterson, L., Rexford, J., Shenker, S., & Louis, S., (2008). *Sigcomm08_Openflow.Pdf., 38*(2), 69–74. https://doi.org/10.1145/1355734.1355746.

Medved, J., Varga, R., Tkacik, A., & Gray, K., (2014). OpenDaylight: Towards a model-driven SDN controller architecture. *Proceeding of IEEE International Symposium on a World of Wireless, Mobile and Multimedia Networks 2014, WoWMoM 2014.* https://doi.org/10.1109/WoWMoM.2014.6918985.

Mininet, (2014). *Mininet: An Instant Virtual Network on Your Laptop (or other PC)-Mininet.* Mininet.Org.

Ns-3 Training. https://www.nsnam.org/consortium/activities/training/ (accessed on 25 February 2021).

Shalimov, A., Zuikov, D., Zimarina, D., Pashkov, V., & Smeliansky, R., (2013). Advanced study of SDN/OpenFlow controllers. *ACM International Conference Proceeding Series.* https://doi.org/10.1145/2556610.2556621.

Shirali-Shahreza, S., & Ganjali, Y., (2018). Delayed Installation and expedited eviction: An alternative approach to reduce flow table occupancy in SDN switches. *IEEE/ACM Transactions on Networking, 26*(4), 1547–1561. https://doi.org/10.1109/TNET.2018.2841397.

Ting-Yu, M., Ala, A. F., Khaled, S., Farag, M. S., & Junaid, Q., (2017). SDN flow entry management using reinforcement learning. *Journal: ACM Transactions, 123*(Xx), 174–181. https://doi.org/10.1002/elan.

Varga, A., (2010). OMNeT++. In: *Modeling and Tools for Network Simulation.* https://doi.org/10.1007/978-3-642-12331-3_3.

Wang, C., & Youn, H. Y., (2019). Entry aggregation and early match using hidden Markov model of flow table in SDN. *Sensors (Switzerland)*, *19*(10). https://doi.org/10.3390/s19102341.

Wang, D., Li, Q., Wang, L., Sinnott, R. O., & Jiang, Y., (2017). A hybrid-timeout mechanism to handle rule dependencies in software defined networks. In: *2017 IEEE Conference on Computer Communications Workshops, INFOCOM WKSHPS* (pp. 241–246). https://doi.org/10.1109/INFCOMW.2017.8116383.

Wang, M., Zhou, H., & Chen, J., (2018). PoTiA: A popularity and timeout analysis based SDN controller protection approach. *IEEE Access*, *6*, 59253–59267. https://doi.org/10.1109/ACCESS.2018.2875164.

Wang, S. Y., Chou, C. L., & Yang, C. M., (2013). EstiNet OpenFlow network simulator and emulator. *IEEE Communications Magazine*. https://doi.org/10.1109/MCOM.2013.6588659.

Xiao, P., Qu, W., Qi, H., Xu, Y., Li, Z., Chhabra, A., & Kim, H. J., (2017). A hybrid-timeout mechanism to handle rule dependencies in software defined networks. *IEEE Access*, *5*(3), 241–246. https://doi.org/10.1109/INFCOMW.2017.8116383.

Yan, B., Xu, Y., Xing, H., Xi, K., & Chao, H. J., (2014). Cab: A reactive wildcard rule caching system for software-defined networks. *HotSDN*, 163–168. https://doi.org/10.1145/2620728.2620732.

Yoshioka, K., Hirata, K., & Yamamoto, M., (2018). Flow-based routing for flow entry aggregation in software-defined networking. *IEICE Transactions on Communications*, *E101B*(1), 49–57. https://doi.org/10.1587/transcom.2017ITP0007.

Zhang, L., Lin, R., Xu, S., & Wang, S., (2014). AHTM: Achieving efficient flow table utilization in software defined networks. In: *2014 IEEE Global Communications Conference, GLOBECOM, 2014*, 1897–1902. https://doi.org/10.1109/GLOCOM.2014.7037085.

Zhang, L., Wang, S., Xu, S., Lin, R., & Yu, H., (2015). TimeoutX: An adaptive flow table management method in software defined networks. In: *2015 IEEE Global Communications Conference, GLOBECOM*, 1–6. https://doi.org/10.1109/GLOCOM.2014.7417563.

Zhang, S., Shen, Y., Herlich, M., Nguyen, K., Ji, Y., & Yamada, S., (2015). Ryuo: Using high level northbound API for control messages in software defined network. In: *17th Asia-Pacific Network Operations and Management Symposium: Managing a Very Connected World, APNOMS*, 115–120. https://doi.org/10.1109/APNOMS.2015.7275412.

Zhang, X., Cheng, Z., Lin, R. P., He, L., Yu, S., & Luo, H., (2017). Local fast reroute with flow aggregation in software defined networks. *IEEE Communications Letters*, *21*(4), 785–788. https://doi.org/10.1109/LCOMM.2016.2638430.

Zhu, H., Fan, H., Luo, X., & Jin, Y., (2015). Intelligent timeout master: Dynamic timeout for SDN-based data centers. *Proceedings of the 2015 IFIP/IEEE International Symposium on Integrated Network Management, IM*, 734–737. https://doi.org/10.1109/INM.2015.7140363.

CHAPTER 5

Micro-Service Provisioning in the Multi-Tier SDN-Fog Architecture for IoT Applications

PRASENJIT MAITI, BIBHUDATTA SAHOO, ASHOK KUMAR TURUK, and HEMANT KUMAR APAT

Cloud Computing Research Lab, Department of Computer Science and Engineering, National Institute of Technology, Rourkela–769008, Odisha, India, E-mail: pmaiti1287@gmail.com (P. Maiti)

ABSTRACT

As the need for fast processing and reply increases, the requirement for high response system increases. It is expected that the internet of things (IoT) devices will be more than two times in number as they are now in a time span of less than 20 years, which makes it harder to deliver services with the same speed existing now rather than faster. Fog Computing provides a distributed platform to data processing and resource provisioning for IoT services, and ensuring quality of services (QoS) in terms of energy and low-latency for these services is essential taking into consideration that deploying IoT services in the Fog computing infrastructure is a difficult process due to heterogeneous fog nodes (FNs). The rapid development of the IoT applications makes human life comfortable, but the IoT applications such as Health-care, Smart Home, Smart Transportation, and Industry have different needs concerning latency, real-time response, makespan, computing capability, etc. Recently, proposed Fog-to-Cloud multi-tier computing model aims to enhance the execution of IoT applications through harmonizing management of underlying resources. In this research, we are proposing a new architecture that can minimize the total makespan of the scheduling algorithms. The four-tire architecture proposed in this chapter, i.e., (Cloud, SDN-Controller, Fog-Controller, Fog) might consume relatively more energy, but we aim to prove that it can do the scheduling tasks in less amount of time and less servicing miss ratio compared to the existing architectures, i.e., (Fog-Cloud). In continuation of our work, we propose a services provisioning approach to reduce makespan for IoT applications having service dependency in a multi-tier fog computing architecture.

5.1   INTRODUCTION

Upon request for IoT services, smart sensor data must be processed and efficiently retrieved. IoT devices are growing rapidly and about 50 billion devices are projected to be deployed by 2020. Current cloud system offers a wide range of data services. In many applications, the integration of IoT and cloud services is done in the cloud. However, due to lack of resources in the cloud, increased network-wide traffic, and delay in processing the services, it can cause various challenges. Various types of IoT services such as Healthcare, Smart Transportation, Smart Home, Smart Grids, Face Recognition, Military, and Disaster Management required a very low latency real-time response. The gateway is such an edge device type that collects data from smart sensors, but has no capabilities for preprocessing or decision-making. The gateway must therefore be made more intelligent with the capabilities of Fog and named fog smart gateway (FSG). Fog computing, therefore, is taking care of these problems. Fog computing is a phenomenon at the edge of the network that provides services. In order to handle the facilities, fog nodes (FNs) must be installed on the network near the customers. The major architecture design problems and challenges for edge-centered IoT services are the public and safe discovery of edge nodes, data storage, partitioning, and offloading tasks using edge nodes. Resource allocation is the task of architectural design that satisfies the quality of service (QoS) and Service Level Agreement (SLA) due to resource limitations, resource discovery (Maiti et al., 2018). The location and scheduling aspect of an architecture plays a major role in keeping track of the available resources (information provided by the Monitoring Service) to identify the best candidates to host a FN. Virtualization of data sensors is an IoT services feature that allows an application to access and manipulate data with the discovery and monitoring of live data. Service allocation or coordination of all services to reduce the wait for each allocation of services by taking into account both the availability of resources and the state of the equipment. Providing an efficient service, service node placement, service node selection, and service placement with a balanced and efficient pairing or matching strategy in an edge node sensor-virtualization environment crucial to the achievement of Service Level Agreement (SLA) and QoS. For the different types of IoT services, different pricing models are required. We need to propose an edge-centric model for IoT that provides real-time IoT services. Containers handle processing of IoT traffic hosted by distributed FNs. For edge centric architecture design for IoT services with above-mentioned parameters, only a few literatures are available. Good infrastructure needs to be developed to reduce service response time, overall network traffic, and economically feasible.

5.2   RELATED WORK

IoT related services, including e-Health, smart cities, smart transportation systems, and industrial scenarios challenge cloud computing efficiency, often due to volatile and often high communication latency, privacy gaps, and based traffic loads from networks connecting cloud computing to end-users. As a result, computing service requests that are prone to real-time and latency to be answered by remote cloud centers often experience significant round trip delays, network congestion, loss of service quality, etc.

A new concept called "Edge Computing" or "Fog Computing" has recently been introduced to solve these problems in addition to centralized cloud computing. On both sides, Fog-Cloud gateways and Sensor-Fog gateways can collect and process huge data generated from sensor nodes through the gateways (Sahoo et al., 2019a).

The Sensor-Fog Cloud provides a platform for the execution of services in such a publish/subscribe system that operates on sensed data and also satisfies and ensures the derived confidence and security requirements. A Sensor-Fog allows users to easily capture, view, process, and search the Sensor-Fog infrastructure's complex behaviors to enable the automated delivery of their services as required by users.

Bonomi et al. (2012) claimed that Fog computing is a highly virtualized platform offering services for processing, storing, and networking between end devices and conventional data centers (DCs) for cloud computing. It is possible to classify IoT data into three groups: (i) continuous data; (ii) periodic data; and (iii) event data. IoT gateway is an intermediary tool between smart devices and applications that produce data and access value. The gateway allows you to collect data from computers, remote users, and applications easily and safely to meet a specific need. With interconnectivity and the ability to share data, today's industrial devices and other systems are often built. Intel, Dell, Huawei, Redhat, and AMD IoT gateways allow businesses to interconnect industrial infrastructure devices seamlessly and secure data flow between devices and cloud. It also enables safe collection, sharing, and filtering of data analysis by customers. Intelligent IoT gateways make local decisions and give the application real-time resources. A key component for gathering data from different smart sensor nodes (SSNs) is the smart gateway. Optimal gateway positioning is required to have full network coverage with reduced service latency, resources, and overall deployment cost. In fog computing, the fog layer is known to be situated between the cloud and the edge, and while it depends on the concept, the core network router nodes and gateways, the WAN switch nodes, and even the fog layer includes wireless AP and smartphones.

Fog computing is a distributed framework supplying the network with cloud-like services. Three-layer architecture was suggested by many researchers, consisting of cloud DCs, FNs as at the edge of the network and computers as endpoints (Sahoo et al., 2019b). This provides the customer with micro-services. Cisco created a FN, defining a fog computing system as a mini-cloud, positioned at the edge of the network and implemented via a variety of edge devices, interconnected by a variety of, mainly wireless communication technologies. The FNs can be router in the core network, turn in the WAN, depending on the concept, and even wireless APs and smartphones are included in the fog layer. The smart gateway is proposed as a FN (Aazam et al., 2014; Gia et al., 2015), the micro DCs proposed (Aazam et al., 2015), or the suggestion of FNs serving as caches in Information Centric Networking developed (Abdullahi et al., 2014). FNs suggested by Skala et al. (2015) and Tang et al. (2015), as mini-clouds. All applications are distributed across different layers and are assumed to collect and process the raw data collected from sensors.

Today, the key aspect is the positioning of FNs. Aazam et al. (2014); Gia et al. (2014); Aazam et al. (2015); Rahmani et al. (2015); Tiwary et al. (2018) suggested that FNs should be placed in highly capable devices such as routers or smart gateways. Bonomi et al. (2012, 2014) suggested intermediate computation nodes as FNs that are not reliant on particular computers.

Tang et al. (2015) are proposing the use of three layers of fog computing in smart cities for large data analysis. The first layer of fog, called intermediate computing nodes, consists of intermediate computer powered computers. Small computing nodes (e.g., mobile phones) construct the second fog layer, called edge-computing nodes. Ultimately, the third layer, called the lowest layer of fog, only consists of sensors with sensing capabilities. Fog computing was implemented in the industrial environment in a separate application (Gazis et al., 2015). Fog computing is implemented in Cisco edge routers in that article, as was first suggested by Cisco. Abdullahi et al. (2014) and Skala et al. (2015) are proposing to install fog computing in routers that are responsible for providing services for processing, storing, and applications closer to data-producing edge devices.

Depending on the facilities and resource management approach, different solutions are possible. For example, computing skills can be accessed on demand in emergency situations (natural disasters, etc.), from volunteer sources such as cars parked nearby, or individuals supplying emergency personnel with their mobile tools if they happen to be close by. The sharing of mobile computing resources was given an interesting example only when phones are connected to the grid (Busching et al., 2012). Therefore, adding processing capabilities to edge devices does not seem adequate to manage these highly demanding situations, so it is important to implement additional concepts.

Fogs are not limited to either executing a function or transferring it to the cloud, but they also have the ability to work with other nearby fogs. The total end-to-end latency will be decreased. The fog layer is made up of several independent fogs, containing each fog. A container is made up of various storage and processing capacities. Whenever a node in the IoT layer submits a job to be processed or stored in the Fog to Cloud scenario, the node first contacts the fog with which it is associated, rather than directly submitting the job to the cloud. The fog when it wants to do the job itself or to forward it for transmission to the cloud. The fog has lower storage and processing capabilities than the cloud, it could often refuse to take on new jobs if it had reached its maximum capacity, thus introducing the idea of fog availability (Masri et al., 2017). The authors mentioned in this chapter that fogs are no longer limited to either conducting a function or uploading it to the cloud, but also to communicate with other fogs to process the job request. This minimizes the total latency of the network. Kumar et al. (2016) have built a distributed cloud DC called mini-clouds that can be used to duplicate data. Masip-Bruin et al. (2016) implemented a Fog-to-Cloud architecture consisting of a layered management structure that incorporates into hierarchical architecture specific heterogeneous fog layers.

To select the best fog available to meet such service requirements, a management system is responsible for identifying a collection of available fogs. Authors do not clarify the parameters used in selecting the best fog by the management system. In Fog-to-Cloud settings, Souza et al. (2016) suggested a QoS-conscious management approach. The goal of the work is to achieve a low delay in the allocation of service by using service atomization in which services are decomposed into separate sub-services called atomic services to allow parallel execution.

There is a control plane (CP) within the architecture of Fog-to-Cloud which is responsible for the distribution of the atomic resources among the available edge nodes. The purpose of the service allocation process is to reduce the delay in service allocation, providing load balance and energy use balance between the different fogs. While comprehensive cloud resource sharing research exists, it is still premature to work on fog resource sharing and cooperation.

A service flow is generated between a data source and users when one or more users request a service that involves data for one service that occurs in the same data source. The computing power should be considered to assess the location of FNs, service latency, and network traffic. It is quite common that the service latency is drastically reduced when fog computing is implemented as compared to data processing using the cloud, but the service response time can be further reduced depending on which nodes are deployed as FNs.

Based on the deployment location of the FN, network traffic can also be reduced. The number of services running in common scenario and the available computing resources of each system can differ in time. It is therefore necessary to find the place where service latency and network traffic can be minimized, taking into account the deployment role among the edge devices currently capable of executing the FNs.

Network service flows are constantly changing because the same service is not always used by consumers. Even if the FN is deployed, the data flow changes constantly, so processing the service on the same fog server will result in inefficient results at all times. Narendra et al. (2015) proposed optimal mini-cloud placement to minimize IoT device data collection latency; and mini-cloud data migration to address storage capacity issues while minimizing access latency. Malandrino et al. (2016) work shows that high server usage and low latency of operation, but the best strategies will rely on the implementation strategy and geographic details of the cities of the individual network operator.

Fog computing architecture eliminates most studies on fog computing (Hu et al., 2017; Chen et al., 2016; Brogi et al., 2017; Sarkar et al., 2016) service latency, network traffic and power consumption. Nonetheless, deploying the FNs near to the user is hypothetical only, and there is no thought as to which devices will actually be installed on the fog server. The idea of fog computing was defined by Luan et al. (2015); and Hong et al. (2013) as mobile fog and showed that mobile users can use fog computing to boost QoS, reduce bandwidth and energy consumption, end-to-end delay and network traffic. However, there is no thought as to where the FNs should be deployed or mounted.

5.3 FOG MODEL IN CONTEXT OF SDN

There are many existing models and architectures representing fog and cloud environment. As per our study and research, we gained thorough understanding of the service placement problem and its approaches. Hence, we proposed our own multi-tier fog computing architecture (Figure 5.1) (Maiti et al., 2019) for both the independent and dependent sections of service placement problem shown as follows:

1. **Tier 1:** This is the lowest tier that includes the entire SSNs to which unique IPv6 addresses have been allocated, compressed according to the 6LoWPAN protocol, and forms a mesh network. SSN is a sensor and actuator array. We are responsible for sensing and transmitting data from the atmosphere to its immediate upper layer. There may be instructions to perform an operation from the upper layer to the actuator. IoT devices or IoT nodes are a series of SSNs (smart meters, mobile phones, smart vehicles, etc.). SSN is distributed at random randomly. Increasing SSN is given a co-ordinate value. In a smart city setting, we consider the transmission range as a SSN loop. A typical smart city scenario

has hundreds of networks across its geographic area, linked to the different domains. A coordinating device (CD) coordinates each of these networks. Across different networks, cluster head (CH) across sensor networks, Access Point (AP) in Wi-Fi networks and reader in radio frequency identification (RFID) network, etc., a CD is identified differently.

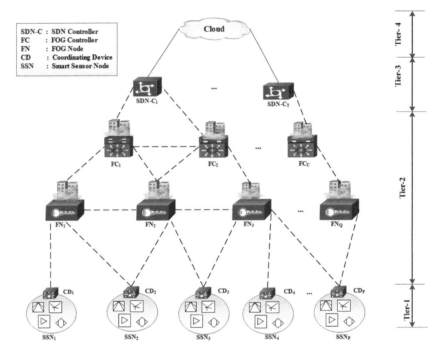

FIGURE 5.1   Multi-tier fog computing architecture.

Source: Reprinted with permission from Maiti et al., 2019. © Elsevier.

2. **Tier 2:** For the efficient execution of their applications, CDs must send their data to the Internet. The system known as FNs enables this data transmission. This tier is made up of edge devices such as switches, routers, gateways, access points. Such tools take care of temporary data storage, storing, and analyzing the information obtained. SSN mobility is provided by the fog computing devices. FNs receive CD data. The fog tier is responsible for running all applications prone to latency as well as monitoring them in real time. Within its vicinity, each FN serves multiple CDs. A FN

group is setting up a Fog Cluster (FCL). The FN, which acts as access points, enables the control and monitoring of underlying IoT devices such as sensor and actuator nodes. Notations of work requests are used for computational tasks to be done using the tools of fog.

The individual program instances are referred to as utilities where these requests are performed. Map Some potential examples of these facilities are code reduction, distributed data storage or stream processing. However, a limit is put by the computational resources on the number of devices that needs to be controlled by the FN. A request is received by each FN for the service placement and corresponding actions as per the placement plan for the service are taken by the fog controller (FC) node. Service execution is observed and the required computational resource for deploying and executing the service is provided by FN. A set of API are exposed by FNs for development and deployment of application as well as control and management of resources. A seamless access is allowed by these APIs to various OS, service containers, and hypervisors on a physical machine. Remote monitoring and management of different physical resources like memory, network interfaces, and CPU is also enabled by them. Heterogeneous and hierarchically deployed fog resources simplify the IoT application development by adoption of mobile fog programming model. The same application code is run by mobile fog on different devices constituting the heterogeneous fog infrastructure. The application is comprised of multiple processes performing separate tasks with respect to their position in the hierarchy of network as well as the capabilities of the device. A number of FNs are managed by a connecting FC. Exactly one FC manages each FCL. The management of resources offered by the subordinate FNs and provisioning of these resources for execution of task requests is carried out by FC. It can also propagate these task requests to some other FCL via its FC or the SDN Controller (SDN-C) in case it cannot be handled by the current FCL. A mechanism of resource management for vertical stability is needed for the identification of task request delegation process in the whole fog landscape. Apart from provisioning of resources, other tasks like performing infrastructural changes in the FCL, analysis of the resource utilization in the

FCL, creation of a plan for resource provisioning for allocation of resources for task requests and monitoring the FNs and IoT devices. A plan for providing resources to the FCL is produced by FC that is needed for the execution of task requests received. The services are selected according to this plan to fulfill the task requests. The plan also determines the location for deployment of these services as well as which FN should be used. If the current FN does not have the required resources or there is a need for further processing, the task request is propagated to a different FCL via the FC. The FN database is monitored by FC for comparison with the expected level of QoS, i.e., measurement of resource consumption and QoS parameters such as the execution time of each FN. The decision-making in FC is influenced by this information. The service implementation is hosted by FC that enables the search of services by the FN and their deployment on the FN. A higher level of fault tolerance is given by a decentralized FC. The approach of resource provisioning has a goal of optimization with respect to the FN utilization and delay minimization.

3. **Tier 3:** Traffic control is performed by SDN-C as OpenFlow (OF) controller and connectivity management for FCs and IoT devices. As SDN-C is placed on a higher level in the network hierarchy, region with multiple FCs are covered by a single SDN-C. OF switches are used for interconnection of network partitions that enables data exchange between controllers. It is required to schedule traffic flow between IoT devices and FCs located across various partitions. FCs and FNs have local SDN agents running on them to which some control tasks may be delegated. FC at the network edge may control FNs to IoT devices multi-hop wireless communication in their coverage region based on their local knowledge and policy rules obtained from the SDN-C. Other routes in the system are determined by SDN-C like the inter-region routes, the routes towards the other autonomous systems with data intended for the cloud. The IoT tasks that are time-critical need the installation of flow rules in advance which results in reduction in efficiency of SDN-C in resource allocation. The traffic can be separated into delay-insensitive traffic and emergency traffic by exploiting the granular traffic control provided by Overflow. Therefore, the latter must be scheduled giving the highest priority

in comparison to the proactively installed routes where the route determination and reservation of resources for other categories of traffic may be completed in a reactive manner. The SDN-C is regularly informed by the FCs about the position and capabilities of FNs as well the IoT devices being served. Thus, a whole connectivity graph can be built by the SDN-C that can run optimization algorithms periodically to achieve better utilization of network resources and QoS enhancement. For instance, SDN-C can start a re-routing process in order to improve the utility of network and bring reduction in congestion on discovering unbalanced network load as a result of proactive routing that causes focus on few selected nodes. Along with routing optimization, a time-window basis connectivity management by SDN-C is also desired. The implementation of optimal access point selection algorithm to work in a multi-network IoT environment is done on SDN-C to assign access point for set of newly joined devices on the basis of the radio access technologies supported the types of services requested by the devices and the current multi-network capacity in the controlled partition. At the end of each time window, an assignment process is triggered that aims to find access point set to satisfy the bandwidth requirement of the FNs, FCs, and IoT devices and guarantee an optimal performance for the system. The application traffic needs to pass through the component before being sent that enables the identification of traffic flow access in the network by the CP elements, i.e., FNs, and FCs. Information about FCs is collected and maintained by SDN-C in a controlled domain like software applications, secondary storage, running OSs and available RAM. It also collects information about capabilities, state, and inter-connectivity of the network elements, including: wireless technology of the access points (e.g., 3G/4G/5G, LTE, Wi-Fi, etc.), links capacity and residual bandwidth, the flow table content and neighbor list of each network node. The controller may even store environment road map and information related to speed and positions of the vehicles involved besides the list of neighbors to be used for high-mobile vehicular applications.

4. **Tier 4:** The topmost tier is the cloud that manages and stores massive amounts of data to high-end servers and DCs. A DC has several physical servers, and each physical server has a high-speed

LAN network interconnection and a high bandwidth connection to the Internet. Every IGW is connected via a wired network to a cloud DC. The cloud computing system is in a DC with the number of physical heterogeneous hosts.

5.4 FOG SERVICE PROVISIONING

5.4.1 *SERVICE PROVISIONING FOR INDEPENDENT SERVICES*

For the last couple of years, service placement problem is a major research challenge in both industry and academia. The problem addresses the number of services required and their placement with considering different performance metrics. Service placement architecture proposed by Velasquez et al. (2017) to reduce latency using a smart service placement system that facilitates the location of services in the appropriate position according to specific needs. Service orchestrator as well as some implementation details was discussed using ILP. Yousefpour et al. (2018) introduced the issue of dynamic fog service delivery that dynamically deploys services on FNs or releases services already deployed on FNs to fulfill the required QoS constraints. INLP is used to formulate the problem and simulation is used with heuristic solutions. The provision of quality-of-service (QoS) is an essential feature of the networks of the next generation. Skarlat et al. (2017) present a conceptual framework for fog computing and then model the problem of service placement over fog resources for IoT applications as an optimization issue. Figure 5.2 represents the workflow for independent services.

Genetic algorithm is used for attaining the optimal placement of services in order to minimize the communication delay and better utilization of fog resources. The optimization approach generates a service placement plan that is more effective in the use of fog landscape resources, resulting in lower execution costs compared to the average service placement plan generated by the genetic algorithm (with the cost of the service placement plans provided by the genetic algorithm representing just 40%). The genetic algorithm generates solutions that face a lower delivery delay on average by taking advantage of more cloud resources (on average 36%-the services were run in the cloud).

Minh et al. (2017) proposed an approach to optimize the service placement on fog landscape. A multilayer fog computing architecture is presented that optimize service decentralization on fog landscape and also improved the latency, energy consumption and network load if we compared with traditional cloud computing. The approaches are not only cost effective but also improve the utilization of virtual resources. Redowan et al. (2018) proposed a quality of experience (QoE)-aware application placement policy that prioritizes different application placement request according to users' expectation and calculate the capacities of fog instances considering their current status. It also facilitates placement of applications to suitable fog instances so that users QoE is maximized in respect of utility access, resource consumption, and service delivery.

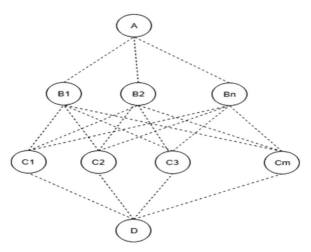

FIGURE 5.2 IoT applications workflow represented as a graph.

Brito et al. (2017) proposed an architecture called fog orchestration architecture to deliver the services to the end users. Fog orchestration efficiently handles the infrastructure management node selection and service placement in fog computing paradigm. In this chapter, they present architecture for service orchestration based on the core requirements of Fog Computing. Based on a virtualized environment, where FNs are capable of running virtualized and containerized applications and services, offering them access to attached/connected devices, over different communication technologies, to accomplish their task. Santos et al. (2017) tried to improve the performance metrics by adopting fog computing in place of fog computing. Allocation of services to appropriate nodes is an important criterion while evaluating the performance of global file systems, so multiple optimization objectives have been resolved, such as low latency and energy efficiency have been taken into consideration for the evaluation of performance.

5.4.2   SERVICE PROVISIONING FOR DEPENDENT SERVICES

The heterogeneous earliest finish time (HEFT) approach suggested by Topcuoglu et al. (2002) is one of the most well-known workflow management strategies in heterogeneous environments. This consists of a phase of task selection and a selection step of the processor. Tasks are prioritized by their position in the workflow graph during the task selection process and the task with the highest priority is selected. Subsequently, the selected task is allocated to the processor in the processor selection step, which can provide it with the earliest finish time, using idle time slots in the schedule of the processor. The 'predict earliest finish time' (PEFT) strategy is suggested in by Arabnejad and Barbosa (2014), which is basically an enhanced version of the HEFT approach. It introduces a look forward feature based on a cost table that is optimistic. The authors show that in terms of the scheduling length ratiometric, their proposed approach outperforms HEFT. Figure 5.3 depicts the DAG model for dependent services of IoT applications, and Figure 5.4 represents the processor graph of virtual machines (VMs).

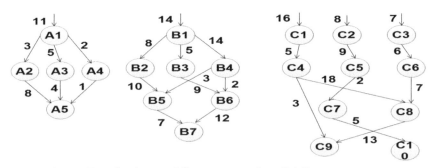

FIGURE 5.3   IoT applications workflow represented as a DAG.

Jiang et al. (2011) present the path clustering heuristic with a distributed gap search (PCH-DGS) novel clustering algorithm for scheduling multiple workflows in a heterogeneous cloud. Their proposed method aims to insert each task group into the first schedule gap available in the schedule of a processor. Workflow activities are split into groups in an attempt to minimize the cost of contact between them. If the time gap cannot accommodate all of the group's tasks, the rest of the group's tasks will be inserted recursively into the next available gap in the system's schedule of the same or other processors. Although all of the above algorithms are ideal for scheduling workflows in a heterogeneous environment, the characteristics of a fog and cloud architecture are not taken into account. Most significantly, they are static and no time constraints are taken into account. More and more attention has been paid to scheduling in hybrid fog and cloud environments (Chen, 2018; Shah-Mansouri, 2018; Taneja, 2017). Deng et al. (2016) are proposing a workload allocation strategy in a fog-cloud system. The authors analyze the trade in the two-tiered system between power consumption and transmission delay. Based on these two variables, their method aims to determine the optimal distribution of workload between fog and cloud layers.

Based on simulation experiments and theoretical approaches, it is shown that fog computing can dramatically improve the performance of cloud computing by sacrificing modest computational resources to save communication bandwidth and reduce transmission latency through the proposed approach. Nevertheless, the proposed solution cannot be extended to workflow applications as there is no consideration of data dependencies and precedence constraints between workload tasks.

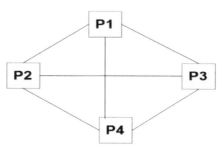

FIGURE 5.4   Processors graph.

Nan et al. (2016) propose an online algorithm for scheduling applications in a three-tiered architecture, called Unit slot Optimization, consisting of an IoT layer, a fog layer, and a cloud layer. The FNs do not require any monetary costs, but have minimal computational power.

The cloud nodes, on the other hand, are more analytical, which entail monetary costs. In an attempt to find a balance between the average application response time and the average monetary expense, a portion of the applications that arrive at the fog layer is offloaded to the cloud layer. The suggested solution changes the tradeoff between these two variables dynamically, based on the optimization technique of Lyapunov. The suggested solution is shown to be able to provide cost-effective processing while maintaining an average response time. Although the application response time is included in this job, however, no real-time constraints (i.e., deadlines) are taken into consideration. Furthermore, as no inter-task dependencies are considered, the proposed policy is not suitable for scheduling workflow applications. On the other hand, Pham et al. (2017) present in a first attempt to schedule workflows based on collaboration between cloud and fog computing.

The main goal of the proposed heuristic, cost-makespan conscious scheduling (CMaS), is to achieve a trade-off between application time and cloud resource consumption cost, under user-defined limitations. While this method is both fog-conscious and cloud-conscious and ideal for real-time workflows, the use of empty time slots during the scheduling cycle has the following drawbacks:

- It is static and therefore not suitable for the dynamic nature of IoT applications.
- Only one process is considered for scheduling.
- The connectivity costs incurred by transferring data from the IoT layer shall not be taken into account during the scheduling process.

On the contrary, the heuristic fog and cloud-aware suggested in this chapter is ideal for the complex scheduling of several real-time workflows, using possible time gaps. In addition, the communication costs incurred by transferring data from the sensors and devices in the IoT layer to the VMs in the fog layer are taken into account during the scheduling process.

5.5 PERFORMANCE METRICS FOR MICRO-SERVICE PROVISIONING

The efficiency metrics used to assess the performance of scheduling algorithms applications are discussed in subsections.

5.5.1 DEADLINE MISS RATIO (DMR)

DMR is the ratio of the number of applications that have not finished their execution during their deadline over the number of applications that have been submitted to the scheduler over the time period observed.

5.5.2 SCHEDULE LENGTH RATIO (SLR)

A scheduling algorithm's efficiency is its output schedule's day length (makespan). Thanks to the use of a large set of service graphs with different properties, the schedule length must be averaged to a lower bound, called SLR.

5.5.3 SPEEDUP AND EFFICIENCY

The speed-up value for a given graph is calculated by dividing the sequential execution time (i.e., the accumulated cost of the tasks in the graph) by the concurrent execution time (i.e., the makespan of the production schedule). The sequential execution time is determined by assigning all tasks to a single processor to minimize the total cost of the calculation.

5.6 CONCLUSION

This research has established a mixed real-time schedule of multiple DAGs-based applications on heterogeneous multi-core processors. Considering that the timing constraint is not to schedule high-priority applications earlier and that there is a time span between the lower bound and the application deadline, the authors presented algorithms to meet the high-priority applications deadlines and reduce the overall makespan of the system.

ACKNOWLEDGMENTS

This research was supported by Media Lab Asia (Visvesvaraya PhD Scheme for Electronics and IT, Project Code-CSVSE) under the department of MeitY Government of India and carried out at Cloud Computing Research Laboratory, Department of CSE, National Institute of Technology Rourkela, India.

KEYWORDS

- **cost-makespan conscious scheduling**
- **deadline miss ratio**
- **fog cluster**
- **fog computing**
- **fog smart gateway**
- **heterogeneous earliest finish time**
- **IoT services**

REFERENCES

(2015). *Cisco Fog Computing Solutions: Unleash the Power of the Internet of Things*, http://www.cisco.com/c/dam/en_us/solutions/trends/iot/docs/computing-solutions.pdf (accessed on 16 December 2020).

Aazam, M., & Huh, E. N., (2014). Fog computing and smart gateway-based communication for cloud of things. *International Conference on Future Internet of Things and Cloud* (pp. 464–470). Barcelona.

Aazam, M., & Huh, E. N., (2015). Fog computing micro datacenter based dynamic resource estimation and pricing model for IoT. *IEEE 29th International Conference on Advanced Information Networking and Applications*, 687–694.

Abdullahi, I., Arif, S., & Hassan, S., (2014). Ubiquitous shift with information centric network caching using fog computing. *Computational Intelligence in Information Systems* (pp. 327–335). Chapter of volume-331 of the series advances in intelligent systems and computing, Springer.

Arabnejad, H., & Barbosa, J. G., (2014). List scheduling algorithm for heterogeneous systems by an optimistic cost table. *IEEE Trans Parallel Distrib Syst., 25*(3), 682–694.

Bonomi, F., (2013). *The Smart and Connected Vehicle and the Internet of Things,* http://tf.nist.gov/seminars/WSTS/PDFs/1-0_Cisco_FBonomi_ConnectedVehicles.pdf (accessed on 16 December 2020).

Bonomi, F., Milito, R., Natarajan, P., & Zhu, J., (2014). Fog computing: A platform for internet of things and analytics. *Big Data and Internet of Things: A Roadmap for Smart Environments* (pp. 169–186). Chapter of volume-546 of the series studies in computational intelligence, Springer.

Bonomi, F., Milito, R., Zhu, J., & Addepalli, S., (2012). Fog computing and its role in the internet of things. In: *Proceedings of the First Edition of the MCC Workshop on Mobile Cloud Computing.* ACM.

Brito, M. S. D., (2017). A service orchestration architecture for Fog-enabled infrastructures. *Second International Conference on Fog and Mobile Edge Computing (FMEC)* (pp. 127–132). Valencia.

Brogi, A., & Stefano, F., (2017). QoS-aware deployment of IoT applications through the fog. *IEEE Internet of Things Journal.*

Busching, F., Schildt, S., & Wolf, L., (2012). Droid cluster: Towards smartphone cluster computing-the streets are paved with potential computer clusters. *32nd International Conference on Distributed Computing Systems Workshops (ICDCSW).*

Chen, N., Chen, Y., You, Y., Ling, H., Liang, P., & Zimmermann, R., (2016). Dynamic urban surveillance video stream processing using fog computing. *IEEE Second International Conference on Multimedia Big Data (BigMM)*, 105–112.

Chen, Y., (2018). *Service-Oriented Computing and System Integration: Software, IoT, Big Data, and AI as Services* (6th edn.). Kendall Hunt Publishing, Dubuque.

Deng, R., Lu, R., Lai, C., Luan, T. H., & Liang, H., (2016). Optimal workload allocation in fog-cloud computing toward balanced delay and power consumption. *IEEE Internet Things Journal, 3*(6), 1171–1181.

Gazis, V., Leonardi, A., Mathioudakis, K., Sasloglou, K., Kirikas, P., & Sudhaakar, R., (2015). Components of fog computing in an industrial internet of things context. *Proceedings of 12th Annual IEEE International Conference on Sensing, Communication, and Networking-Workshops (SECON Workshops).*

Gia, T. N., Jiang, M., Rahmani, A. M., Westerlund, T., Liljeberg, P., & Tenhunen, H., (2015). Fog computing in healthcare internet of things: A case study on ECG feature extraction. *IEEE International Conference on Computer and Information Technology; Ubiquitous Computing and Communications; Dependable, Autonomic and Secure Computing; Pervasive Intelligence and Computing* (pp. 356–363). Liverpool.

Hong, K., Lillethun, D., Ramachandran, U., Ottenwälder, B., & Koldehofe, B., (2013). Mobile fog: A programming model for large-scale applications on the internet of things. *ACM SIGCOMM Workshop on Mobile Cloud Computing,* 15–20.

Hu, P., Ning, H., Qiu, T., Zhang, Y., & Luo, X., (2017). Fog computing-based face identification and resolution scheme in internet of things. *IEEE Transactions on Industrial Informatics, 13*(4), 1910–1920.

Jiang, H. J., Huang, K. C., Chang, H. Y., Gu, D. S., & Shih, P. J., (2011). Scheduling concurrent workflows in HPC cloud through exploiting schedule gaps. In: *Proceedings of the 11th International Conference on Algorithms and Architectures for Parallel Processing (ICA3PP'11),* 282–293.

Kumar, A., Narendra, N. C., & Bellur, U., (2016). Uploading and replicating internet of things (IoT) data on distributed cloud storage. *IEEE 9th International Conference on Cloud Computing (CLOUD),* 670–677.

Luan, T. H., Gao, L., Li, Z., Xiang, Y., Wei, G., & Sun, L., (2015). *Fog Computing: Focusing on Mobile Users at the Edge. arXiv* preprint arXiv:1502.01815.

Maiti, P., Apat, H. K., Sahoo, B. D., & Turuk, A. K., (2019). An effective approach of latency-aware fog smart gateways deployment for IoT services. *Internet of Things Journal* (pp. 1–19). Elsevier.

Maiti, P., et al., (2018). Smart gateway based multi-tier service-oriented fog computing architecture for achieving ultra-low latency. In: *2018 International Conference on Information Technology (ICIT)*. IEEE.

Malandrino, F., Kirkpatrick, S., & Chiasserini, C. F., (2016). How close to the edge? Delay/ utilization trends in MEC. *ACM Workshop on Cloud-Assisted Networking, ACM,* 37–42.

Masip-Bruin, X., Marín-Tordera, E., Tashakor, G., Jukan, A., & Ren, G. J., (2016). Foggy clouds and cloudy fogs: A real need for coordinated management of fog-to-cloud computing systems. *IEEE Wireless Communications, 23*(5), 120–128.

Masri, W., Ridhawi, I. A., Mostafa, N., & Pourghomi, P., (2017). Minimizing delay in IoT systems through collaborative fog-to-fog (F2F) communication. *Ninth International Conference on Ubiquitous and Future Networks (ICUFN)* (pp. 1005–1010). Milan, Italy.

Minh, Q. T., Nguyen, D. T., Van, L. A., Nguyen, H. D., & Truong, A., (2017). Toward service placement on fog computing landscape. In: *4th NAFOSTED Conference on Information and Computer Science* (pp. 291–296). Hanoi.

Nan, Y., Li, W., Bao, W., Delicato, F. C., Pires, P. F., & Zomaya, A. Y., (2016). Cost-effective processing for delay sensitive applications in cloud of things systems. In: *Proceedings of the IEEE 15th International Symposium on Network Computing and Applications (NCA'15)*, 162–169.

Narendra, N. C., Koorapati, K., & Ujja, V., (2015). Towards cloud-based decentralized storage for internet of things data. *IEEE International Conference on Cloud Computing in Emerging Markets (CCEM)*, 160–168.

Pham, X. Q., Man, N. D., Tri, N. D. T., Thai, N. Q., & Huh, E. N., (2017). A cost- and performance-effective approach for task scheduling based on collaboration between cloud and fog computing. *Int. J. Distrib. Sens. Netw., 13*(11), 1–16.

Rahmani, A., Thanigaivelan, N., Gia, T., Granados, J., Negash, B., Liljeberg, P., & Tenhunen, H., (2015). Smart e-health gateway: Bringing intelligence to internet-of-things based ubiquitous healthcare systems. *Proceedings of the 12th Annual IEEE Consumer Communications and Networking Conference (CCNC)*.

Redowan, M., Narayana, S. S., Ramamohanarao, K., & Buyya, R., (2018). Quality of experience (QoE)-aware placement of applications in fog computing environments. *Journal of Parallel and Distributed Computing*.

Sahoo, K. S., et al., (2019a). ESMLB: Efficient switch migration-based load balancing for multi-controller SDN in IoT. *IEEE Internet of Things Journal*.

Sahoo, K. S., et al., (2019b). Improving end-users utility in software-defined wide area network systems. *IEEE Transactions on Network and Service Management*.

Santos, J., Wauters, T., Volckaert, B., & De Turck, F., (2017). Resource provisioning for IoT application services in smart cities. *13th International Conference on Network and Service Management (CNSM)* (pp. 1–9). Tokyo.

Sarkar, S., & Misra, S., (2016). Theoretical modeling of fog computing: A green computing paradigm to support IoT applications. *IET Networks, 5*(2), 23–29.

Shah-Mansouri, H., & Wong, V. W. S., (2018). Hierarchical fog-cloud computing for IoT systems: A computation offloading game. *IEEE Internet of Things, 5*(4), 3246–3257.

Skala, K., Davidovic, D., Afghan, E., & Sojat, Z., (2015). Scalable distributed computing hierarchy: Cloud, fog and dew computing. *Open Journal of Cloud Computing (OJCC), 2*(1).

Skarlat, O., Nardelli, M., Schulte, S., Borkowski, M., & Leitner, P., (2017). Optimized IoT service placement in the fog. *Service Oriented Computing and Applications, 11*(4), 427–443.

Souza, V. B., Masip-Bruin, X., Marin-Tordera, E., Ramirez, W., & Sanchez, S., (2016). Towards distributed service allocation in fog-to-cloud (F2C) Scenarios. *IEEE Global Communications Conference (GLOBECOM)*, 1–6.

Taneja, M., & Davy, A., (2017). Resource aware placement of IoT application modules in fog-cloud computing paradigm. In: *Proceedings of the IFIP/IEEE Symposium on Integrated Network and Service Management (IM'17)* (pp. 1222–1228).

Tang, B., Chen, Z., Hefferman, G., Wei, T., He, H., & Yang, Q., (2015). A hierarchical distributed fog computing architecture for big data analysis in smart cities. *Proceedings of the ASE Big Data and Social Informatics*.

Tiwary, M., et al., (2018). Response time optimization for cloudlets in mobile edge computing. *Journal of Parallel and Distributed Computing, 119*, 81–91.

Topcuoglu, H., Hariri, S., & Wu, Y. M., (2002). Performance-effective and low-complexity task scheduling for heterogeneous computing. *IEEE Trans Parallel Distributed System, 13*(3), 260–274.

Velasquez, K., Perez, A. D., Curado, M., & Monteiro, E., (2017). Service placement for latency reduction in the internet of things. *Annals of Telecommunications*, 105–115.

Yousefpour, A., Patil, A., Ishigaki, G., Kim, I., Wang, X., Cankaya, H. C., Zhang, Q., Xie, W., & Jue, J. P., (2019). *QoSaware Dynamic Fog Service Provisioning*. Accepted for publication in IEEE Internet of Things Journal, arXiv:1802.00800v2.

CHAPTER 6

Blockchain-Supported Cloud Architecture for Software-Defined Industrial IoT

KSHIRA SAGAR SAHOO[1], BATA KRISHNA TRIPATHY[2],
ABINAS PANDA[3], and BROJO KISHORE MISHRA[4]

[1]*Department of Computer Science and Engineering, SRM University, Amaravati, AP, 522502, India, E-mail: kshirasagar12@gmail.com*

[2]*School of Electrical Sciences, Indian Institute of Technology, Bhubaneswar–752050, Odisha, India*

[3]*Department of Computer Science and Engineering, National Institute of Technology, Rourkela–769008, India*

[4]*Department of CSE, GIET University, Gunupur, Odisha, India*

ABSTRACT

The recent development of industrial Internet of things (IIoT) and the huge data explosion from the smart devices create a major concern to the data centers (DCs). Although few dedicated approaches exist, efficient data management is still a big question. High availability, low latency, optimized response time, real time data delivery are the major concern in IIoT. To address this issue, this chapter discussed cloud architecture that supports blockchain with Software-defined networking (SDN) enabled IIoT (SD-IIoT). Software-defined networking (SDN) is an emerging network architecture, which separates the control logic from the hardware switches and router. With this separation, the network layer devices turn into packet forwarding devices and the control logic transferred to a central entity called control plane (CP). The proposed architecture based on blockchain technology, provides a secured, and on-demand access to the most essential and computing resources in IIoT network. Similarly, blockchain is a promising technology that carries no transaction cost that allows passing the information in a fully automated environment and a safer manner. During transaction, one party initiates the process by creating a block. The created block is verified by thousands of computers distributed around the Internet, which later added to a chain after verification. Particularly, this chapter discusses a cloud architecture in which the computing resources available nearer to the IIoT network through edge computing. Further, large amounts of data can access securely with minimum latency, with the help of both SDN and blockchain techniques.

6.1 INTRODUCTION

Internet of things (IoT) is that concept in which a group of animated devices can sense, collect, analyze, and transfer data over the Internet without human intervention (Sahoo et al., 2019a; Puthal et al., 2018). *Nowadays, a*ll the data available on the Internet at first captured by human beings. Since the human being has limited time, capturing real time data is a difficult task. At the same time analysis of captured data, accuracy on analysis from the captured data is more difficult. If we have an intelligence system which can know about the things and gathered data without any human interference, it will be easy to track and get the things simple. This is what the concept of "IoT" came. It is often referred to a smart object. Starting from smartphone to smart home all are belong to smart objects (Sahoo et al., 2016).

The arena of IoT is the system of interconnected heterogeneous objects which comprises of sensors, actuators, RFID, embedded computing system that uniquely identifiable and run over a standard communication protocols. Figure 6.1 depicts about the application of IoT in different sectors.

Smart devices have a major role for transforming the physical surroundings around us to a digital world using the IoT system. A smart device can contain a dozen of application logic that sense the local environment and interact with human users.

Other than IoT, there is another analogous concept called Industrial IoT (IIoT). At the first time, the term IIoT was coined by General Electric, mentioning it is the subset of IoT. The underlying idea of both the architecture is same. The prime difference is that, the usage of IIoT in the field of large-scale industries such as manufacturing, supply chain management, health care, energy, etc. Whereas, the IoT concept is commonly used in consumer usage such as smart watch, smart glass, etc. The idea behind of this concept is that how smartly the dumb machines can capture and analyze the real time data and at the same time take the business decision more accurately.

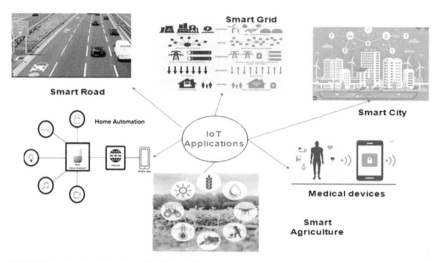

FIGURE 6.1 Application of IoT in different sectors.

The newly emerged IIoT is a collection of different technologies including automation, machine learning, big data, sensor data that have existed in the industrial background for many years. IIoT improves the visibility and increase the efficacy of the productivity as we as reduce the complex processes within the industry. The major aspect covers safety, quality, and productivity. The origin of IIoT revolutionalized from Industry 4.0. The Industry 4.0 concept primarily focuses more on industrial assets which can construct a smart factory. It also lets for the growth of novel business models which may supplement to fundamentally new ways of communication from corner to corner in the entire chain. This term was originated by the German government which encourages the computerization of manufacturing industry. The related technologies use the methodologies that support self-configuration, self-diagnosis, and enough intelligent support of workers in their complex system. In other words, IIoT allows manufacturing companies to pay more priority to their customers at the same time, ensures cost-effective internal operations. It promotes adaptability with open architectures that carry higher customization across thousands of devices. For instance, Kaa is a cloud-assisted IoT platform that can easily fit with a variety of sensors used in industrial machines, hardware controllers, and gateways. Figure 6.2 illustrates a typical IIoT scenario and different usage of it.

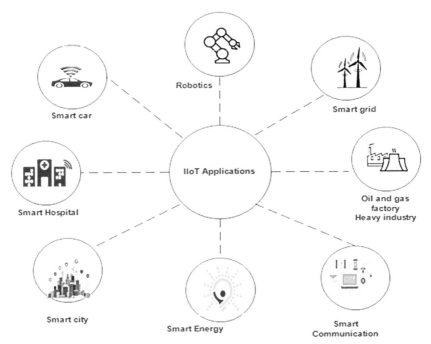

FIGURE 6.2   A typical IIoT scenario.

Nowadays, major industrial sectors now can be visible in IIoT system. The industrial sector includes the energy industry (oil and gas), healthcare industry, transportation, manufacturing, and many more. Apart from that, many other government use cases can be seen as IIoT such as in smart cities, smart energies, smart irrigations, etc. The significant advantages by implementing of IIoT have been outlined below:

1. IIoT system can help to predict any machinery defect, requirement of any prior maintenance by collecting real data from the machines.

2. Field services can be improvised with the help of IIoT. For instance, the field engineer can recognize the potential issues that exist in the customers' equipment.

3. The asset Management system can easily be handled through this system. In the supply chain, suppliers, customers, and manufacturers can track their status of the product, delivery details, and current location of the product effectively.

4. The manufacturing industries can produce customer-centric product through IIoT.

5. End to end manufacturing process of a product can effectively be monitored through this system, which reduces the operational cost. In the manufacturing industry, the close monitoring system of IoT can eliminate unnecessary labor cost and wastage of products.

6. The integration of big data analytics and IIoT can enhance the safeness of operators, craftsmen, engineers, laborers, drivers, etc. The security and safety of a worker can be decided by monitoring different parameters, such as the number of absent days, injury incidents, property damage, etc. Therefore, efficient monitoring assures better safety. Table 6.1 discusses the key difference between IoT and IIoT system.

Similar to IoT, these days blockchain technology draw a heavy attention from many sectors including heath care, governance, settlement, finance, e-governance, etc., (Fernández-Caramés, Tiago and Paula, 2018), (Available: https://coinmarketcap.com/). All the application in blockchain runs in a decentralized fashion. The central authority is not requiring monitoring the transactions among different parties. (Available: https://www.treasury.gov/initiatives/fio/Documents/McKinsey_FACI_Blockchain_in_Insurance.pdf). In short, blockchain technology can be defined as a mathematical model which holds transactional records by ensuring a secured, and transparently with a decentralized method. All the records are stored in the form of blocks which are guarded by no solitary authority. In other words, it is a distributed ledger that is entirely unlock to everyone working over the network. Although the storing process is not simple, but once the information are stored, it is really hard to modify it (Attaran, Mohsen, and Angappa, 2019; Esposito et al., 2018).

In another end, software defined networking (SDN) is one more novel technology enables to held the control plane (CP) separately from the

TABLE 6.1 Key Differences between IoT and IIoT

Difference Parameter	IoT	IIoT
General Usage	Meant for consumer usage.	Meant for industrial purpose.
	Example: smart green house, smart farming, wearable devices such as smart watch, smart glass, etc.	*Example:* Heavy industry, oil, and gas industries, robotics, smart city, smart supply chain, aero space, etc.
Degree of Application	It can use in the less risk areas, where low cost sensors and actuators are used.	It can handle more important machineries for which sophisticated sensors and analytics required inside the plants, supply chain, heavy industries.
Production volume	Since low cost sensors are used, the production volume is much higher.	Since precise sensors are used for production sector, the production volume is less.
Risk factor	IoT deals with consumer devices with low cost sensors. Usage of IoT, usually in low risk areas such as irrigation, smart farming, etc. Hence, the risk factor is low.	IIoT deals with heavy machineries, health care, defense like critical sectors with high cost sensors, hence the risk factor is high.
Security	Security is major factor for IoT system.	For IIoT system, security as well as robust and correct sensing data is required.
Operations technology (OT)	Legacy OT is not compulsory.	Legacy OT like SCADA and M2M (Machine to Machine) must exist to operate IIoT.
ERP system	ERP system is not compulsory	For IIoT, integrated back end ERP system is essential
Latency	For conserving power low latency is required.	In terms of safety, decision making in supply chain like areas, IIoT solution must support low latency.

underlying rigid data plane (DP) (Sahoo et al., 2019b). It becomes one of the popular technologies for organizing and deploying various applications running over the network. SDN is becoming instrumental that allow the enterprises to deploy applications at a faster rate, in turn the overall deployment cost become reduced. For securing the transactions in SDN, many cryptographic applications start using blockchain technology. This makes a fast reconciliation among the different involved parties because it does not consider any intermediary body in transaction activities. The prime reason behind the great interest in blockchain is that, with this technique applications can be operated in distributed manner, rather rely on a trusted intermediary. It is widely believed that this technology can overcome problems faced by the cloud system previously. For instance, companies as if Amazon provides a decentralized storage cloud infrastructure with a minimal charge. With this offer organizes host their own important data to cloud server. This move decreases the maintenance of the company. However, it bound us to believe on third party for transaction. With the parallel development of cloud and financial sector, the existing system can be replaced with blockchain technology.

This chapter proposes a secured distributed cloud infrastructure for IIoT system that uses two different emerging technologies such as blockchain and SDN with edge computing. This framework can gather, and analyze IIoT data at edge server in a distributed cloud system. In this framework the key role of SDN is that, it facilitates easy management and flexible orchestration. The proposed distributed cloud architecture provides a secured edge server platform with the help of SDN and blockchain technologies. It helps to IIoT network, in such a way that the required resources are available and executed at the edge server securely.

6.2 PRELIMINARIES

6.2.1 BLOCKCHAIN

As demonstrated in Figure 6.3, the construction of blockchain is consisting of a series blocks. The hash values are used to inter-link the blocks. In blockchain, a public ledger retains the digitally signed transactions of the involved parties. A user has two keys, such as a public key and a private key (Amine et al., 2018; Biswal, 2020). For encryption purposes, a private key is used to read the encrypted message. The importance of private and public keys has been demonstrated in Figure 6.4. In a blockchain network, the transactions are being signed by the private key whereas public key used for unique address.

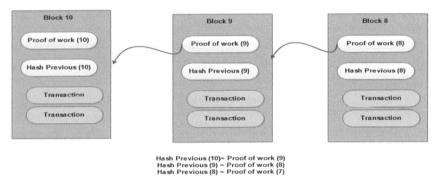

FIGURE 6.3   A basic structure of a blockchain.

A block is a digital item which consists of three parts:

1. It keeps information about the transactions conducted by the user. It can store data like date, Rupees amount of the recent purchased from Flipkart website (For example);
2. Further, it stores helpful information like who is engaging in transactions. Instead of using an actual user name, a unique "digital signature," is associated with the transaction. Data stored by the blocks differ from other block; and
3. Each block keeps a unique key called a 'Hash' by which blocks can be identifiable.

In the preliminary stage, a user has to sign on a transaction with the help of its private key, later the signed transaction have intimates it to its peers (Ivánkó, NatáliaRéka, and Max, 2018). Upon receiving the signed transaction, the peers authenticate the transaction. Further, the authenticated transaction circulates over the network. The involved parties in the transactions authenticate the transaction to convene a consensus agreement. After reaching of the distributed consensus agreement, a special node called minor takes in the valid transaction into a time stamped block. The used block, then broadcast back to the network. After validating and hash function matching with the previous block, the broadcast block is attached to the blockchain. Figures 6.4(a) and (b) illustrate the blockchain working principles.

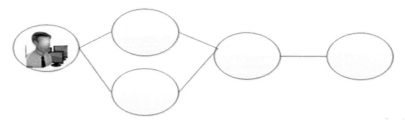

(a) Transaction signing by the user.

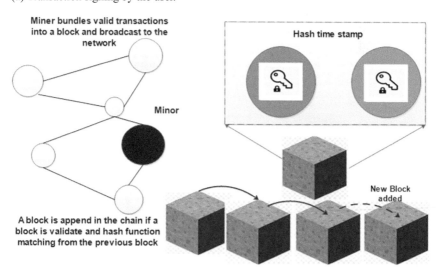

(b) Adding block in the chain.

FIGURE 6.4   Blockchain working principle.

Depending on the application, blockchain technology can be categorized into the public or private blockchain. The execution process of the consensus protocol, authorization mechanism, preservation of the ledger are different in the above two types of blockchains. Further, in the context of IIoT, it can be broadly classified based on authentication. In a public blockchain there is no involvement of any intermediary for the selection of minor and adding as a block to the chain system. Particularly, the consensus protocols are the key structure of the blockchain mechanism. Hence, security to various consensus protocols becomes a major research issue in this field.

As discussed above, blockchain is a data structure which is a collection of transactional records by ensuring a secured mechanism in a decentralized fashion. In other words, it is immutable transactions that are time stamp based and controlled by cluster of system. However, it is not handled by a single entity. Blocks in the chain are secured with strong cryptographic beliefs. The immutable ledger concept is unlocked for everyone in the network. Therefore, anything occurs within the chain it will reflect other parties involved in the transactional activities.

The blockchain principle can be visualized with an example. For instance, we are going for booking ticket through a mobile application. While we are paying the amount through credit card, the credit card company imposes charges as processing fees. However, using blockchain the third party cannot levied the charge. Now, two parties are railway operator and fellow passenger (Bahack, 2013). Here, the booked ticket is treated as a block and added into the ticket blockchain. Like bitcoin, transactions in blockchain are verifiable, immutable, and unique (Conti et al., 2018). The important fact is all the process is free.

6.2.2   SOFTWARE-DEFINED NETWORK

Software-Defined Networks (SDN) is a network paradigm whose objective is to build an adaptable and flexible network. In other words, SDN aims to improve network control in a better way by investing in enterprises and service providers for responding fastly on the basis of business requirements (Xia et al., 2017).

In a legacy network, both packets forwarding tasks and managing the flow are handled by a single and expensive hardware unit, generally called router (Sahoo et al., 2018b, c). Conventionally few router vendors allow the flexibility to manage the queue size such that congestion control and traffic control can be maintained efficiently. However, the underlying devices pose a low performance for the changeable traffic demand. Moreover, in the traditional IP-based network, in case of any modification to the topology, it is an expensive task. It can be simplified by performing all decision at a centralized software unit, instead of embedding in a hardware device. In this way, the administrator can get ample opportunity to handle network traffic.

This decoupling feature is called Software Defined Network (SDN). In SDN, both control and DPs are separated. In the CP, the controller has a major role in making a decision on the incoming flows into the network (Sahoo et al., 2019b). The decoupled architecture provides numerous benefits such as centralized control provisioning, better enterprise management, lower operating cost, and granular security. Depending upon the size of the network topology, there can be more than one controller that can handle the entire network.

There are numerous benefits of SDN. Few of them are highlighted below:

1. The underlying network resources can be utilized efficiently.
2. Due to the programmability nature of SDN, network administrators can manage the network efficiently.
3. Multi-tenant data centers (DCs) are well suited to the SDN.
4. SDN can facilitate better traffic engineering, fine-grained security rules, and adopting congestion control like major advantages.
5. SDN can reduce the CAPEX, due to the use of inexpensive devices.
6. The centralized network management can have the entire view of the network. Due to this centralized monitoring, the DDoS like potential security issues can be checked.
7. Fine-grained security rules can be imposed on the underlying devices through SDN-C.
8. Being capable of automating the traffic, SDN enhances the quality of services (QoS) and multimedia transmissions. Streaming high-quality video content becomes more accessible due to SDN.

SDN has three-layer such as CP layer, DP layer, and application layer (Sahoo et al., 2019c). Similarly, there are three different interfaces such as: northbound, southbound, and east-west bridge. Figure 6.5 illustrates basic three-layer SDN architecture.

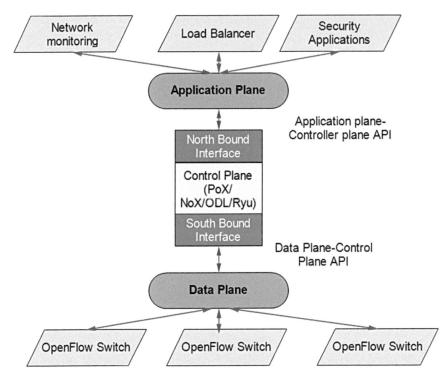

FIGURE 6.5 Basic SDN architecture.

Source: Reprinted with permission from Sahoo et al., 2016.

6.2.3 EDGE COMPUTING

Nowadays, edge computing is a very prevalent technology that facilitates computations such as analytics, storage, processing nearer to the source of data. Instead of relying on cloud always, the generated data are processed near to the source itself (Biswal et al., 2020; Tomovic et al., 2017). In other words, the edge can be distinguished by its proximity and geographical distribution to the Cloud computing system (Stojmenovic, Ivan, and Sheng, 2014). Edge computing provides services by introducing a new intermediate layer composed of geographically distributed micro datacenters. Each micro DC is an extremely virtualized platform hosted on committed computing devices. In order to get faster services, the IIoT generated data sent to the nearby edge server for processing, instead of to the remote cloud.

However, edge computing filter out non-actionable data and further send them to the remote cloud for batch analytics. This technology improves QoS for a variety of IIoT applications and reduces bandwidth consumption in the network. Although edge computing has many benefits, however, its internal communications are very complex. A few reasons are service synchronization, service delivery, soft state, etc.

6.2.4 APPLICATIONS OF BLOCKCHAIN OVER IIoT

The applications of blockchain over IIoT are numerous. Few of them are listed below:

1. The practice of IIoT in healthcare sector is numerous. It allows storing the clinical data related to patients and their respective healthcare service providers. The electronic medical record (EMR) is such a system that helps to maintain such data efficiently by the healthcare provider (Liang et al., 2017; Lei et al., 2017). After storing the sensible patients and healthcare data, blockchain technology can promise the security on these data. A typical authorizing access to confidential medical records, provided by blockchain. As a distributed trust method, this technology tackle various issues related to a distributed database of patient records. Since these patients' data are maintained by different parties including hospital, insurance companies, etc., (Kang et al., 2017; Li et al., 2018). Blockchain can track records in a secured manner.

2. Nowadays, Internet of vehicles, it is also termed as IoV is a promising approach. IoV let the amalgamation of vehicles into the IoT concept. Though this integration vehicles can set up a smart communication among various heterogeneous networks such as v2v, v2r (road), v2h (human), v2s (sensors), etc. On the other hand, few researchers have tried to incorporate blockchain in IoV system for more security (Xia et al., 2017). The decentralized security model of blockchain ecosystem helps to add more security into the IoV (Yang et al., 2017).

3. The dispersion of rich content from IIoT, becoming a challenging task for ISP which conceives a new concept called collaborative video delivery. However, researchers have added blockchain mechanism for an efficient collaborative video delivery mechanism (Xu, 2017).

4. In IIoT billion of smart devices send the sensing information to the remote cloud server with the help of Internet. This concept is popularly known as Internet of cloud (IoC), which utilizes the virtualization concept of cloud. For less energy consumption in IoC, few researchers have utilized blockchain technology. In order to reduce the utilized energy, Xu et al. devised an intelligent technique that supports blockchain technology (Xu, 2017). In another work, Sharma and their co-authors projected a distributed cloud system that utilizes three different promising technologies such as: SDN, fog computing, and blockchain technology. Blockchain-based MeDshare framework has proposed by Xia et al. (2017). This proposed framework share the data among cloud service providers efficiently.

5. For a proficient use of IoT system's bandwidth, authors have utilized SDN paradigm. The controller, the brain of the SDN, can provide an easy decision making process for the efficient use of IIoT bandwidth. However, DistBlockNet framework featured a distributed IoT architecture that follows the blockchain technology (Sharma et al., 2017).

6. In the earlier edge-computing paradigm, the edge servers communicate among themselves via third party. However, with the introduction of blockchain technology there is no need of any third party for the communication. A novel payment scheme has proposed by Huang et al. (2018). The proposed scheme can help for outsourcing the computations of Fog devices.

7. The blockchain technology can be used in crowdsensing applications. The mobile crowdsensing is the combination of geo-crowdsourcing and volunteered geographic information. In this mechanism, mobile users utilize their mobile computing and collect the local data through the in-built sensors, process it, and further delivered it to other users for supporting their mobility. For secured communication in crowdsensing, Wang et al. proposed a mechanism that uses the blockchain framework (Xu et al., 2017).

8. Storing and sharing a large volume of IoT data in a secured manner is a big challenge. Jiang et al. proposed a decentralized storage mechanism based on blockchain technology which is termed as Searchain (Sahoo et al., 2019a).

6.3   INTEGRATION OF SDN AND EDGE COMPUTING

The SD-IIoT is integration of IIoT devices with access points, SDN-C, cloud server, and edge nodes. Edge nodes exhibit a set of application programming interfaces (APIs) for the deployment of applications and resource management. Such APIs provide seamless access to hypervisors and service containers on a physical machine. In addition to this, they can monitor the physical resources (Sahoo et al., 2018a).

For instance, jobs of large-scale video surveillance applications in an industry may be organized as follows. Like, face recognition in IP camera conduct at edge and aggregation at the remote cloud server. It is assumed that each of the devices has information about its geophysical location. Here, a major challenge inflicted by edge server, i.e., service orchestration. It involves replication, migration of service instances on a large volume, etc. In a typical case, all different applications should be scaled up transparently at the runtime without any over-provisioning. In order to realize the centralized orchestration SDN will help extensively. To achieve these tasks the controller requires an up-to-date illustration of the entire system.

6.4   INTEGRATION OF SDN AND BLOCKCHAIN

It is already realized that with the increasing demand of network traffic, clouds cannot meet the desired requirement. Hence, edge computing is an alternative to this problem, which brings the computing capabilities nearer to the distributed IIoT network. Instead of transferring the raw IIoT data to the cloud, the edge server can play a major role in between. Edge computing helps to gather, categorize, and analyze data nearer to the industrial setup itself, which can ultimately enhance the processing speed of the network. However, the addition of blockchain technology in the cloud server can enhance the security of the IIoT system more effectively. Figure 6.6 shows a proposed architecture that combines three different emerging technologies such as SDN, edge computing, and blockchain for accessing data through the cloud.

In the previous section, it has discussed that SDN-C can effectively take the decision for executing IIoT data either by edge server or cloud server. Here, the edge server can offer localization, whereas the cloud layer can offer wide-area monitoring. Each controller deployed in the edge network is authorized with various analysis functions on the flow rule and migration module for secure communication during any kind of attack (Sharma et al., 2017; Sahoo et al., 2019c). All base stations (BS) are equipped with OpenFlow (OF) enabled switches, which act as a forwarding plane. These are meant for aggregating raw data coming from IIoT devices. Further, the controller deployed over edge provides programming interfaces to network operators to carry out a variety of networking utility.

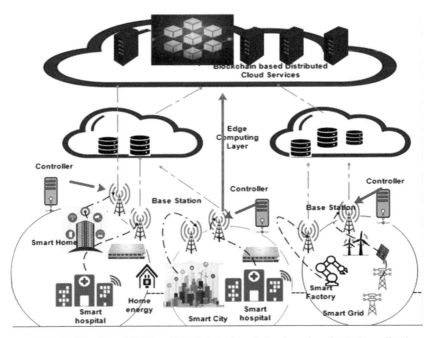

FIGURE 6.6 Distributed SDN and blockchain-based cloud services for IIoT applications.

The proposed blockchain-based cloud architecture comprises of four steps:

1. **Step 1:** In the initial step, the cloud user selects the essential resources from the SP pool available in the blockchain-enabled cloud server.
2. **Step 2:** When the assortment has finished, the particular SP puts forward the desired services to the user. For instance, services like task execution, and provision of servers, etc., provide to that user.
3. **Step 3:** Upon providing the requested services, the registered SP records the transaction in the form of blockchain and shares it with all participated SP in the particular cloud service.

4. **Step 4:** At last, the user will disburse and made payment to the provider. To make a secured transaction, the proposed SDN and blockchain-based architecture can provide a transparent and reliable solution to the SP.

Here, SP denotes Service Provider. Further, the proof-of-work can be done with the available protocol, for instance, Etherium. It would promise that a vast number of approves token exchanges are happening in the blockchain of nodes that utilize cryptographic challenges.

6.5 CONCLUSION

Recently integration of both SDN and blockchain technology has drawn heavy attention from many sectors. All the application in blockchain runs in a decentralized fashion. The central authority is not required to monitor the transactions among different parties. In short, all the records are stored in the form of blocks which are guarded by no solitary authority. Moreover, the central visibility and programmability nature of SDN change the characteristic of network management. Having realized a significant potential of these two technologies, in this chapter, we have discussed a new blockchain-based cloud Computing model for the Industrial IoT system. The raw data generated from IIoT devices are managed in the cloud and at the edge server. The discussed model can support large-scale IIoT application for accessing secured data with low latency and fast delivery.

KEYWORDS

- base stations
- blockchain
- edge devices
- electronic medical record
- internet of cloud
- internet of things
- operations technology
- quality of services

REFERENCES

Ali, M., et al., (2016). Blockstack: A global naming and storage system secured by blockchains. In: *2016 {USENIX} Annual Technical Conference ({USENIX}{ATC} 16)*.

Amine, F. M., et al., (2018). *Blockchain Technologies for the Internet of Things: Research Issues and Challenges*. arXiv preprint arXiv:1806.09099.

Attaran, M., & Angappa, G., (2019). Blockchain principles, qualities, and business applications. *Applications of Blockchain Technology in Business* (pp. 13–20). Springer, Cham.

Bahack, L., (2013). *Theoretical Bitcoin Attacks with Less than Half of the Computational Power (draft)*. arXiv preprint arXiv:1312.7013.

Biswal, A. K., Maiti, P., Bebarta, S., Sahoo, B., & Turuk, A. K., (2020). Authenticating IoT devices with blockchain. In: Kim, S., & Deka, G., (eds.), *Advanced Applications of Blockchain Technology* (Vol. 60). Studies in Big Data. Springer, Singapore.

Conti, M., et al., (2018). A survey on security and privacy issues of bitcoin. *IEEE Communications Surveys and Tutorials, 20*(4), 3416–3452.

Crypto-Currency Market Capitalizations. [Online]. Available: https://coinmarketcap.com (accessed on 16 December 2020).

Dorri, A., et al., (2017). Blockchain: A distributed solution to automotive security and privacy. *IEEE Communications Magazine, 55*(12), 119–125.

El-Sayed, H., et al., (2017). Edge of things: The big picture on the integration of edge, IoT and the cloud in a distributed computing environment. *IEEE Access, 6*, 1706–1717.

Esposito, C., et al., (2018). Blockchain: A panacea for healthcare cloud-based data security and privacy? *IEEE Cloud Computing, 5*(1), 31–37.

Fernández-Caramés, T. M., & Fraga-Lamas, P., (2018). A review on the use of blockchain for the internet of things. *IEEE Access, 6*, 32979–33001.

Garcia, L. P., et al., (2015). Edge-centric computing: Vision and challenges. *ACM SIGCOMM Computer Communication Review, 45*(5), 37–42.

Guo, R., et al., (2018). Secure attribute-based signature scheme with multiple authorities for blockchain in electronic health records systems. *IEEE Access, 6*, 11676–11686.

Huang, X., et al., (2018). LNSC: A security model for electric vehicle and charging pile management based on blockchain ecosystem. *IEEE Access, 6*, 13565–13574.

Ivánkó, N. R., & Max, M., (2018). Towards blockchain-based collaborative intrusion detection systems. *Critical Information Infrastructures Security: 12th International Conference, CRITIS 2017* (Vol. 10707). Lucca, Italy, Revised Selected Papers, Springer.

Kang, J., et al., (2017). Enabling localized peer-to-peer electricity trading among plug-in hybrid electric vehicles using consortium blockchains. *IEEE Transactions on Industrial Informatics, 13*(6), 3154–3164.

Lei, A., et al., (2017). Blockchain-based dynamic key management for heterogeneous intelligent transportation systems. *IEEE Internet of Things Journal, 4*(6), 1832–1843.

Li, L., et al., (2018). Creditcoin: A privacy-preserving blockchain-based incentive announcement network for communications of smart vehicles. *IEEE Transactions on Intelligent Transportation Systems, 19*(7), 2204–2220.

Liang, X., et al., (2017). Integrating blockchain for data sharing and collaboration in mobile healthcare applications. In: *2017 IEEE 28th Annual International Symposium on Personal, Indoor, and Mobile Radio Communications (PIMRC)*. IEEE.

McKinsey and Company, (2017). *Blockchain Technology Report to the US Federal Advisory Committee on Insurance.* [Online]. Available: https://www.treasury.gov/initiatives/fio/documents/mckinsey_faci_blockchain_in_insurance.pdf (accessed on 16 December 2020).

Puthal, D., et al., (2018). The blockchain as a decentralized security framework [future directions]. *IEEE Consumer Electronics Magazine, 7*(2), 18–21.

Sahoo, K. S., & Bibhudatta, S., (2019). CAMD: A switch migration-based load balancing framework for software defined networks. *IET Networks.*

Sahoo, K. S., Bibhudatta, S., & Abinas, P., (2015). A secured SDN framework for IoT. In: *2015 International Conference on Man and Machine Interfacing (MAMI).* IEEE.

Sahoo, K. S., et al., (2016). A comprehensive tutorial on software defined network: The driving force for the future internet technology. *Proceedings of the International Conference on Advances in Information Communication Technology and Computing.* ACM.

Sahoo, K. S., et al., (2018a). A learning automata-based DDoS attack defense mechanism in software defined networks. *Proceedings of the 24th Annual International Conference on Mobile Computing and Networking.* ACM.

Sahoo, K. S., et al., (2018b). On the placement of controllers in software-Defined-WAN using meta-heuristic approach. *Journal of Systems and Software, 145*, 180–194.

Sahoo, K. S., et al., (2019a). ESMLB: Efficient switch migration-based load balancing for multi-controller SDN in IoT. *IEEE Internet of Things Journal.*

Sahoo, K. S., et al., (2019b). Improving end-users utility in software-defined wide area network systems. *IEEE Transactions on Network and Service Management.*

Sahoo, K. S., et al., (2019c). Toward secure software-defined networks against distributed denial of service attack. *The Journal of Supercomputing*, 1–46.

Sharma, P. K., et al., (2017). Distblocknet: A distributed blockchains-based secure SDN architecture for IoT networks. *IEEE Communications Magazine, 55*(9), 78–85.

Sharma, P. K., Mu-Yen, C., & Jong, H. P., (2017). A software defined fog node based distributed blockchain cloud architecture for IoT. *IEEE Access, 6*, 115–124.

Stojmenovic, I., & Sheng, W., (2014). The fog computing paradigm: Scenarios and security issues. In: *2014 Federated Conference on Computer Science and Information Systems.* IEEE.

Tomovic, S., et al., (2017). Software-defined fog network architecture for IoT. *Wireless Personal Communications, 92*(1), 181–196.

Xia, Q., Sifah, E. B., Asamoah, K. O., Gao, J., Du, X., & Guizani, M., (2017). MeDShare: Trust-less medical data sharing among cloud service providers via blockchain. *IEEE Access, 5*, 14757–14767.

Xu, C., Kun, W., & Mingyi, G., (2017). Intelligent resource management in blockchain-based cloud datacenters. *IEEE Cloud Computing, 4*(6), 50–59.

Yang, Z., et al., (2017). A blockchain-based reputation system for data credibility assessment in vehicular networks. In: *2017 IEEE 28th Annual International Symposium on Personal, Indoor, and Mobile Radio Communications (PIMRC).* IEEE.

Zyskind, G., & Oz, N., (2015). Decentralizing privacy: Using blockchain to protect personal data. In: *2015 IEEE Security and Privacy Workshops.* IEEE.

CHAPTER 7

DDoS Attack Detection in Software-Defined IoT: A Big Picture

MOIN SHARUKH[1], DURGA PRASAD VARMA[1], JANGILI NARENDRA[1], and KSHIRA SAGAR SAHOO[2]

[1]Department of Information Technology, VNR Vignana Jyothi Institute of Engineering and Technology, Hyderabad–500090, Telangana, India

[2]Department of Computer Science and Engineering, SRM University, Amaravati, AP, 522502, India

ABSTRACT

With the emergence of smart devices and the declining market value of sensing systems, the implementation of the internet of things (IoT) is gaining momentum. IoT has become an integral part of many smart systems such as smart buildings, smart cities, and smart heath, etc. Despite many advantages, from its inception, IoT system is vulnerable to many threats. Such systems are more likely to be attacked and breached, by denial of service (DoS) or distributed denial of service (DDoS) attacks. DDoS attacks are one of the Internet security's most disruptive threats. The towering volume of smart devices with a greater level of heterogeneity increases the severity of this attack. To date, there is no protocol that guarantees complete protection of IoT systems. To enable the resiliency, continuous monitoring, along with an adaptive decision-making system, is essential. These challenges can be addressed with the help of software-defined networking (SDN), which can effectively handle the IoT devices. Moreover, the centralized provisioning of SDN enables a secured and adaptive IoT environment that can effectively handle the DDoS attack. The software-defined internet of things (SDIoT) framework based on SDx paradigm consists of a controller pool, SD-IoT switches integrated with an IoT gateway, and IoT devices. In this chapter, a broad range of various DDoS attacks and detection methods for the IoT environment used in the SDN paradigm have been analyzed. Finally, different future scopes of this evolving field have been discussed.

7.1   INTRODUCTION

Software-defined networking (SDN) was initially introduced to resolve the complicated issues faced by the traditional network like traffic monitoring, cloud abstraction, granular security, and many more issues (Dargahi, 2017; Sahoo et al., 2016). The major goal of the software-defined network was to centralize the network and also to reduce the cost of hardware (Alsmadi, Iyad, and Mohammed, 2017). In this chapter, we are discussing about software-defined network and how it is useful to detect the DDoS (distributed denial of service) attacks.

Firstly, we are trying to understand the traditional networking architecture and the limitations faced by the current network. To overcome the limitations of the traditional network SDN has introduced. By discussing about the architecture of the SDN and its benefit over the traditional network has highlighted. To launch a DDoS attack the intruders generally use the devices connected to internet and more often IoT (internet of things) devices. The IoT devices are equipped with lower levels of security; hence they are prone to DDoS attacks. We discuss about the IoT with some mere examples.

Once we have a clear picture of the architectures and working mechanisms of both the SDN and IoT we then discuss about SDIoT. It is a combination of SDN and IoT. The Principle of SDIoT is discussed to explain the role of SDN in IoT. The relationship between the SDN and IoT is clearly explained in the role of SDN in IoT. The DDoS is been discussed in the further portion of the chapter. To understand the DDoS attack we have explained the architecture of DDoS and how the attack is launched. The various types of phases in the DDoS and their variations in different levels along with the types of DDoS attacks are discussed in the last portion of the chapter. The detection and mitigation techniques are then proposed after the phases of distribute denial of services and thus the optimal solution is also discussed in the end of the chapter.

Overall, this chapter summarizes about the traditional networks, software defined networks, IoT, software-defined internet of things (SDIoT) and its role and principles and finally about the DDoSs its phases and detection and mitigation techniques.

7.2 BACKGROUND

7.2.1 TRADITIONAL NETWORK

Traditional networking is embedded in fixed networking devices, such as a switch or a router. Each of these devices has certain features that work well together and serve the network (Sahoo et al., 2019a). Flexibility of these conventional networks is a recurrent obstacle. They are not useful for new business ventures, possess little agility, and are also static in nature. Most of the switching hardware and software in the conventional network are proprietary, but the software used cannot be quickly modified as needed. Figure 7.1 depicts the component of a traditional network device.

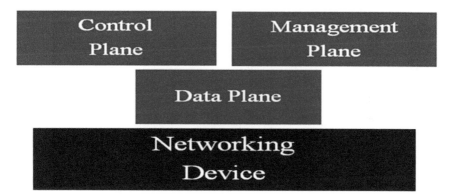

FIGURE 7.1   Traditional networking device.

> ➤ **Traits of Traditional Networking:**
>
>   1. Traditional networking mechanisms are operated mainly from dedicated devices, utilizing one or more switches, as well as routers or controls for software execution (Tripathy et al., 2016).
>   2. Within dedicated hardware, such as application-specific integrated circuits (ASIC), the design of mainstream networking is mostly incorporated. Limitations are one of the negative

aspects of this conventional hardware-centered networking. Figure 7.2 illustrates the architecture of a traditional network.

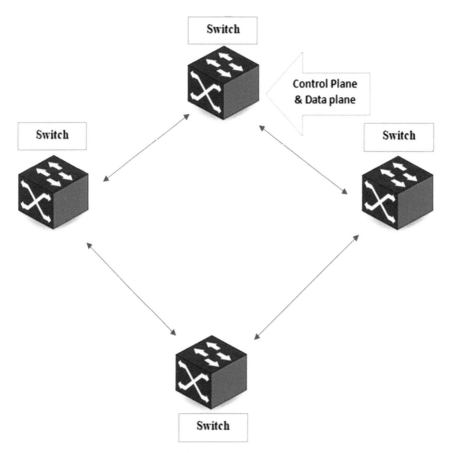

FIGURE 7.2   Simple architecture of a conventional network.

> **Limitations of Traditional Network:**
>
> 1. Since the data plane (DP) and control plane (CP) are mounted on same plane, there is a need to introduce new protocol for every service.
> 2. Manual configuration and reconfiguration consume lot of time.
> 3. The traditional network provides limited information about networks.

4. All the packets are leaded in the same way.
5. It becomes difficult to replace the existing program with new ideas and works according to packet forwarding tables.
6. Network management turns out to be difficult as the changes are implemented separately at each device.
7. The maintenance cost is higher.
8. The resource utilization is very low.

7.2.2 SOFTWARE DEFINED NETWORKING (SDN)

Software-defined networking (SDN) technology is a network management technique that allows for flexible, programmatically efficient network configuration to enhance network performance and monitoring, making it more like cloud computing than conventional network management (Sahoo et al., 2018c, 2019b). SDN is intended to address the fact that conventional networks static architecture is hierarchical and complicated, whereas modern networks require greater mobility and simpler trouble-shooting. SDN aims to centralize the network intelligence in one network component by detaching the forwarding process of network packets present in the DP from the routing process in the CP. The CP comprises of one or more controllers which are known to be the heart of the SDN network where the whole information is embedded.

SDN allows users to virtualize their hardware equipment like switches and routers and construct a computer network by splitting the network into the following separate planes:

1. The CP provides NetFlow's performance, efficiency, and fault management, it is often used to handle system configurations that are remotely connected to a software-defined network.
2. The DP directs the network traffic to its desired destination, before the data packets enter the DP; the CP determines the direction it will follow by using the flow protocol.

SDN controllers (SDN-Cs) have a northbound interface (NBI) that communicates to APIs (Liyanage, Mika, and Andrei, 2014). As a conse-quence of this interaction, application developers may specifically code the network, rather than using the protocols provided for conventional networking. SDN allows users to use software to provide new devices instead of using physical infrastructure, so that IT administrators can direct network paths and proactively manage network services. Unlike traditional switches, SDN also has the ability to communicate better with devices using the network.

Virtualization is the key difference between traditional networking and SDN. Once SDN virtualizes the entire network, it creates an imaginary replica of your physical network and enables you to provide services from a centralized location. Figure 7.3 depicts the structure of a software-defined network and the different planes in it.

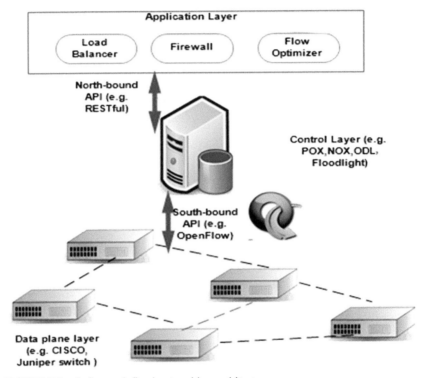

FIGURE 7.3   Software defined networking architecture.

Through SDN, the CP turns software-based, enabling it to be accessible through the connected device. Such control helps IT managers to monitor traffic flow in greater detail from a single user interface (UI) (Kalkan, Gurkan, and Fatih, 2017). Such centralized environment gives users greater flexibility over how their networks operate as well as how their networks are designed. It is advantageous for network segmentation to be able to rapidly process different network configurations from a centralized UI. SDN has now become a prominent alternative to traditional networking because it enables IT managers to provide the services and bandwidths required without needing additional physical infrastructure to spend. To enhance the network capacity, conventional networking requires new hardware. For generalization, the framework of SDN versus traditional networking could be distilled: One of them includes further expansion of hardware and the other needs only keystrokes.

7.2.2.1 BENEFITS OF SOFTWARE DEFINED NETWORKING (SDN)

SDN provides the following brief advantages in addition to centralizing and simplifying the management of enterprise network management:

1. **Cloud Abstraction:** SDN controllers have the capability to manage all of the networking components that constitute large data centers (DCs).
2. **Centralized Network Provisioning:** Through providing a single view throughout the entire network, SDN help to centralize business management and procurement. It can also accelerate service delivery and enhance agility in providing a central location for virtual and physical network devices.
3. **Holistic Enterprise Management:** Upon order, business networks need to set up new software or virtual machines (VMs) to accommodate new demands for storage such as big data queries. SDN allows IT administrators to deal with network design without the network being compromised. SDN also facilitates the administration from a single controller of both physical and virtual switches and network devices; which you cannot do with SNMP.
4. **Granular Security:** Centralized security is one of the major benefits of SDN that most appeals to IT managers. With virtualization coming into the picture network management has become more complex. It is harder to consistently apply firewall and content filtering policies to VMs.
5. **Lower OPEX:** Server utilization improvements, better virtualization control, Administrative productivity and other benefits should lead to operational savings.

6. **Reduced Hardware Cost:** SDN adoption also brings new life to existing network devices. SDN makes it even easier to optimize commoditized hardware. Existing equipment can be reused using guidelines from the SDN-C, and inexpensive hardware can be implemented more easily because new equipment are simply "white box" switches with all information based on the SDN-C.

7. **Efficient Content Delivery:** One of the key advantages of software-defined networking is the ability to mold and control network traffic.

7.2.3   INTERNET OF THINGS (IoT)

The internet of things (IoT) is a collection of interlinked smart devices, physical or virtual devices, with unique identifiers (UIDs) and the ability to access information over a network without human-to-human or computer-to-computer interference (Ma et al., 2015). Due to the integration of numerous innovations, like real-time analytics, machine learning, deep learning (DL), and embedded systems, the concept of the IoT has evolved (Zhang et al., 2019). The IoT technology is mostly associated with products that support one or more specific ecosystems and can be regulated through devices associated with that ecosystem, such as smartphones and smart speakers, such as lighting fixtures, thermostats, home security systems and cameras and other home appliances. Figure 7.4 depicts the simplified architecture of IoT.

7.2.3.1   EXAMPLES OF INTERNET OF THINGS (IoT)

1. **Autonomous Vehicles:** The autonomous vehicle has become one of IoT's most innovative applications. These vehicles have no operators and are flexible enough to drive you to your own destination. Configured with lots of devices such as sensors, gyroscopes, cloud architecture, internet, and more, these automobiles detect vast amounts of traffic data, pedestrians, road conditions such as speed breakers, potholes, corners, and sharp turns and process them quickly at great speeds. This information is transmitted on to the controller which takes the appropriate driving decisions. The key aspects of autonomous vehicles are artificial intelligence and machine learning.

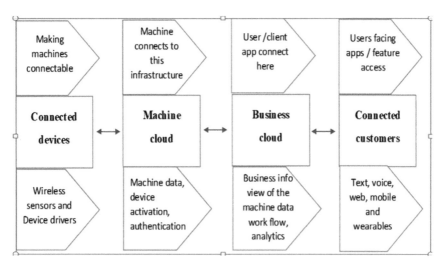

FIGURE 7.4   Simplified architecture of internet of things.

2. **Wearable Devices:** IoT comprises anything you carry that is connected to the internet, including fitbits to smartwatches. These wearable devices consist of sensors through which they communicate data to give you the most precise information you require at the moment (Figure 7.5).

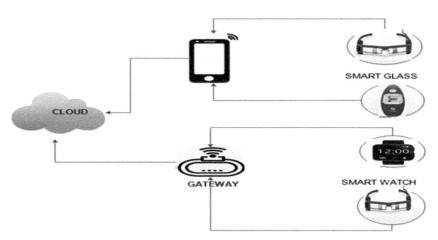

FIGURE 7.5   Smart wearable device.

7.2.3.2   APPLICATIONS OF IoT

1. **End-User Applications:** For consumer usage, a handful variety of IoT devices are being developed, including connected automobiles, smart homes, wearable devices, connected health, and security monitoring devices.
2. **Corporate Applications:** The Internet of Health Things (also known as the Internet of Medical Things) is an implementation of IoT for health and medical specific uses, information gathering and processing for research and analysis.
3. **Smart Agriculture:** It is very often ignored in IoT applications. Nevertheless, since the amount of farming operations are typically remote and the huge number of animals that farmers rely on, all of these can be tracked through the IoT and can fundamentally change the way farmers work every day. However, this proposal still has to reach a large-scale exposure. It is one of several IoT technologies that shouldn't be overlooked. Smart agriculture seems to have the potential to become an exciting field of operation, especially in the countries exporting agricultural products.
4. **Smart Retail:** Companies have begun to implement IoT technologies and also use IoT embedded devices across a number of applications that optimize market operations, increase sales, minimize vandalism, enable inventory management, and enhance the shopping experience of the client.
5. **Industrial Internet:** Another way of looking at things about the Global Network is by gazing at interconnected computers and appliances in sectors such as generating electricity, coal, gasoline, and healthcare. This also enables use of circumstances where unplanned interruption or device instability can lead to life-threatening situations.

7.2.3.3   SOFTWARE-DEFINED INTERNET OF THINGS (SDIoT)

The increasing number of devices in the IoT network makes it difficult to match the large number of things connected to the internet with the conventional IP specifications. Such devices may also have different characteristics and attributes, and therefore it is necessary to converge another routing protocol to accommodate this growth in the IoT environment.

To deal with the increasing amount of IoT devices in the current network IPv6 can be considered as a good choice, but it is not capable to address the heterogeneity of the underlying devices. Therefore, SDN has been used to enable communication between different devices from different networks using IPv6. The SDN-C is coupled with an IoT controller to simplify the management and control operations (Figure 7.6).

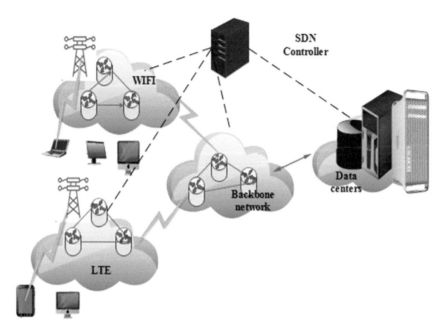

FIGURE 7.6 Schematic view of software-defined internet of things.

7.2.3.4 PRINCIPLES OF SOFTWARE-DEFINED INTERNET OF THINGS (SDIoT)

Traditionally, software-defined relates to the concept of extracting low-level elements, e.g., hardware devices and allowing them to be distributed and handled through a well-defined API. It helps the existing architecture to be refactored into finer-grained resource components, the configuration of which can be specified in the code after being deployed. Software-defined IoT systems include a collection of cloud-hosted resource components that can be supplied and managed at runtime.

The major principles of software-defined IoT systems include:

- **API Encapsulation:** IoT infrastructure and applications are integrated in well-defined APIs to provide a centralized view of application access and IoT cloud service configurations.
- **Fine-Grained Consumption:** To enable flexible usage and self-service consumption, IoT tools and technologies need to be available at different levels of granularity.
- **Policy-Based Specification and Configuration:** The units are specified declaratively, and their functionality is defined programmatically in software, using the well-defined API and available, familiar software libraries.
- **Automated Provisioning:** Key provisioning processes have to be streamlined to allow large-scale (e.g., hundreds of gateways) flexible, on-demand installation and application of software-defined IoT systems.
- **Cost Awareness:** To allow their utility-oriented use, they must be able to allocate and monitor the costs of distributed IoT services and capabilities.
- **Elasticity Support:** By providing runtime control of elastic resources through well-defined API, we must help elasticity governance.

7.2.4   ROLE OF SDN IN IoT

Billions of devices are projected to be used globally in a decade or so through the use of IoT technologies. It is therefore apparent that enormous information will be produced from the smart devices that need to be analyzed and processed in a seamless and efficient manner. Network management would seem to be a critical factor in handling such a huge collection of devices and the tremendous data they produce. For load balancing and reducing network latency, appropriate technology are required to transmit and monitor traffic flows in the network. The SDN-based technology can satisfy these criteria, as it centralizes the global view of the network. The SDN-based architectures can therefore be used to control IoT networks, such as load balancing, fine-grained packet forwarding, and enhanced bandwidth utilization (Puthal et al., 2016).

Ultimately, protecting systems and networks is an important factor to consider for the inclusion of multiple devices, suppliers, and consumers in a single platform. For instance, a group of devices are linked with a specific service provider.

As mentioned in the above section, IoT is meant to link billions of devices. In fact, the device holders should always be able to access them from anywhere and at any moment so that they can monitor or adjust the functionality of their devices in a smooth way, based on the specifications. These smart devices can be operated in the network, utilizing SDN-based technology while protecting others privacy.

Consequently, only the specific service provider should be allowed to access the equipment. Additionally, even though they have the information, certain service providers should not be able to gain access to the data generated by the devices. At the same moment, for the consumers participating in an IoT network, confidentiality is a major concern. Numerous agencies may have the data about who is doing what, leading to the convergence of multiple devices into a single platform, which in effect breaches users 'confidentiality. Researchers therefore need to recognize such situations to protect user's confidentiality when incorporating multiple devices into a single platform. Fine-grained flow control via SDN improves network traffic security and privacy. It is clear from the above-mentioned evidence that SDN-based technology will have a massive impact from the facets of edge, connectivity, core, and DC networks in the management of the IoT network.

7.3 DDoS ATTACK

DDoS attacks are perhaps the most challenging threats faced by the internet today (Mahjabin et al., 2017). The DDoS attacker depends on transmitting an excessive number of fake packets to overload the victim's resources such as CPU, memory, and bandwidth of the network (Mishra et al., 2018). Therefore, because of the flooded system resources, requests from genuine clients cannot be handled and the services may not be provided. Tremendous prevention methods have been developed to deal with this type of attacks. Nonetheless, owing to their implementation complexity as well as prohibitive operating costs, only few of them have been fully deployed. Some of the key reasons are that these methods typically require large network connection, state tables or high-end hardware to be mounted on routers or switches, and sometimes even require human interaction, which raises additional storage space or computing costs. It is therefore desirable to model certain standardized, lightweight, and flexible DDoS mitigation methods. Figure 7.7 shows the basic DDoS scenario.

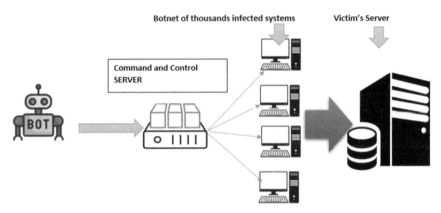

FIGURE 7.7   Distributed denial of service attack.

Botnets are used to conduct distributed denial-of-service attacks, they are capable to steal data, send spam, and allow the intruder to access the computer and its links. The undetectable attribute in coordinated attacks is just what hackers or attackers are hoping for their illegal activities to exploit a device or network. A botnet's originator is commonly known as a "bot herder" or "bot master."

The bot master operates the botnet remotely, often through intermediate machines known as the command and control servers. Increasing incidents and attacks against genuine internet activities such as data theft, click fraud, denial of service (DoS) or email spam, etc., has now become a very serious issue. Such victims are labeled as zombies or bots operated by organized attackers that stem from the term "robot." Software applications operating as an automatic process over the web are commonly referred to as the word bots. A community of bots may create a self-propagating, self-organizing, and autonomous framework called botnet under a command and control (C2, or C&C) infrastructure. In particular, the controller of the botnet (also named as herder) can remotely control bots to download worms, Trojan horses, and backdoors on them to exploit a set of machines.

7.3.1 TYPES OF DDoS ATTACKS

DDoS attacks can be classified based on the protocol layers:

- **Network-Level Flooding Attack:** Attacks at the transport or network level are typically carried out through various control packets such as ICMP, UDP, or TCP. An attacker tries to interrupt the authorized user's normal communication stream by using TCP or voice over internet protocol (VoIP) flooding in the network layer and transport level. The Attackers delivers some false requests to the reflectors in a reflection-based attack. The reflectors, in turn, deliver the responses to the target and the victim's available resources get depleted. The best example of the reflector-based attacks is the Smurf attacks (Swain and Bibhudatta, 2009).

  An intruder tends to compromise the victim's infrastructure in an amplification-based attack by sending a large volume of requests or messages. The traffic towards the victim is intensified on receiving a text message. The Smurf attack is carried out to deliver a huge volume of packets with the help of reflection and amplification.

- **Application Level Flooding Attack:** Generally, this type of attack is launched with the intention of compromising the operations of the legitimate user by decimating the resources of server. These resources are nothing but the input and output bandwidth, allotted memory, processing speed of the central processing unit, and the bandwidth between main memory and secondary memory.

  Since the application-level breaches are equivalent to legitimate traffic, they utilize fewer resources. For interrupting the session, hackers exploit certain characteristics of the application such as session initiation protocol (SIP), hypertext transfer protocol (HTTP), or DNS related characteristics. SIP and domain name systems are by far the most prominent methods of launching flooding attack.

  The VoIP attack is a similar kind of application-level attack. The intruder transfers a huge volume of spoofed VoIP packets at an alarming rate to the target network. The target database requires a considerable amount of time and resources to distinguish between the bogus VoIP packets from benign traffic for a proper link. If the intruder has been using the same origin address for a prolonged period of time, it will appear like a legitimate traffic; thus, it is very hard to identify.

7.4   HTTPS FLOODING

An HTTP flood attack is indeed a form of denial-of-service (DDoS) attack intended to overload a specific database with HTTP requests. Only when the target is flooded with requests and therefore cannot react appropriately to regular traffic, there will be denial-of-service for additional requests from real users.

HTTP flood attacks are a DDoS attack form "layer 7." Layer 7 is the OSI model's software layer, relating to internet protocols like HTTP. HTTP is the foundation of browser-based internet applications and is widely used to load web pages or transfer data from the application over the network. Since malicious traffic is difficult to distinguish from normal traffic, mitigating layer attacks is particularly complex. Figure 7.8 depicts the HTTP flooding attack.

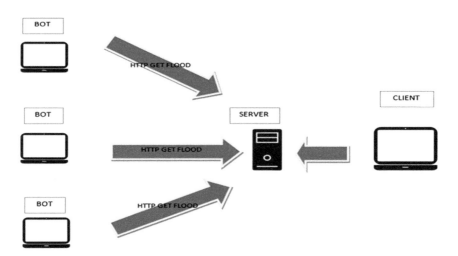

FIGURE 7.8   HTTP flooding scenario.

7.5   ATTACK PHASES OF DDoS

Various pathways involved in various phases of attack were discussed in this paragraph. There seem to be three different phases of DDoS attacks that can be labeled as Phase I-recruiting attack armies, Phase II-propagation, and Phase III-attack. The specifics of these steps will be described below:

1. **Phase I: Recruiting Attack Armies:** The very first stage of DDoS attacks would be to activate the botnet or attack army. The intruder utilizes worms for this purpose which corrupts users' computers by taking full advantage of their security flaws. The botnet army is formed by several various techniques. The major theme is to scan across networks to locate defective devices or devices with flaws. The three key methods for infecting a device are discussed as follows:

   - **Random Scanning:** Throughout the random scanning approach, the botnets for infecting new machines they probe with random IP addresses from the IP address space. For instance, the popular worm Code-Red (CRv2) could be utilized for this scanning. Such screening generates immense congestion because the machines are very prone to be placed in different networks. However, the lack of coordination between multiple compromised machines creates a significant number of redundant reports from the infected machines.
   - **Hitlist Scanning:** Hitlist testing tries to minimize the initial infection period to infect a large number of devices. The intruder generates an initial list of devices considered extremely insecure in this method. Whenever a worm is launched, it scans through the list and then when it infects a machine, it spreads huge chunk of the list to the infected computer. In this way, an active worm can infect most of the vulnerable machines in its list in just a few seconds.
   - **Permutation Scanning:** It is an intelligent scanning mechanism that introduces self-coordination to prevent numerous tests of the same IP address. It could also evaluate whether a minimal benefit will be obtained or not, by any further scanning. Through evaluating the development of new infection, it can also determine when and where to stop the process. A commonly shared list of IP address space pseudo-random permutation is being used in this technique.
   - **Topological Scanning:** The hit list scanning has many alternatives and topological scanning is considered one among the scanning techniques. In this process of scanning, when the computer has been corrupted, a worm chooses its new target from those in the information provided by the compromised system.

Peer-to-peer systems, where a virus may corrupt a program, may have a database of peers who are very enticing targets for the next infection. Topological scanning therefore does not involve a pre-produced set of devices and can build its own database, which allows this test desirable for the initial spread of the worm.

- **Local Subnet Scanning:** In case of local subnet scanning, the new targets are being searched by the compromised devices in its very own local subnet and attempts to break down these devices. Certain techniques which are mentioned initially may be utilized jointly in order to boost the range of compromised systems. The major objective of such a scanning technique is to target as much of the local machines as possible on a sub-network that is usually found to be encased by firewalls.

2. **Phase II: Propagation:** The next step after the development of the attack army is to transmit the attack code to the compromised computers. The attack code gives information on the target, the timing, and length of the attack, and so on.

- **Central Source Propagation:** Throughout the centralized source distribution mechanism, the attack code progresses from the central server to the compromised computer Since every compromised system interacts and receives a version of the attack code from some central points, this generates a tremendous amount of data traffic that could ultimately lead to an intrusion detection.

  As well, this approach does have the capability for single-point failure. Therefore, if an intrusion is identified, the elimination of the central point can avoid further infection and the intervention of the botnet or attack army.

- **Back-Chaining Propagation:** In the back-chaining process, the vulnerable computer extracts the intrusion software from the infected machine. Essentially, during the infection process, the intruder uses a mechanism that creates a link between the intruder and the infected computer. In this process, the trivial file transfer protocol (TFTP) can be utilized. A popular worm, namely Ramen utilizes this transmission technique in the process of creating an army attack.

- **Autonomous Propagation:** In the case of decentralized propagation, as its title implies, all attack codes are transmitted directly from the intruder to the compromised device throughout the process of infection, no further contact with any more devices is required to pass the attack codes.

  Throughout the case of decentralized propagation, the traffic needed to transmit the software is significantly diminished relative to the other two approaches and therefore poses a small risk of detecting the threat.

3. **Phase III: Attack Processes:** In terms of understanding the research on DDoS attacks, it is necessary to understand DDoS attack mitigation processes. Various classifications of DDoS attacks have been seen in the literature over the last decades. In the whole study, our goal is to examine all of these attack categorizations and to create a completely covered, simple-to-understand classification system.

   The differentiation depends on the effect of the attack on victims' networks or property. In reality, a web server or proxy server is the key victim of an assault by DDoS and requires limited resources to do so.

7.5.1 DDoS ON IOT INFRASTRUCTURE

IoTs interconnect network devices of various kinds, varying from a refrigerator at home to a cardiac surveillance device embedded in a human body, a smart grid framework, or a desktop camera. Therefore, the IoT objects are called "extremely heterogeneous" networked entities.

In the work of Strategy and Unit, the International Telecommunications Union (ITU) has described its dream for the IoT environment as "software to provide access to anything." DuBravac and Ratti185 have stated that in 2015, the amount of connected devices has risen to 10–20 billion, while in 2003 there were only 500 million connected devices and in 5 years, the number of C phones. This example illustrates the tremendous growth of the IoT system that is both positive and bad at the same time. This is because too many of these IoT systems are not protected at all, as the suppliers or producers of these products are not worried about the safety issues of these devices. In contrast, certain vendors have hardcoded less stable IoT phones, which cannot be modified but are very easy to guess.

As a consequence, the cyber world has experienced some of the biggest (in-size) DDoS assaults in its history in the last few months of 2016. All of these assaults included millions of IPs from all of these smart devices. As we have already mentioned that it is very important to ensure the safety of devices through the actions of device manufacturers and end-users. On the other side, when IoT systems run in a range of complex fields, such as health care, rescue services, connected cars, where these devices face a DoS assault, a catastrophic event could occur if the devices fail to interact and provide services in critical situations.

So far, encryption is the workaround for DoS attacks on such phones. It is therefore very important to pay more attention to this massively growing field of internet. The increasing size of DDoS attacks today is bad enough, but things are about to get worse with the widespread adoption of 5G. That's because the implementation of 5G will usher in an age of unprecedented data speeds and significantly lower latency, meaning that DDoS attacks will have to be mitigated in a matter of seconds, not minutes.

With Ericsson estimating that the number of IoT devices with a cellular connection will reach 4.1 billion by 2024, it's plain to see why vulnerable 5G-connected IoT devices will pose a serious threat to organizations around the globe. If left unchecked, the scale of 5G-connected IoT DDoS attacks is likely to make even the biggest attacks of today pale in comparison. To combat the next generation of 5G DDoS attacks, it's imperative that organizations implement advanced DDoS threat intelligence that combines real-time threat detection and automated signature extraction. Only then can organizations effectively defend themselves against the colossal, hyper-fast DDoS attacks of the future.

7.5.2 *DDoS ATTACK ON SDN*

Ever since SDN has been introduced, the DDOS attack has been challenging the security of SDN and has become a popular research area (Kuan-Yin et al., 2016; Dong et al., 2016). The relationship between SDN and DDoS attack has always been contradictory. The attributes of SDN such as centralized control of the network and programmability make it easy for conventional networks to detect and respond to DDoS attacks, which depict the security supported by the SDN. SDN of its own can be a target for DDoS attacks.

SDN is divided into three basic structural planes, i.e., the application plane (AP), the CP, and the DP. Depending on potential targets, DDoS attacks are often segmented into three categories in SDN that are application-layer DDoS attacks, control layer DDoS attacks, and data layer DDoS attacks.

7.5.2.1   APPLICATION LAYER DDoS ATTACKS

There seem to be two possible ways to execute DDoS attacks onto the application layer. The first is the attacks on certain SDN applications; another is the intrusion on the SDN Northbound API. In addition, it is difficult to recognize the separation of applications, an attack of the DDoS application layer might have an impact on another application that is not the objective. Such corrupted applications may lead to legitimate security breaches in the SDN. Braga et al. suggest a self-organizing map (SOM) approach to differentiate DDoS-based attacks utilizing machine-learning techniques (Jin and Bing, 2013).

The SOM system is educated in this approach by gathering factual information from OpenFlow (OF) switches. SOM training features are average packets per flow, normal bytes per stream, average duration per flow, and percentage of bi-directional flows, single-flow growth, and single-port growth.

7.5.2.2   CONTROL LAYER DDoS ATTACKS

Control layer is the core of SDN and the least effective linkage in all SDN security due to a single point of failure. CP DDoS attacks could also be managed by three techniques attacking the server, attacking the northbound APIs and attacking the southbound APIs. Distinct and unique implementations can result in a number of alternative flow laws that can cause DDoS attacks in the control layer (Sahoo et al., 2018a).

Now that the controller decides to forward the streams based on the current flow rules, when the network device finds a new network packet in the DP, and there are no flow rules to match the current flow information in the flow table for new packets. Either the entire packet or part of the packet header is sent to the controller to address the request. With an enormous amount of internet traffic, sending a total packet to the controller may lead to high-data bandwidth. The plan is to use centralized control of SDN for the detection of DDoS attacks and to provide a solution that is effective and light in terms of the resources needed (Sahoo et al., 2018b).

7.5.2.3   DATA LAYER DDoS ATTACKS

Multiple potential activities are performed by that of the SDN switch, such as dumping or transmitting the file. Therefore, the assessment of the controller relies on the flow principles of the switches. In this context, one of the major issues facing the operator is to differentiate between a benign flow rule from a dishonest flow rule/Information theft is yet another threat to the SDN DP for instance, Instants several vSwitch (logic switch) on the top of an OF-enabled hardware switch. Suppose for each vSwitch is allocated to that of a different client. If the related authentication, such as certification and password, is not sufficiently separated, there may be a chance of information leakage. In fact, the underlying conceptual network may be corrupted. DP hardware failure is yet another security issue that may manipulate and control the integrity of the system. This can be restricted by the use of high-level protection strategies.

7.5.3   DDoS ATTACK ON SDIoT

The SDx framework makes use of software to regulate hardware configurations types. SDN is amongst the most extensive applications of the SDx framework and one of the most major areas of software innovation. SDN systems are programmable and therefore the infrastructure itself is more complex, scalable, price-effective, and adaptable. SDN detaches the DP and the CP. Controllers and switches are indeed the major components of SDN. The SDN-Cs are responsible for the operation of the entire network and the SDN switches are liable for the transfer of the internet traffic on the basis of instructions provided by the SDN controllers (SDN-Cs). SDN aims to be tailored for evolving traffic patterns, high latency, the complex complexity of today's devices, and is also an emerging technology which can provide safety protection options since it is sensitive enough to detect threats. Numerous studies have shown that SDN is known to be a vital enabler for the protection of IoT infrastructure. SDN will optimize IoT's plug-and-play predetermined protocols for network devices, dynamically identify and address security flaws, automate edge computing, and evaluate low data conditions. The process of DDoS attacks can be explained as follows:

- The DDoS attacker transmits a new packet to a different SD-IoT switch in which the attack packet is created by that of the attack script.
- Where there is no correlation throughout the flow table objects of the SD-IoT switch, the SD-IoT switch encapsulates the packet header in the packet-in text and transfers it to another controller in the SD-IoT collection.
- The SD-IoT controller unwraps the packet-in text and creates a unique flow table item that will be sent to SD-IoT switch.

Whenever a DDoS intruder creates a large proportion of unmatched packets, the SD-IoT controller throughout the controller pool obtains a huge number of packet-in texts that not only take up the network resources between the SD-IoT controller and the SD-IoT switch, but it also ingest the CPU, memory, and other resources of the SD-IoT controller, leading to increased delay and even downtime.

7.6 DDoS ATTACK DETECTION

The IIoT systems are interconnected with various heterogeneous devices. For instance, smartwatch, smart glass, heart-monitoring system, webcam of a computer all are heterogeneous devices. With the boom of IoT, using all these devices increases exponentially. A study of Trend Micro, Inc envisioned that most of IoT vendors are not security concerned (Trend, 2016). Due to this reason, from the last 2 years cyber world as faced a sizable DDoS attack. Hence, a prevention-based awareness is required from the IoT manufacturer's perspective. Moreover, IoT devices are operating in different sensitive places like the health sector, connected vehicles, etc. If these devices face a massive DDoS attack, then it would be a disaster to the entire network system. Hence, it is necessary to pay more attention to the security aspect of IIoT devices, particularly for DDoS attacks.

Since the last couple of years, there are many research articles addresses the DDoS attack on SDN network. The research was carried out in two different directions. Few researchers are going for an efficient technique for detecting DDoS attacks on the CP, DP, and application layer of SDN system. In another direction, researchers are put forward their research on SDN as a tool against DDoS mitigation and prevention. Nevertheless, the development of powerful mechanisms of these researches towards DDoS attacks using SDIoT environment is in the initial stage.

Throughout our study, we have investigated a few of the research work that has used SDN as a tool for DDoS detection in IoT environment, which have highlighted in Table 7.1.

TABLE 7.1   SDN Using as a Tool for DDoS Detection in IoT Environment

Description	References
An ultra-lightweight integrity verification method has been developed using Walnut signature for IoT Devices. However, two major disadvantages are there in this method. First, the implementation environment is too costly. Second, novel constructions are not always a wise choice.	Atkins et al. (2016)
An SDN solution has been proposed to protect IoT devices. The framework consists of a set of controllers; Software-defined IoT enabled switches, gateway, and IoT devices. For DDoS detection, the controller runs an algorithm that is based on the cosine similarity of the vectors of the incoming packet rate at boundary switch ports.	Yin et al. (2018)
A SDN framework has been proposed for detecting DDoS attacks for large-scale smart city projects, where IIoT devices are being used.	Bawany et al. (2017)
A secured SDN framework has been proposed for IoT-based Wireless Sensor Networks.	Sahoo et al. (2015)
A scheduling-based structure has developed for the SDN control plane by Lim et al.	Lim et al. (2015)
The authors proposed the SoftThings framework for DDoS detection. It is an SDN-based DDoS framework for IoT system for detecting unusual behaviors of the incoming traffic by using Machine Learning techniques.	Bhunia et al. (2017)
The proposed DDoS framework is the integration of SD Network and IoT. In the detection module, the deep learning (DL) technique has been adopted. In addition, it uses restricted Boltzmann machines (RBM).	Dawoud et al. (2018)
Discuss various security architecture for SD-IoT	Krishnan et al. (2017)
Authors have used the entropy technique for detecting DDoS attacks in an SDN environment.	Mousavi et al. (2015)
Authors have used the information distance technique for detecting DDoS attacks in an SDN-based data center network.	Sahoo et al. (2018c)

Throughout our review, we draw a few challenges that are helpful to the researchers:

1. In the last couple of years, most of the DDoS attacks carried out through IoT devices. Hence IoT and associated sensor devices are a significant threat to the cyber world. Hence device-level security is a challenging task.
2. Preventing the IoT botnets, identifying their location, detection can be implemented through SDN like novel technology.
3. To stop the variety of DoS attacks, real-time implementation is essential. Therefore, in this sense, scalability is a bigger challenge. With efficient flow management capabilities, SDN could be one solution, where less research was conducted.

7.7 CONCLUSION

The growing size of DDoS attacks nowadays is a serious concern; however, things are about to get more serious with the extensive use of IoT, Industrial IoT, and 5G. To fight against the next generation 5G DDoS attacks, it is important to note that organizations need to implement some advanced, automated, and intelligent DDoS detection mechanism. In this chapter, we have highlighted different attack types seen so far. Further, we analyzed the DDoS attack in IIoT and IoT scenarios. We also provided some reviews on DDoS detection and mitigation solutions to the Software-Defined IoT environment. Finally, we have concluded the chapter with a future scope on detection of DDoS attacks using the SD-IoT framework. Still, there endures the chance to see new invisible attacks with new features.

KEYWORDS

- **application-specific integrated circuits**
- **control-plane**
- **deep learning**
- **denial of service**
- **distributed denial of service**
- **hypertext transfer protocol**
- **International Telecommunications Union**

REFERENCES

Alsmadi, I. M., Iyad, A., & Mohammed, A., (2017). A systematic literature review on software-defined networking. *Information Fusion for Cyber-Security Analytics* (pp. 333–369). Springer, Cham.

Atkins, D., Anshel, I., Goldfeld, D., & Gunnells, P., (2016). *Walnut Digital Signature Algorithm: A Lightweight, Quantum-Resistant Signature Scheme for Use in Passive, Low-Power, and IoT Devices*. In NIST Lightweight Cryptography Workshop, NIST.

Bawany, N. Z., Shamsi, J. A., & Salah, K., (2017). DDoS attack detection and mitigation using SDN: Methods, practices, and solutions. *Arabian Journal for Science and Engineering, 42*(2), 425–441.

Bhunia, S. S., & Mohan, G., (2017). Dynamic attack detection and mitigation in IoT using SDN. In: *2017 27th International Telecommunication Networks and Applications Conference (ITNAC)*. IEEE.

Dargahi, T., et al., (2017). A survey on the security of stateful SDN data planes. *IEEE Communications Surveys and Tutorials, 19*(3), 1701–1725.

Dawoud, A., Seyed, S., & Chun, R., (2018). Deep learning and software-defined networks: Towards secure IoT architecture. *Internet of Things, 3*, 82–89.

Dong, P., et al., (2016). A detection method for a novel DDoS attack against SDN controllers by vast new low-traffic flows. In: *2016 IEEE International Conference on Communications (ICC)*. IEEE.

Jin, R., & Bing, W., (2013). Malware detection for mobile devices using software-defined networking. In: *2013 Second GENI Research and Educational Experiment Workshop*. IEEE.

Kalkan, K., Gurkan, G., & Fatih, A., (2017). Defense mechanisms against DDoS attacks in SDN environment. *IEEE Communications Magazine, 55*(9), 175–179.

Katta, N., et al., (2016). Cacheflow: Dependency-aware rule-caching for software-defined networks. *Proceedings of the Symposium on SDN Research*. ACM.

Krishnan, P., Jisha, S. N., & Krishnashree, A., (2017). SDN framework for securing IoT networks. *International Conference on Ubiquitous Communications and Network Computing*. Springer, Cham.

Kuan-Yin, C., et al., (2016). SDN shield: Towards more comprehensive defense against DDoS attacks on SDN control plane. In: *2016 IEEE Conference on Communications and Network Security (CNS)*. IEEE.

Lim, S., Yang, S., Kim, Y., & Yang, S., (2015). Controller scheduling for continued SDN operation under DDoS attacks. *Electronics Letters, 51*(16), 1259–1261.

Liyanage, M., Mika, Y., & Andrei, G., (2014). Securing the control channel of software-defined mobile networks. *Proceeding of IEEE International Symposium on a World of Wireless, Mobile and Multimedia Networks*. IEEE.

Ma, H., et al., (2015). On networking of internet of things: Explorations and challenges. *IEEE Internet of Things Journal, 3*(4), 441–452.

Mahjabin, T., et al., (2017). A survey of distributed denial-of-service attack, prevention, and mitigation techniques. *International Journal of Distributed Sensor Networks, 13*(12), 1550147717741463.

Mishra, A. K., et al., (2018). Analytical model for Sybil attack phases in internet of things. *IEEE Internet of Things Journal, 6*(1), 379–387.

Mousavi, S. M., & St-Hilaire, M., (2015). Early detection of DDoS attacks against SDN controllers. In: *2015 International Conference on Computing, Networking and Communications (ICNC)*. IEEE.

Puthal, D., et al., (2016). Threats to networking cloud and edge datacenters in the internet of things. *IEEE Cloud Computing, 3*(3), 64–71.

Sahoo, K. S., Bibhudatta, S., & Abinas, P., (2015). A secured SDN framework for IoT. In: *2015 International Conference on Man and Machine Interfacing (MAMI)*. IEEE.

Sahoo, K. S., et al., (2016). A comprehensive tutorial on software defined network: The driving force for the future internet technology. *Proceedings of the International Conference on Advances in Information Communication Technology and Computing*. ACM.

Sahoo, K. S., et al., (2018a). A learning automata-based DDoS attack defense mechanism in software defined networks. *Proceedings of the 24th Annual International Conference on Mobile Computing and Networking*. ACM.

Sahoo, K. S., et al., (2018b). A machine learning approach for predicting DDoS traffic in software defined networks. In: *2018 International Conference on Information Technology (ICIT)*. IEEE.

Sahoo, K. S., et al., (2018c). An early detection of low-rate DDoS attack to SDN based data center networks using information distance metrics. *Future Generation Computer Systems, 89*, 685–697.

Sahoo, K. S., et al., (2019a). ESMLB: Efficient switch migration-based load balancing for multi-controller SDN in IoT. *IEEE Internet of Things Journal*.

Sahoo, K. S., et al., (2019b). Improving end-users utility in software-defined wide area network systems. *IEEE Transactions on Network and Service Management*.

Swain, B. R., & Bibhudatta, S., (2009). Mitigating DDoS attack and saving computational time using a probabilistic approach and HCF method. In: *2009 IEEE International Advance Computing Conference*. IEEE.

Trend M., Inc. (2016). *The Internet of Things Ecosystem is Broken. How Do We Fix it?* https://blog.trendmicro.com/trendlabs-security-intelligence/internet-things-ecosystem-broken-fix/ (accessed on 16 December 2020).

Tripathy, B. K., et al., (2016). A novel secure and efficient policy management framework for software defined network. In: *2016 IEEE 40th Annual Computer Software and Applications Conference (COMPSAC)* (Vol. 2). IEEE.

Yin, D., Lianming, Z., & Kun, Y., (2018). A DDoS attack detection and mitigation with software-defined internet of things framework. *IEEE Access, 6*, 24694–24705.

Zhang, X., et al., (2019). Intrusion detection and prevention in cloud, fog, and internet of things. *Security and Communication Networks*.

CHAPTER 8

SDN-Enabled Fog Computing Architecture

HEMANT KUMAR APAT, BIBHUDATTA SAHOO,
PRANITHA MADAPATHI, and PRASENJIT MAITI

Department of Computer Science and Engineering,
National Institute of Technology, Rourkela, Odisha, India,
E-mail-hemant.rimt@gmail.com (H. K. Apat)

ABSTRACT

The rapid growth of internet and communication technology, and rapid adaption internet of things (IoT) devices which generate different applications, put pressure on Cloud computing Infrastructure which leads to high latency and high energy consumption for latency-sensitive applications. Designing an architecture based on IoT applications has a lot of inevitable issues that must be taken consideration for enhancing the performance of the system the issues are security, massive traffic, high availability, high reliability, and energy constraints. The latest distributed computing paradigms, such as Fog computing, and Edge computing, software-defined networking (SDN), network virtualization (NV), and block-chain has been implemented in IoT networks to swamped the aforementioned challenges while fulfilling the expected quality of service (QoS). In this chapter, we proposed the architecture of fog computing along with the IoT devices, how IoT devices access the virtual resources in the virtual environment. IoT devices are very much capable of capturing data using the sensors, collection of the data over the network and perform some analysis for better decision making for improvement of the productivity of current processes as well as to cater to new types of services to the multiple geographical locations. Fog computing architecture consists of IoT layer moves the data generated by the IoT devices to the upper layer that consists of fog nodes (FNs) which are controlled by software-enabled devices which we call as Software-defined Network(SDN) to achieve better reliability and availability for latency-sensitive application. The SDN based network architecture is equipped with controllers and resource-constrained devices. The existing cloud computing technology has certain drawbacks which could enforce to develop new distributed computing which we referred here as fog computing which is based on collaboration with cloud computing and has become the next generation of the cloud computing which is placed between cloud and IoTs to meet the requirement of IoTs based application. Fog computing helps to reduce transmission latency because it is available locally to the IoT layer, i.e., at less distance, it can be accessed and substantially decrease monetary cost for accessing resources. In this chapter, we study the various issues related to network services delivered to the application request by users. A Software-Defined Networking (SDN) is an emerging architecture that enables dynamic manageable, cost-effective adaptable to provide high bandwidth to the dynamic nature of the application. It also decouples the network control and forwarding the functions. So by using this, management of the network became easy. IoT and SDN are complementing each other to enhance the system architecture for big data management, etc. In this chapter, we are trying to propose a service architecture model in fog computing, which is SDN enabled.

8.1 INTRODUCTION

Over the years, the computing paradigm has transformed from distributed, parallel, Grid, and Cloud computing. Cloud computing (Salman et al., 2015) has emerged as a new computing environment with several promising capabilities such as Scalability, Robustness, On-demand access, Resource management, and service provisioning (Vaquero et al., 2008). It comprises three fundamental services IaaS (Infrastructure as service), PaaS (platform as a service), and SaaS (software as a service) but it has some limitations when latency and QoS are taken into consideration. With the advent of internet of things (IoT), a vast network of vehicles, home use appliances, physical gadgets, and other electronics, sensors, and connectable software which enables these gadgets to exchange data with the internet and other gadgets which wants to access resources over network with low latency Cloud computing fails to deliver the services efficiently because the communication link between end device and cloud server is not close some time due to link failure or another hardware failure. Monitoring the failure of link and recovery from failure is not an easy task to implement in the architecture hence a new computing architecture has been framed which is termed as Fog Computing by CISCO in 2012. The fog computing market is expected to grow from USD 22.28 Million in 2017 to reach USD 203.48 million by 2022, at a CAGR of 55.6% between 2017 and 2022. The fog computing market is expected to be dominated by the Americas, followed by APAC and Europe during the forecast period. The Top 5 players in the fog computing market in 2017 would be Cisco Systems, Inc. (USA), Microsoft Corporation (USA), Dell Inc. (USA), Intel Corporation (USA), and PrismTech Corporation (USA). At the same time, IoT market is projected to grow CAGR of 20.55% between the forecasted periods of 2016 to 2024 according to data compiled by Transparency Market Research. IoT platforms help create and manage applications that can run analytics, store, and secure data (Vangelista et al., 2015). IoT effectively contributes to cloud computing platforms by helping combat storage space and energy-related problems (Zhang et al., 2010). To handle these diverse and multidimensional data efficiently there is a critical need of some distributed environment which extends the feature of cloud and very close to the edge of the network and the term Fog computing came into the pictures which overcome the existing cloud computing technology without violating the SLA with the strong support of IoT application (Chen et al., 2016). Indeed, significant amounts of data can be stored, controlled, and computed over the fog networks that are configured and managed by end-user nodes. However, to reap the benefits of fog networks many architectural and operational challenges must be addressed.

Fog computing is considered the promising extension of the cloud computing paradigm to handle IoT-related issues at the edge of the network (Dastjerdi et al., 2016). It is a distributed computing environment introduced by CISCO in 2012 that acts as an intermediate layer between the cloud data centers (DCs) and IoT devices (Fog computing provides services like computing, networking, and storage. The ultimate goal of fog computing is to provide end-users with considerable processing power and computing resources that allow them to run the applications and other user's requirements. In fog computing architecture, clients have access to the resources provided by the fog provider as described in their Service

Level Agreement (SLA) (Mouradian et al., 2017). Fog using virtualization technology and DCs to allocate distributed resources for clients as they need. Different research challenges of fog computing have been identified and researcher continuously working on this area to improve the computing architecture, here we try to summarize the challenges and issues while designing architecture of fog computing with special focus on IoT devices. Several surveys and tutorials related to fog computing have been published over the past years.

Cloud computing is considered as the cerebrum of Internet applications. It has been widely accepted and applicable in every fields of internet based applications. Cloud computing is integrated into traditional network to enhance the performance and intelligent of the devices used. However, with the rapid adaption and development of IoT, 50 billion "things" will be connected to internet by 2020 (Syst et al., 2016). Due to this large IoT device large volume of data are generated which required further processing for executing their application, we need special software that controls the devices used in the architecture efficiently so to manage the requirements of vast IoT devices cloud computing technologies cannot meet the following requirements:

1. **High Latency:** The cloud computing DCs are usually a far away from IoT devices, and the service response and transmission latency will be in minute's level. Due to the above mentioned, when an application with an emergency, the cloud-computing server cannot be able to collect data immediately and send the corresponding results back to the IoT devices then, so the system will suffer from high latency and this denotes the fault of cloud system.

2. **Low Bandwidth:** As the bandwidth is fixed the application generated data needs to transmit the packet into the cloud server for analyzing, storing, and monitoring is time consuming.

3. **Low Security:** During the execution processes, the IoT data will be transmitted, analyzed, computed, and stored on exterior cloud computing servers. These sensitive IoT data packets should be protected to avoid leakage.

To mitigate the above drawbacks, fog computing is presented. The benefits of internet with fog computing in contexts of IoT are given below:

1. **Lower Latency:** As the fog computing node are close to the IoT devices the data generated by the IoT devices gets processed

easily with less time and gives the result back to IoT devices in comparison to cloud computing server.

2. **Better Network Utilization and Cost:** The analysis and computation of IoT data can use local fog computing servers rather than exterior cloud computing servers. The exterior network bandwidth and cost can be reduced.

3. **Security:** By using a local fog-computing server to analyze and compute sensitive IoT data, the data packets can avoid from leakage.

4. **Greater Scalability:** Fog applications can be quickly deployed into industrial environments and the manufacturer can offer machine as a service (MaaS) to customers. According to the customers' requirements, new products will improve the service level through fog applications. A comparison of different aspects of fog computing and cloud computing in industrial internet is presented in Table 8.1.

TABLE 8.1 A Comparison of Different Aspects of Fog Computing and Cloud Computing in Industrial Internet

Metrics	Fog Computing	Cloud Computing
Response Time	Millisecond	Minutes, Hours or day
Storage Time	1 or 2 hours transient storage	May take months
Geographical Awareness	Local	Global
Bandwidth Cost	Very less	more
Protocol	Any protocol	IP protocol
Application Example	M2M communication	Big data Analytics

As the IoT is the next generation of internet and as per the IDC projection billions of heterogeneous devices will be connected in nearby future. This large number of devices puts high constraints on the system architecture in terms of the following terms:

• Network coverage;
• Security and privacy;
• High System reliability;
• Integration;
• Traffic load;
• Latency.

To get rid of this problem and to achieve more efficient system which is capable of connecting more devices latest technology cum communication paradigm can be included to support the underlying networks. SDN and Fog computing is one of them which facilitates the efficient usage and better performance. The primarily aims to cater the cloud services whether it may be computation, storage, and processing at the edge of the access network, i.e., one or two hops distance from the endusers. By this approach, we are moving large centralized DC to distributed cloud units having limited capabilities. Moreover, edge computing for IoT network achieves better benefits like reducing the communication latency and provides data offloading, etc.

Fog computing is another form of edge computing that is suitable for IoT networks. Fog computing is an extension of cloud computing to provide processing, computing, and storage capabilities. Fog computing supports different types of heterogeneous devices that can connect and communicate with distributed fog nodes (FNs) including sensor devices and wireless gateways. It has a significant advantage over the cloud and edge computing like the reduced end-to-end latency, higher system reliability, and control traffic congestion and overhead. Fog computing was proposed, firstly by Cisco in 2012 to provide a complement to the existing cloud computing paradigm (Chen et al., 2015). As the application was processed on the cloud there are high latencies between the users and server, now by using fog computing, we can process them at the fog layer where the number of heterogeneous FNs is available. A FN may be switches, routers, embedded servers, surveillance cameras, etc. Placing resources at the edge of the network helps data spend very low time to reach the processing station, so latency-based tasks are optimized. However, the processing capacity of FN is limited, so small and sensitive latency tasks are prioritized to be processed in the fog-computing layer, while the cloud still takes the major responsibility for latency-tolerant and large-scale tasks. Eventually, fog computing complements the cloud to form a new computing paradigm, cloud-fog computing.

According to Gartner reports the connected object increasing in exponential way so it's very difficult to manage the data generated by these diverse devices so there is a critical need to provide the elasticity and flexible network to get rid of high congestion network and flood of data and that leads to leave the network paralyzed. To achieve such goals, emerging technologies such as software defined networking (SDN) and network function virtualization (NFV) come into the existence to provide adequate solution. It has recently added and attention among the researcher and has been proved in centralized network. The current computing paradigm of processing the data and storing is not feasible so we must think a better ways to analyze, and to aggregate the data at the network layer which may be the upcoming IoT solution to handle big data. Big data does not imply the volume data generated, it is about the multivariate form of data.

8.2 FOG COMPUTING ARCHITECTURE WITH SDN

Fog computing architecture is one of the key technologies to achieve ubiquitous network connectivity in contexts of IoT that is used to connect distributed sensors, controllers, and network transmission devices, gateways, and other subsystem. At the same time for large-scale IoT device connection the requirements of low bandwidth low delay and low energy consumption also need to be met. The present cloud computing architecture is not able to cater the latency sensitive application, based on this feature of traditional network, the network designers believe to integrate some software with the underlying network architecture that is suitable for large-scale IoT devices.

However using a centralized network cloud-computing infrastructure SDN has lot of advantage due to the separation of control plane (CP) and data plane (DP) (Sahoo et al., 2019a, b). By comparing a traditional network and SDN enable networking the following are the advantages:

1. **Improved Performance:** Network utilization is the main purpose of centralized traditional computing architecture SDN integrated cloud computing substantially reduces the network cost and use reliable network devices to perform routing function through software. The system will be simplified due to the adoption of software to control the centralized routing scheme. Also management of security quite simple by adding SDN into the centralized Cloud computing architecture.
2. **Configuration:** In traditional computing infrastructure like cloud computing network configuration and management is one of the most important functions. When a new devices is added to the existing network some manual configuration need to take place. During this manual configuration process errors are inevitable.

Hence Cloud computing architecture with SDN can effectively prevent unnecessary errors with the help of automated controlling.

3. **Scalability:** It is important issues when we think about the computing architecture the architecture should be enough scalable to the large scale IoT based application. The traditional network has less scalable which reduce the robustness of the architecture. So SDN based computing architecture is required to meet the current demand of IoT devices.

The architecture we proposed here is based on the hierarchy, i.e., our architecture has three main components IoT, Fog, and Cloud there is interface called cloud-fog control middleware which control the fog and cloud layer and make available as per the requirements of IoT applications. In the fog layer fog devices are deployed to process the data coming from IoT devices as per their priority which is gain by a fog control manager (FCM) and the last level of hierarchy is IoT devices (Maiti et al., 2018) that consists of large number of IoT devices which makes request to FCM for a particular service:

i.   It performs infrastructural changes in the fog cluster;
ii. Analyze resource utilization within the fog;
iii. Compute a service placement plan for service requested;
iv. Monitoring of fog nodes.

Fog computing can be defined as an open platform for computing and storing applications at data source devices. Using a fog-computing server, an algorithm can be quickly deployed to calculate bandwidth allocation. The SDN is defined as a network in which the network CP is separated from the network-forwarding plane. An SDN-C can centrally control multiple SDN switches. Using SDN, the centralized control architecture easily replaces the traditional one in NUMFabric to obtain the flow rate fast, and the flow rate acquisition speed will directly affect the bandwidth allocation recovery time. To this end, we propose an industrial Internet characterized by fast bandwidth allocation. To the best of our knowledge, this is the first work that deploys SDN and fog computing to address the issue of reducing bandwidth allocation recovery time in industrial internet (Figure 8.1) (Chen et al., 2014):

1. **IoT Device Layer:** An IoT application consists of well-defined tasks generated by an IoT device by sensing some events that occurred, which may be medical-related data, traffic-related or

temperature of vehicle, etc., required to process and execute and get the result back to clients in distributed environments.

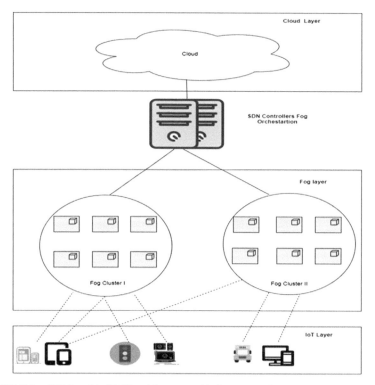

FIGURE 8.1 SDN enabled IoT architecture with fog computing.

2. **Fog Layer:** These consist of heterogeneous FNs Fog is another layer of a distributed network environment and is closely associated with cloud computing and the IoT. Public infrastructure as a service (IaaS) cloud vendors can be thought of as a high-level, global endpoint for data; the edge of the network is where data from IoT devices is created (Byers et al., 2017).

3. **Cloud Layer:** Cloud is the topmost level/tier of a typical fog-computing environment. This level consists of centralized DCs, which have the capacity to store all the data of the FNs/servers. It usually has the capacity to store a huge amount of data. It causes huge network congestion and also it causes high latency in quality of services (QoS) (Botta et al., 2015).

4. **Software Defined Network (SDN):** The network also enabled SDN technology and that are deployed to assist the system and provide control, management, and security issues to the introduced system (Sahoo et al., 2017). The end-to-end system structure of the proposed IoT system is presented in Figure 8.2.

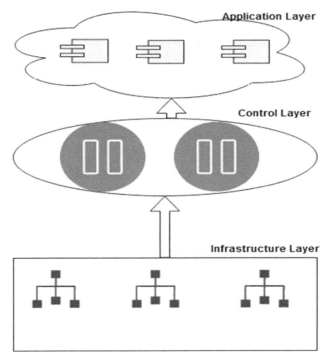

FIGURE 8.2   SDN architecture figure.

8.3   IoT AND SDN

The IoT is a promising technology which describes smart ecosystem hold diverse technologies. The physical devices equipped with RFID tags actuators sensors and wireless communication devices are connected to the internet to form IoT network (Borgia et al., 2016). These devices are generally deployed in application contexts to participate the smart environment form machine-to-machine communication from vehicular networks to cellular network and embedded system. Some of the application scenarios are remote health monitoring, smart agriculture monitoring and safety system, smart homes and buildings, nifty, traffic control and management (Atzori et al., 2010).

8.4 SDN ARCHITECTURE WITH FOG COMPUTING

SDN is an approach to reduce the complexity of network configuration and management. Different Network control management can easily be deployed on existing architecture to install new program on the computer. In SDN network management operation are controlled by centralized and physically separated from forwarding operation. SDN switches classify and forward packets according to the flow rules decided by the SDN-Cs (Figures 8.3–8.6).

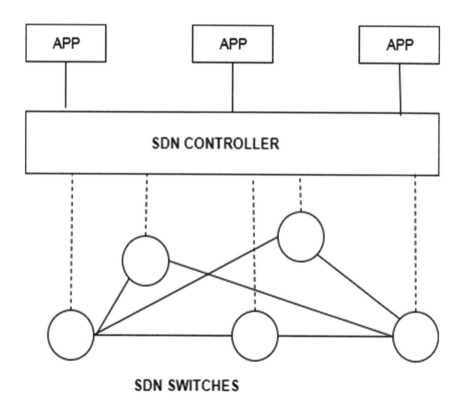

FIGURE 8.3   SDN-WISE infrastructure.

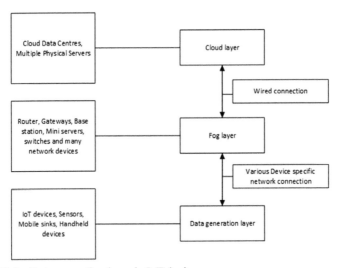

FIGURE 8.4   Data generation layer in IoT devices.

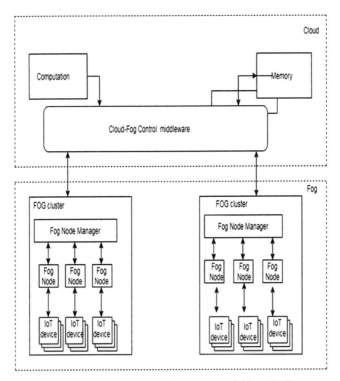

FIGURE 8.5   Fog computing architecture with internet of things (IoT).

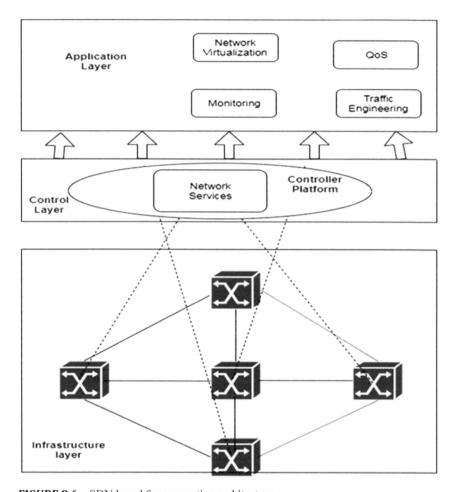

FIGURE 8.6 SDN based fog computing architecture.

8.5 BACKGROUND AND RELATED WORK

The prevalence of cloud computing and Fog computing among the researchers has been increasing due to the interoperability with IoT devices. In this section, we are discussing the limitation of cloud computing versus fog computing with the context of SDN.

8.6 IoT SURVEY SUMMARY

Subject	Contributions	Limitations
IoT based applications and opportunities (Zeng et al., 2011)	The main benefits of IoT application (Smart Homes, Healthcare, and connected vehicle) are presented.	Without enabling SDN technology
IoT Infrastructure (Gaur et al., 2016)	Different components of IoT Infrastructure have been discussed.	SDN and Fog are not included.
IoT based Security (Conti et al., 2018)	IoT security issues are presented and different protocol are proposed for implementing security	SDN security is missing.
IoT Standardization (Al-Fuqaha et al., 2015)	Different IoT domain is reviewed.	Standardization effort for fog and SDN are not included
IoT with SDN controller (Sood et al., 2016)	Different application of SDN are explained	Not scalable architecture

8.7 IoT CHALLENGES, BENEFITS, AND LIMITATIONS

Scalability	New Devices can be Connected Easily	• **Network Capacity** • **QoS**
Big Data	Enabling, new Application for Big data management	High latency, redundancy, etc.
Heterogeneity	combined different IoT vertical silos Integrating different communication technologies, devices' types, data types, etc.	Interoperability
Security and privacy	Enabling innovative applications using sensitive data	• New types of attacks • Private data inspection

8.8 SDN-BASED IoT MANAGEMENT FRAMEWORKS

Architecture	Management	Architecture	Control Plane/ Data Coupling	Protocol Used	Scalability	Benefit	Limitation
SDN-WISE (Galluccio et al., 2015)	Localization of distributed sensor, energy management,	Centralized controller with dumb sensor node having flow table like Open Flow table which is preinstalled flow rules	Centralized controller, dumb data plane	Open Flow	Medium	The state-full approach, reducing information exchange. Mobility, reconfiguration, and localization of	In-depth architectural details are missing and Lacking security and reliability.
WSN-SDN (Gante et al., 2014)	Sensor network flow management	WSN cluster with centralized controller monitored and controlled by Master SDN controller	Centralized master controller	Open Flow/ distance aware routing protocol	Low	Optimal path selection, routing strategy adjustment	Implementation of master and central controller is not clear, No proof of validation,
SD-WSN (Miyazaki et al., 2014)	Infrastructure management and reconfiguration	FPGA	Microcontroller	COAP	Low	Programmable reconfiguration of network	Hardware bounded and device dependency
Integrate WSDN (Leontiadis et al., 2012)	Management platform for using virtual machine (INNP)	Local controller in each sensor node which interacts with a centralized controller. INNP is done through VM in the node platform	Centralized controller and local controller	Contiki OS on each local controller	Low	Flexibly using commodity off the shelf device, reducing cost	Missing evaluation for behavior and performance of WSN
SOF (Luo et al., 2012)	Flow management	INNP in data plane and flow-based packet forwarding	Centralized controller and distributed data plane	Sensor Open Flow (SOF)	Low	handling peer compatibility, address classification,	Theoretical idea and not experimentally proved

8.9 SDN FOR WIRELESS SENSOR-BASED IoT DEVICES

Approach	Security Parameter	Network	Description	Limitations
Secured SDN framework (Leontiadis et al., 2012)	Authentication	Ad hoc network	SDN controller block all switch port on receiving new flow and start authentication	Not prove implementation or simulation, only a theoretical framework
DISFIRE (Luo et al., 2012)	Authentication and authorization	Grid network	hierarchal cluster network with multiple SDN controllers implement a dynamic firewall to ensure authorization	Evaluation of framework is lacking. The protocol used is opflex which is not practically tested
Black SDN (Wu et al., 2015)	Location Security, Confidentiality, Integrity, Authentication, and Privacy.	Generic IoT/M2M communication	secure the meta-data and the payload by encryption in the link layer and use SDN controller as TTP	Scalability in black network will create hazard in providing complete security
SDP (Chakrabarty et al., 2016)	Authentication	Ad hoc network/M2M communication	SDP collect the IP addresses of all M2M communication capable devices and store into a logical network. Authenticate based on information stored	Scalability will encounter performance in case of IoE.

KEYWORDS

- fog control manager
- infrastructure as a service
- internet of things
- machine as a service
- network function virtualization
- service level agreement
- software-defined networking

REFERENCES

Alaba, F. A., Othman, M., Hashem, I. A. T., & Alotaibi, F., (2017). Internet of things security: A survey. *J. Netw. Comput. Appl., 88*(C), 10–28.

Al-Fuqaha, Guizani, M., Mohammadi, M., Aledhari, M., & Ayyash, M., (2015). Internet of things: A survey on enabling technologies, protocols, and applications. *Commun. Surv. Tutorials, IEEE 17*(4), 2347–2376.

Atzori, L., Iera, A., & Morabito, G., (2010). The internet of things: A survey. *Comput. Networks, 54*(15), 2787–2805.

Bonomi, F., et al., (2012). Fog computing and its role in the internet of things. *Proceedings of the First Edition of the MCC Workshop on Mobile Cloud Computing*. ACM.

Borgia, E., (2014). The internet of things vision: Key features, applications and open issues. *Comput. Commun., 54*, 1–31.

Botta, A., De Donato, W., Persico, V., & Pescapé, A., (2016). Integration of cloud computing and internet of things: A survey. *Future Gener. Comput. Syst., 56*, 684–700.

Byers, C. C., (2017). Architectural imperatives for fog computing: Use cases, requirements, and architectural techniques for FOG-enabled IoT networks. *IEEE Commun. Mag., 55*, 14–20.

Chakrabarty, S., & Daniel, W. E., (2016). A secure IoT architecture for smart cities. In: *2016 13th IEEE Annual Consumer Communications and Networking Conference (CCNC)*. IEEE.

Chen, N., Chen, Y., Song, S., Huang, C. T., & Ye, X., (2016). Poster abstract: Smart urban surveillance using fog computing. In: *2016 IEEE/ACM Symposium on Edge Computing (SEC)* (pp. 73–78). doi: 10.1109, 2016.

Chen, S., Xu, H., Liu, D., Hu, B., & Wang, H., (2014). A vision of IoT: Applications, challenges, and opportunities with China perspective. *Internet Things J., IEEE, 1*(4), 349–359.

Conti, M., Dehghantanha, A., Franke, K., & Watson, S., (2018). Internet of things security and forensics: Challenges and opportunities. *Future Gener. Comput. Syst., 78*(2), 544–546.

Dastjerdi, A. V., & Rajkumar, B., (2016). Fog computing: Helping the internet of things realize it's potential. *Computer, 49*(8), 112–116.

Díaz, M., Cristian, M., & Bartolomé, R., (2016). State-of-the-art, challenges, and open issues in the integration of internet of things and cloud computing. *Journal of Network and Computer Applications, 67*, 99–117.

Galluccio, L., et al., (2015). SDN-WISE: Design, prototyping and experimentation of a stateful SDN solution for wireless sensor networks. In: *2015 IEEE Conference on Computer Communications (INFOCOM)*. IEEE.

Gaur, P., & Tahiliani, M. P., (2016). Operating systems for IoT devices: A critical survey. In: *Region 10 Symposium (TENSYMP)* (pp. 33–36). Sanur, Bali island, Indonesia.

Leontiadis, I., et al., (2012). SenShare: Transforming sensor networks into multi-application sensing infrastructures. *European Conference on Wireless Sensor Networks*. Springer, Berlin, Heidelberg.

Li, S., Da, X. L., & Zhao, S., (2010). The internet of things: A survey. *Inf. Syst. Front. 17*(2), 243–259.

Luo, T., Hwee-Pink, T., & Tony, Q. S. Q., (2012). Sensor OpenFlow: Enabling software-defined wireless sensor networks. *IEEE Communications Letters, 16*(11), 1896–1899.

Maiti, P., et al., (2018). Smart gateway based multi-tier service-oriented fog computing architecture for achieving ultra-low latency. In: *2018 International Conference on Information Technology (ICIT)*. IEEE.

Mouradian, C., et al., (2017). A comprehensive survey on fog computing: State-of-the-art and research challenges. *IEEE Communications Surveys and Tutorials, 20*(1), 416–464.

Qin, Z., et al., (2014). Software defined networking architecture for the internet-of-things. In: *2014 IEEE Network Operations and Management Symposium (NOMS)*. IEEE.

Ray, P. P., (2018). A survey on internet of things architectures. *J. King Saud Univ. Comput. Inf. Sci., 30*, 291–319.

Sahoo, K. S., & Bibhudatta, S., (2017). SDN architecture on fog devices for real-time traffic management: A case study. *Proceedings of the International Conference on Signal, Networks, Computing, and Systems*. Springer, New Delhi.

Sahoo, K. S., et al., (2019a). ESMLB: Efficient switch migration-based load balancing for multi-controller SDN in IoT. *IEEE Internet of Things Journal*.

Sahoo, K. S., et al., (2019b). Improving end-users utility in software-defined wide area network systems. *IEEE Transactions on Network and Service Management*.

Salman, O., et al., (2015). Edge computing enabling the internet of things. In: *2015 IEEE 2nd World Forum on Internet of Things (WF-IoT)*. Milan, Italy: IEEE.

Salman, T., & Jain, R., (2017). A survey of protocols and standards for internet of things. *Adv. Comput. Commun., 1*(1).

Sood, K., Yu, S., & Xiang, Y., (2016). Software defined wireless networking opportunities and challenges for internet of things: A review. *IEEE Internet Things J., 3*(4), 453–463.

Syst, C., (2015). Cisco systems. *Fog Computing and the Internet of Things: Extend the Cloud to Where the Things Are.*

Vangelista, L., Andrea, Z., & Michele, Z., (2015). Long-range IoT technologies: The dawn of LoRa™. *Future Access Enablers of Ubiquitous and Intelligent Infrastructures.* Springer, Cham.

Vaquero, L. M., Rodero-Merino, L., Caceres, J., & Lindner, M., (2008). A break in the clouds: Towards a cloud definition. *SIGCOMM Comput. Commun. Rev., 39*(1), 50–55.

Zeng, D., Guo, S., & Cheng, Z., (2011). The web of things: A survey. *J. Commun., 6,* 424–438.

Zhang, Q., Cheng, L., & Boutaba, R., (2010). Cloud computing: State-of the-art and research challenges. *J. Internet Serv. Appl., 1*(1), 7–18.

CHAPTER 9

Software-Defined Industrial IoT for Smart City Applications

A. MANISHA[1], G. SURESH REDDY[1], and KSHIRA SAGAR SAHOO[2]

[1]*Department of Information Technology, VNR Vignana Jyothi Institute of Engineering and Technology, Hyderabad–500090, Telangana, India, E-mail: nisha661997@gmail.com*

[2]*Department of Computer Science and Engineering, SRM University, Amaravati, AP, 522502, India*

ABSTRACT

Internet of things (IoT) can be simply referred as a network of physical objects having IP addresses, able to connect and communicate with other devices. IoT plays a vital role in building smart cities and solves different problems from traffic control to environmental issues. Industrial IoT (IIoT) can be referred as an extension that provides the enhancement of infrastructure and delivers the smart connected solutions such as environmental monitoring, smart lights, vehicle parking, etc., and enhances the public transportation, reduces congestion in traffic, provides improved quality of life. Management of smart cities involves big data generated by different IoT devices which is quite difficult and time taking process to handle with traditional administration. Here comes the SDN into picture to solve the problem. SDN enables the cloud computing and provides the facility for network engineers and administrators to respond quickly to the changing business requirements via centralized controller. It is a software-based network, provides more flexibility, and allows users a great management and control of the resources throughout the control plane (CP). It provides an advantage of managing nodes through programming. SDN typically runs on server and with the help of different protocols it indicates switches where the packets to be sent. This chapter discusses the impact of SDN as an innovative approach for smart city development.

9.1   INTRODUCTION

The internet of things (IoT) is a network of interrelated computing devices, digital and mechanical machines, objects, animals, or people that have unique identifiers (UIDs) and the ability to transfer data over a network without requirement of human-to-human or human to computer interaction. IoT offers different new opportunities for cities to make use data in order to manage traffic, to reduce pollution, to make better utilization of infrastructure and to keep citizens safe. A smart city is a framework, predominantly composed of Information and Communication Technologies (ICT), to develop, deploy, and promote sustainable development practices to address growing urbanization challenges. The industrial internet of things (IIoT) began actually for the purpose of enhancing efficiency in the commercial sector, but now its potential for public benefit is increasingly being recognized. In this regard, smart cities are leading the way to a new set of economies around data gathering, infrastructure decision-making, and public utility technology.

In addition to IIoT, the software defined networking (SDN) is the latest innovation whose prime goal is to simplify network management. It improves network functionality by decoupling data and control planes (CPs). The programmability nature of SDN, make service providers and enterprises respond quickly to the changing business requirements. The controller plays an essential role in SDN. The network administrator can manage the traffic through a centralized controller without any physical configuration over the switches.

The controller instructs the data plane (DP) to forward flows according to the traffic requirement. The controller not only instructs to forward the flows but also instructs to drop or modifies the priority of flows if required. Various APIs present in the application layer is used to help the communication process and transfer information between the CP and the application plane (AP). In the following sections we will discuss about IoT, IIoT, SDN, and their application in smart cities.

9.2 BACKGROUND

In this section, we will describe the background details of different cutting-edge network infrastructure.

9.2.1 INTERNET OF THINGS (IoT)

The IoT can be defined as a network of physical objects which are provided with UIDs and ability to transmit the data over the network without human-to-human interaction or human to computer interaction. IoT evolved from M2M technology, i.e., Machine-to-Machine technology, which takes responsibility of connecting devices to cloud, managing them, and collecting data. IoT is a best trending technology nowadays. It is sensor network of huge number of smart devices that can connect people, systems, and other applications for collecting and sharing of data. An IoT system consists of web-enabled smart devices that can make use of sensors, embedded processors, and communication hardware for collecting, sending, and acting on data they acquire from their environments. The IoT technology helps people to work smarter and gets complete control over their lives. It also enables the industries to automate processes and can reduce the labor costs. It also reduces the wastage and enhances the service delivery, makes less expensive to manufacture and deliver goods as well as offers transparency for customer transactions. IoT helps every industry, including finance, retail, healthcare, and manufacturing. Smart cities as a part of IoT can help citizens in reducing the wastage and energy consumption and the connected sensors can even helpful in farming, for example, monitoring the crop and cattle yields, predicting the growth patterns, etc. Thus, IoT technology plays a vital role in our everyday life and can make the companies to be competitive. Figure 9.1 illustrates the example of an IoT system.

9.2.2   SMART CITY

Cities are seeing extraordinary growth, bringing major challenges as they seek to remain sustainable, healthy, and safe places for people to live and works. The IoT offers opportunities for cities to make use data in order to manage traffic, reduce pollution, make better utilization of infrastructure, and keep citizens safe. So, in summary, smart city frameworks are comprised of ICTs to promote and develop sustainable construction practices to approach growing urbanization challenges. The cloud infrastructure helps to accept the IoT data, analyze data and further take efficient decision in real-time.

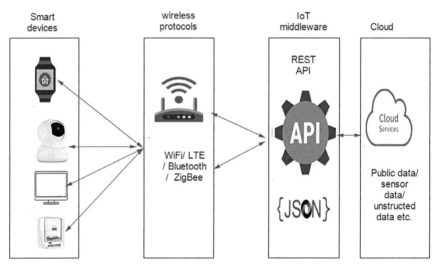

FIGURE 9.1   Example of an IoT system.

For example, consider the next-generation intelligent lighting platforms in smart city. The street light will have integration with solar panel and then it has connectivity with cloud-based central control system. These lights can identify free parking space for the drivers through mobile application. Moreover, it can alert commuters about different disaster information such as weather warnings and fire alarm (Figure 9.2).

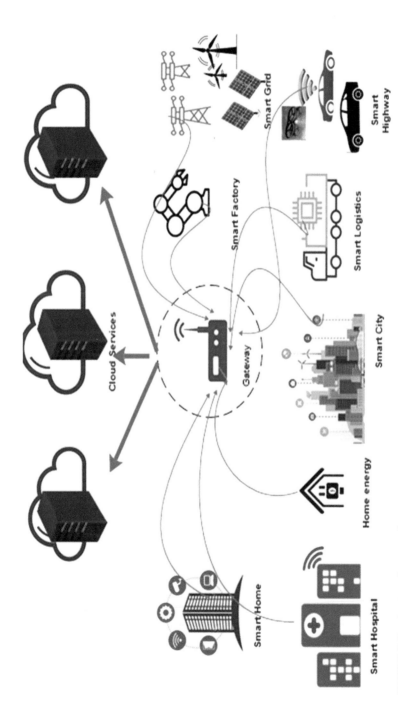

FIGURE 9.2 A smart city scenario.

9.2.3   INDUSTRIAL IoT (IIoT)

The IIoT was began actually for the purpose of promoting efficiency in the commercial sector, but now its potential for public benefit is increasingly being recognized. Smart cities are leading the way to a new set of economies around data gathering, infrastructure decision-making, and public utility technology. In September 2016, the White House created the Smart Cities Initiative, designed to help public, private, and academic institutions work together on improving the nation's cities. Eighty million dollars in new federal investments was announced at the launching of this initiative, with the funds earmarked for an array of research and development areas. Furthermore, the smart city industry is expected to reach $400 billion in value by 2020, as 600 cities are expected to join the connected web.

9.2.4   SOFTWARE DEFINED NETWORKS (SDN)

In a legacy network, both packets forwarding tasks and managing the flow is handled by a single and expensive hardware unit, generally called router (Plotly: Visualize Data, Together). Conventionally few router vendors allow the flexibility to manage the queue size such that congestion control and traffic control can be maintained efficiently (Jain et al., 2013; Ku, You, and Mario, 2014). However, the underlying devices pose a low performance for the changeable traffic demand. Moreover, in the traditional IP-based network, in case of any modification to the topology, is an expensive task. It can be simplified by performing all decision at a centralized software unit, instead of embedding in a hardware device. In this way, the administrator can get ample opportunity to handle network traffic (Usman, Mian, and Deepak, 2019). This decoupling feature is called Software Defined Network (SDN) (Sahoo et al., 2019a–c). In SDN, both control and DPs are separated. In the CP, the controller has a major role in making a decision on the incoming flows into the network (Mohammadi and Al-Fuqaha, 2018; Sahoo et al., 2018a). The decoupled architecture provides numerous benefits such as centralized control provisioning, better enterprise management, lower operating cost, and granular security. Depending upon the size of the network topology, there can be more than one controller can handle the entire network. Figure 9.3 depicts a generic architecture of SDN.

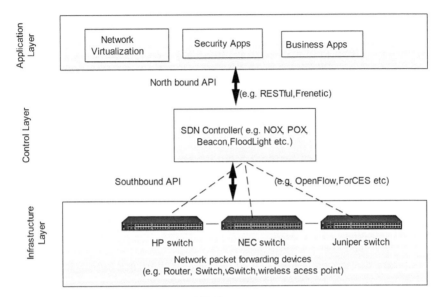

FIGURE 9.3 A generic architecture of SDN.

Source: Reprinted with permission from Sahoo et al., 2016.

SDN architecture comprises of three layers, which are:

- Application layer;
- Control layer; and
- Infrastructure layer.

These three layers communicate among each other through secured API. The CP and DP can communicate with the help of the southbound API. Whereas the CP and application layer can communicate with the help of northbound API. OpenFLow (OF) is one of the examples of southbound API.

9.2.5 WORKING PRINCIPLE OF SDN

SDN supports programmability in different types of technologies, including network virtualization (NV), functional separation, and automation. Basically, SDN technology targets for separation of the CP and DP and centralizes the controller. CP is responsible for sending the packets through the network in an optimized way and the DP is responsible for carrying the actual traffic over the network. CP may differ from DP. In an SDN scenario, when a packet comes to a switch, the rules which are already built in the switch by controller tells the switch to where the packet to be sent. These packet-handling rules are given by centralized controller to switch. The switch can also be called a DP device. SDN uses an operation mode that can also be called dynamic or adaptive, in which switch sends a route request to controller when it doesn't know where to send the packet. This process is different from adaptive routing. In this scenario switch raises route requests through routers and algorithms based on the network topology, not through a controller. SDN uses virtual overlay to attain virtualization, which logically separates the network on the top of a physical network.

9.2.6 *BENEFITS OF SDN*

There are numerous benefits of SDN. Few of them are highlighted below:

1. The underlying network resources can be utilized efficiently.
2. Due to the programmability nature of SDN, network administrators can manage the network efficiently.
3. Multi-tenant data centers (DCs) are well suited to the SDN.
4. SDN can facilitate better traffic engineering, fine-grained security rules, and adopting congestion control like major advantages.
5. SDN can reduce the CAPEX, due to the use of inexpensive devices (Bharill et al., 2019).
6. The centralized network management can have the entire view of the network. Due to this centralized monitoring, the DDoS like potential security issues can be checked.
7. Fine-grained security rules can be imposed on the underlying devices through SDN controller (SDN-C).
8. Being capable of automating the traffic, SDN enhances the quality of services (QoS) and multimedia transmissions. Streaming high-quality video content becomes more accessible due to SDN.

9.2.7 *CHALLENGES WITH SDN*

Security is both pros and cons in SDN technology. If attacker targets the Centralized Controller then it fails at single point, can prove detrimental to the network. Another challenge of SDN technology is there is no specific definition for "SDN" in a network industry. There are various approaches to SDN which are offered by different vendors, ranging from hardware centric models and virtualization platforms to hyper-converged networking designs and controller less methods.

Software defined-wide area network (SD-WAN) technology can distribute the traffic throughout geographically dispersed locations. However, the underlying principle for both the case is same. Both can be programed and have the central provisioning system. In smart city aspect, the importance of SD-WAN is very essential. For instance, South Korea's "Global Digital Seoul 2020" initiative is a 4-year plan to deploy enough free Wi-Fi to cover the entire city by using SD-WAN concept.

9.3 CATALYZING A NEW ERA

The Wall Street Journal points to a set of technological shifts that have together given birth to this age of civic analytics. These shifts include:

- The huge rise of cloud computing, which makes data storage both secure and affordable.
- New techniques of data analysis made possible by machine learning.
- The many sensors that now make it possible to track the behavior of physical objects and environments, such as air pollution, traffic, gunshots, and much more.
- The arrival of the smartphone era, when virtually every citizen has a network portal in their pocket through which they can send and receive information.

9.3.1 *IIoT FOR SMART CITY*

For the government as well as the fellow citizen of a city, the application of IIoT is numerous. It can help to reduce the traffic delay, minimize waste, and improve the transportation system and many more (Sahoo et al., 2018b, c; Tiwary et al., 2018). Nowadays, almost everyone is using smart mobiles. If any damaged road is there on the way, it is informed through their mobile. Room temperature is automated by sensing the presence of the human being inside the room. So smart home initiatives reduce the carbon footprint. The future smart home is coming with relocating the current place by sensing, predict, alerting the situation. With the smart road, smart vehicle the public safety can be improved. With the introduction of sensor-enabled water pipes, parking meter, smart garbage system, the sanitation services of the city can be improved (Amadeo et al., 2015). Crime prevention can also be stopped with the smart city initiatives (Sahoo et al., 2018a). With the wearable sensor, fire fighter can track the people those who are in dangerous zone during firebreak (Tiwary and Sabyasachi, 2020).

9.3.2 SOFTWARE-DEFINED NETWORKING FOR SMART CITY DEPLOYMENT

SDN can support smart city developments in different level such as physical objects level, communications level and data level. In the second level, i.e., communication level, a huge volume of data captured by different sensors over large distributed areas. In such situation, the communication infrastructure has to manage with heterogeneous communications requirements that are difficult to realize with a single configurable network infrastructure. SDN with OF responds very quickly and effectively to these difficulties to achieve required objectives and goals. In effect, SDN deployment in smart city projects can bring many benefits.

Huge volume data generated from IIoT devices of smart city applications. IIoT devices uses in e-heath devices, video surveillance, smart home, smart factories, smart farms, etc. Different traffic has different QoS and QoE requirement. In the smart city project innovatively, a dynamic configurable network can be established with SDN.

Governments of major metropolitan areas and similar cities are considering this SDN and NFV technologies to deliver flexibility and agility needed to support adoption of 'smart' technologies that can enhance the workability, sustainability, and livability in their towns. SDN and NFV reduce hardware requirement, power consumption, and space requirements, and can offer all size cities the scalability and agility to tackle the needs and trends of the future. On the other hand, IoT can help in communication among the devices, with the people. For instance, a refrigerator can communicate with the grocery shop about the items that are running out of the fridge and order more. This technology is not limited to homes but also in terms of both capabilities and scope; it has vast use. In terms of smart cities, it has an impact on everything from lighting to the flow of traffic through the urban areas.

The following are the few ways that can define how this technology is utilizing in today's world:

- Sensors deployed into bridges to detect the things like degradation and effects of seismic forces in the workplace.
- Sensors built into roads to detect the things like traffic flow, wear, and tear, subsidence, etc.
- Sensors built into buildings to sense the things like wind force, seismic activities, foundation subsidence, etc.
- Sensors deployed into the interior of the buildings to sense the things like the presence of people, fire, temperature, and humidity levels and to control the use of lighting, air, and heating, etc., when it not necessary.
- Sensors at the entrance of buildings, offices, etc., can provide security by performing activities like face recognition, speech recognition, etc.

The IoT technology in smart cities is more about achieving important goals, such as improving the quality of life and managing infrastructure properly, enhancing the safety of residents and using the energy in a good and proper way.

9.4 MANAGEMENT OF INFRASTRUCTURE

Many cities are suffering from the issues like decaying infrastructure, degradation of roads, decaying railroad tracks, and aging of bridges which can lead to the unsafety of citizens. IoT can help in the managing and maintenance of infrastructure properly by deploying the sensors into these areas, thereby sensing the issues and intimating the administrator. This can lead to improvement in the safety of citizens and infrastructure.

9.4.1 SECURITY

IoT can provide great security by performing activates like face recognition, speech recognition, biometric, etc., at the entrance of the buildings, offices, homes, etc. (Giordano, Giandomenico, and Andrea, 2016).

9.4.2   REDUCTION IN THE USE OF ENERGY

IoT helps in reducing energy consumption, especially wasted energy lighting and heating or cooling the rooms when the people are not currently using it.

9.4.3   IMPROVEMENT IN THE COMMUNICATION CAPABILITIES

Through IoT is possible for things like traffic lights to communicate their status to the respective administrator or agency.

9.4.4   EMERGENCY AND AWARENESS ON ENVIRONMENT

Smart technology in Smart cities plays a vital role in emergencies and makes people aware of environment.

9.4.5   MONITORING THE TRAFFIC FLOW AND PREVENTING THE CONGESTION

IoT can lead to the prevention of congestion by monitoring and controlling the traffic in urban areas and on highways. IoT Sensors can communicate everything from the total number of vehicles passing a specific spot to the weight of vehicles with their speed. All these factors can be considered as important reasons for the adoption of smart technology in the cities. One of the most immediate impact is better management of traffic can be solved with this smart technology. Smart technology is already having a great impact in the traffic. Many countries including the US and the UK have been using this technology to achieve prime objectives. Smart technology allowed the decision makers to take the instant decisions and react appropriately. For instance, London has been using this technology to improve the parking capabilities for the visitors, residents. By this way, congestion has reduced, further locating the parking spots becomes an easy task. Importantly the time spent for waiting on parking has also reduced.

9.5 IoT PLATFORMS FOR SMART CITY

Table 9.1 discusses a few important IoT platforms used in smart city applications.

TABLE 9.1 Comparison of the Main IoT Platforms

Platform	Services
AWS IoT	It provides services like visualization, monitoring, and analyzing data generating from wired or wireless sensors deployed in smart city.
	Advantage: Provides data transactions security. *Disadvantage:* Private platform.
Echelon	It is suitable for industrial platform such as street lighting, building automation, transportation systems.
	Advantage: Security and automation support. *Disadvantage:* It is high cost.
Oracle IoT platform	It is helpful in real-time data capture.
	Advantage: Can handle millions of device with heterogeneous connectivity. *Disadvantage:* Open source enabled devices does not support.
ThingsBoard	It is an open-source IoT platform for data collection, analytics, etc.
	Support IoT protocols: MQTT, CoAP, and HTTP.
	Advantage: Provide more security in terms of confidentiality and device authentication. Support various protocol like HTTP, MQAT. *Disadvantage:* It might not suit for large-scale network.
KAA	It is an open-source platform. It can be helpful for smart agriculture, smart healthcare, and consumer electronics.
	Advantage: It supports cloud platform and big data application. *Disadvantage:* Partial hardware modules assisted.
Plotly	It supports data visualization and interactive dashboards for smart city application.
	Advantage: visualization tools are available. *Disadvantage:* except visualization no other services.
Kii	Different mobile solution supported such as user and data management, notification facility, etc.
	Advantage: Load balancing supported and open API. *Disadvantage:* latency may be a major constraint.
Open remote	Useful for smart city, home automation services.
	Advantage: Various protocol supported. *Disadvantage:* cost is lofty.

Smart cities can be operated by connecting each and every object wirelessly using WI-FI and other technologies. The main objective of the smart city is to enhance the standard of living of city people by coordinating different technologies. The smart cities could become earning opportunities for the people. It has estimated that more than 50% of the total world population is residing in the cities. It has estimated that by 2025, the urban population would increase to 60% of the total population. For these huge populations, IoT, and smart cities can create potential business opportunities for livelihood. According to Frost and Sullivan, the smart city market is expected to be 1.5 Trillion Dollars throughout the world market. To date, smart home and autonomous vehicle parts of smart city already capture the market. Companies like Cisco spend million dollars into their business for smart city applications.

However, at the same time, certain limitations of a smart city cannot be ignored. Handling huge generated IoT data is a real challenge to smart city applications. At the same SDN is a boon for wireless communication and smart city application. For faster execution with lesser response time SDN can facilitate to process the data either at the edge server or cloud server. In an effective way, SDN can manage the incoming data flow by taking an intelligent decision. In summary, the dynamic nature of SDN is well fit for the smart city network.

9.6 CONCLUSION

The objective of the smart city is to improve the standard of living of the city people by coordinating different technologies such as IIoT, edge computing, cloud computing, etc. Although the advantages of smart cities are numerous, at the same time handling huge volumes of generated data from IIoT devices is a real challenge. The new network paradigm, such as SDN could be a solution to the problem. The programmability, central visibility of the network intelligently handles the smart city application effectively. In addition to this, SD-IIoT can address different real-time challenges such as security, reliability, and energy efficiency. At the same time, the SDN, as well as IIoT in smart city applications, can generate potential business opportunities for livelihood.

KEYWORDS

- **control-plane**
- **industrial internet of things**
- **information and communication technologies**
- **quality of services**
- **software-defined networking**
- **software defined-wide area network**

REFERENCES

Al Nuaimi, E., et al., (2015). Applications of big data to smart cities. *Journal of Internet Services and Applications, 6*(1), 25.

Amadeo, M., et al., (2015). Information centric networking in IoT scenarios: The case of a smart home. In: *2015 IEEE International Conference on Communications (ICC)*. IEEE.

Amazon Web Services, (2021). *AWS IoT.* https://aws.amazon.com/iot/ (accessed on 16 December 2020).

Bharill, N., et al., (2019). Fuzzy knowledge-based performance analysis on big data. *Neurocomputing.*

Echelon, (2019). *Control Networking for the Industrial Internet of Things (IIoT): Gaining the Advantages of IP Enablement Without Starting Over.* https://www.echelon.com/assets/bltf9d13ab4e95c81aa/IoT_April_2014_echelon.pdf (accessed on 16 December 2020).

El-Sayed, H., et al., (2019). A traffic-aware approach for enabling unmanned aerial vehicles (UAVs) in smart city scenarios. *IEEE Access, 7*, 86297–86305.

Giordano, A., Giandomenico, S., & Andrea, V., (2016). Smart agents and fog computing for smart city applications. *International Conference on Smart Cities.* Springer, Cham.

Hakiri, A., Aniruddha, G., & Patil, P., (2017). *A Software Defined Wireless Networking for Efficient Communication in Smart Cities.* Technical report.

Ibrahim, A. T. H., Victor, C., Nor, B., Kayode, A., Ibrar, Y., Abdullah, G., Ejaz, A., & Haruna, C., (2016). The role of big data in smart city. *International Journal of Information Management, 36*(5), 748–758.

IIoT For Smart City. https://www.iiconsortium.org/vertical-markets/smart-cities.htm (accessed on 16 December 2020).

IoT For Smart City, (2020). https://www.gemalto.com/iot/inspired/smart-cities (accessed on 16 December 2020).

IoT, (2020). https://internetofthingsagenda.techtarget.com/definition/Internet-of-Things-IoT (accessed on 16 December 2020).

Jain, S., et al., (2013). B4: Experience with globally-deployed software defined WAN. *ACM SIGCOMM Computer Communication Review, 43*(4). ACM.

Jalali, R., El-Khatib, K., & Carolyn, M., (2015). Smart city architecture for community level services through the internet of things. In: *2015 18*th *International Conference on Intelligence in Next Generation Networks*. IEEE.

Javed, F., et al., (2018). Internet of things (IoT) operating systems support, networking technologies, applications, and challenges: A comparative review. *IEEE Communications Surveys and Tutorials, 20*(3), 2062–2100.

KAA, (2020). *Build Custom Cloud-to-Edge IoT Solutions with a Single IoT Platform.* https://www.kaaproject.org/ (accessed on 16 December 2020).

Khan, Z., Saad, L., & Kamran, S., (2014). A framework for cloud-based context-aware information services for citizens in smart cities. *Journal of Cloud Computing, 3*(1), 14.

KII, (2018). *KII Platform*. https://en:kii:com (accessed on 16 December 2020).

Ku, I., You, L., & Mario, G., (2014). Software-defined mobile cloud: Architecture, services and use cases. In: *2014 International Wireless Communications and Mobile Computing Conference (IWCMC)*. IEEE.

Maiti, P., et al., (2019). QoS-aware service provisioning in heterogeneous fog computing supporting IoT applications. In: *2019 International Conference on Vision Towards Emerging Trends in Communication and Networking (ViTECoN)*. IEEE.

Mazhar, M., et al., (2015). Conceptualization of software defined network layers over internet of things for future smart cities applications. In: *2015 IEEE International Conference on Wireless for Space and Extreme Environments (WiSEE)*. IEEE.

Mishra, S., et al., (2018). Sustainable service allocation using a metaheuristic technique in a fog server for industrial applications. *IEEE Transactions on Industrial Informatics, 14*(10), 4497–4506.

Mohammadi, M., & Al-Fuqaha, A., (2018). Enabling cognitive smart cities using big data and machine learning: Approaches and challenges. *IEEE Communications Magazine, 56*(2), 94–101.

Mukherjee, A., et al., (2019). Distributed aerial processing for IoT-based edge UAV swarms in smart farming. *Computer Networks*, 107038.

OpenRemote, (2018). *OpenRemote is the Open Source Middleware for the Internet of Things.* http://www:openremote:com (accessed on 16 December 2020).

Oracle, (2021). *Oracle Internet of Things Cloud Service.* https://aws.amazon.com/iot/ (accessed on 16 December 2020).

Panigrahi, C., et al., (2019). DATALET: An approach to manage big volume of data in cyber foraged environment. *Journal of Parallel and Distributed Computing, 131*, 14–28.

Plotly, (2021). *Plotly: Visualize Data, Together.* https://plotly.com/ (accessed on 16 December 2020).

Sahoo, K. S., et al. (2016). "A comprehensive tutorial on software defined network: The driving force for the future internet technology." Proceedings of the International Conference on Advances in Information Communication Technology & Computing.

Sahoo, K., Bibhudatta, S., & Abinas, P., (2015). A secured SDN framework for IoT. In: *2015 International Conference on Man and Machine Interfacing (MAMI)*. IEEE.

Sahoo, K., et al., (2018a). A learning automata-based DDoS attack defense mechanism in software defined networks. *Proceedings of the 24*th *Annual International Conference on Mobile Computing and Networking*. ACM.

Sahoo, K., et al., (2018b). A machine learning approach for predicting DDoS traffic in software defined networks. In: *2018 International Conference on Information Technology (ICIT)*. IEEE.

Sahoo, K., et al., (2018c). DSSDN: Demand-supply based load balancing in software-defined wide-area networks. *International Journal of Network Management, 28*(4), e2022.

Sahoo, K., et al., (2019a). ESMLB: Efficient switch migration-based load balancing for multi-controller SDN in IoT. *IEEE Internet of Things Journal*.

Sahoo, K., et al., (2019b). Improving end-users utility in software-defined wide area network systems. *IEEE Transactions on Network and Service Management*.

Sahoo, K., et al., (2019c). Toward secure software-defined networks against distributed denial of service attack. *The Journal of Supercomputing*, 1–46.

Sahoo, S., Bibhudatta, S., & Ashok, K. T., (2019). A learning automata-based scheduling for deadline sensitive task in the cloud. *IEEE Transactions on Services Computing*.

Sahoo, S., et al., (2017). Video delivery services in media cloud with abandonment: An analytical approach. In: *2017 IEEE International Conference on Advanced Networks and Telecommunications Systems (ANTS)*. IEEE.

Santos, J., et al., (2018). City of things: Enabling resource provisioning in smart cities. *IEEE Communications Magazine, 56*(7), 177–183.

Theoleyre, F., et al., (2015). Networking and communications for smart cities special issue editorial. *Computer Communications, 58*(0), 1–3.

ThingsBoard, (2021). *ThingsBoard: Open-source IoT Platform*. https://thingsboard.io/ (accessed on 16 December 2020).

Tiwary, M., & Sabyasachi, D., (2020). *Maintaining Consistency Within a Federated Cloud Environment*. U.S. Patent Application No.: 15/973,859.

Tiwary, M., et al., (2018). Introducing network multi-tenancy for cloud-based enterprise resource planning: An IoT application. In: *2018 IEEE 27th International Symposium on Industrial Electronics (ISIE)*. IEEE.

Usman, M., Mian, A., & Deepak, P., (2019). Paal: A framework based on authentication, aggregation and local differential privacy for internet of multimedia things. *IEEE Internet of Things Journal*.

Yaqoob, I., Ibrar, et al., (2017). Enabling communication technologies for smart cities. *IEEE Communications Magazine, 55*(1), 112–120.

CHAPTER 10

Software-Defined Network and Network Function Virtualization: A Comparative Study

KOPPADA DURGAPRASAD VARMA, G. SURESH REDDY, JANGILI NARENDRA, and MOIN SHARUKH

Department of Information Technology, VNR Vignana Jyothi Institute of Engineering and Technology, Hyderabad–500090, Telangana, India, E-mail: durgaprasadvarma1994@gmail.com (K. D. Varma)

ABSTRACT

Software-defined networks (SDN) is one of the best examples of networking standards aiming towards reaching the goals of overcoming the limitations existing with the traditional networks. SDN enables the software to manage the networks dynamically. Using the software, abstracting of a physical network with virtual networks is possible using SDN. SDN and network functions virtualization (NFV) is that the two of them use network abstraction. SDN tries to separate network control functions from network forwarding functions, while NFV tries to abstract network forwarding and other networking functions from the equipment on which it runs. In this manner, both depend vigorously on virtualization to enable network design and infrastructure to be abstracted in software and then implemented by underlying software across hardware platforms and devices. While both of these new technologies are different in design and implementations, both can enhance network performance effectively. There are various reasons for the growth of both technologies. They can drive big data, smart devices, and distributed servers in an extensive manner. In this chapter, we have highlighted the major significance and difference between these two emerging technologies.

10.1   INTRODUCTION

The cloud is a lot of various sorts of equipment and programming that work by and large to convey numerous parts of figuring to the end-client as online assistance. Cloud computing is the utilization of equipment and programming to convey help over a system. With Cloud computing, clients can get to records and use applications from any gadget that can get to the internet. A case of a Cloud Computing supplier is Google's Gmail. Gmail clients can get to documents and applications facilitated by Google utilizing the web from any gadget. Not at all like customary processing where information is put away on your PC's neighborhood hard drive, the information in the cloud is put away on numerous physical and additionally virtual. A case of a distributed computing document-stockpiling supplier is Dropbox. Dropbox documents can be accessed from any gadget by means of the internet (Agevev et al., 2018).

Cloud computing can be categorized into private, public, and hybrid. A public cloud depends on the standard distributed computing structure, which comprises of different documents, applications, and stockpiling (Li Yoong, Min Chen, 2015). A use case of the public cloud is Gmail. It contains various records, applications, and administrations that are actualized and secured inside a corporate firewall, under the influence of a corporate IT office. Some normal administrations that are facilitated in the cloud are facilitated work area, used by organizations. For instance, e-mail like Gmail, by organizations like Google; distributed storage, gave by organizations like Dropbox; and spilling music, introduce by organizations like Spotify. All these administrations, applications, and documents are put away in the cloud and can be available to clients by means of any gadget. There are a wide scope of organizations and industry verticals that utilize distributed computing; for example, Amazon and Google. Small, medium, and large-sized open and privately owned businesses use the same distributed computing to decrease innovation-obtaining costs.

10.2   DO I NEED CLOUD REGISTERING?

The Cloud Computing market keeps on developing quite a long time after year since organizations are getting increasingly mindful of the cost sparing advantages of embracing the cloud. With Hardware administrations, organizations can utilize the cloud specialist co-op's gear (stockpiling, equipment, servers, and systems administration parts) rather than spending a lot of capital on hardware. With Software benefits, organizations' applications are facilitated by the cloud specialist organization and are made accessible over a system sparing exorbitant arrangement and upkeep costs.

10.3 ARE MY DOCUMENTS SAFE IN THE CLOUD?

While no capacity arrangement is 100% safe, distributed storage suppliers can offer a more secure and progressively open spot for organizations to store information than customary registering techniques. Contingent upon the administration contract, copy duplicates of the organizations' information can be put away on servers situated in various geologies and ensured by reinforcement control supplies on account of a fiasco. Today, numerous organizations are moving to a Hybrid Cloud Computing model. With this model, organizations are given the adaptability of putting away delicate information safely in a private cloud while putting away open information in an open cloud. The two frameworks are kept as discrete, special substances (Wood et al., 2015).

Cloud computing suppliers offer their "administrations" as per various models, of which the three standard models for each NIST are infrastructure as a service (IaaS), platform as a service (PaaS), and software as a service (SaaS). These models offer expanding reflection; they are in this manner frequently depicted as a layer in a stack: framework, stage, and programming as-an administration, yet these need not be connected. For instance, one can give SaaS actualized on physical machines (exposed metal), without utilizing fundamental PaaS or IaaS layers, and then again, one can run a program on IaaS and access it straightforwardly, without wrapping it as SaaS. Typical cloud architecture has been illustrated in Figure 10.1.

10.4 PaaS

Execution runtime, database, web server, development tools:

1. **Iaas:** Virtual machines, servers, storage, load balancers, network.
2. **SaaS:** CRM, E-mail, virtual desktop, communication, games.
3. **Cloud Clients:** Web browser, mobile app, thin client, terminal emulator.

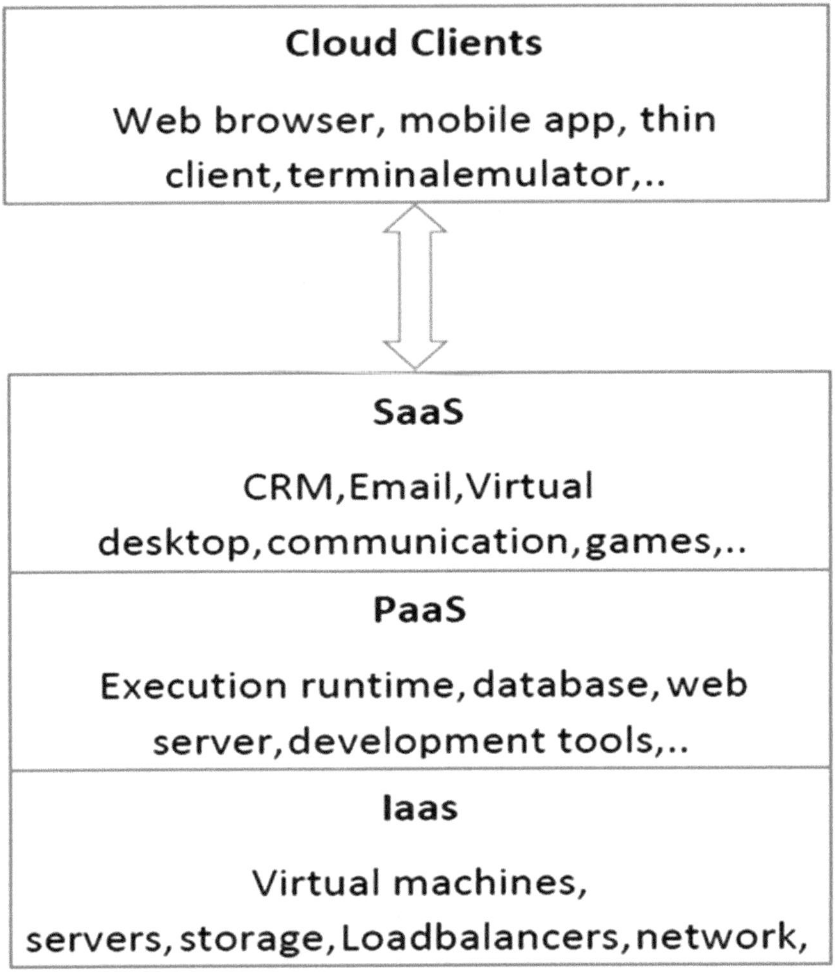

Cloud Clients Web browser, mobile app, thin client, terminalemulator,..

SaaS CRM, Email, Virtual desktop, communication, games,..
PaaS Execution runtime, database, web server, development tools,..
Iaas Virtual machines, servers, storage, Loadbalancers, network,

FIGURE 10.1   A typical cloud architecture.

10.4.1   *INFRASTRUCTURE AS A SERVICE (IaaS)*

"Infrastructure as a service" (IaaS) alludes to online administrations that give elevated level APIs used to dereference different low-level subtleties of basic system framework like physical processing assets, area, information dividing, scaling, security, reinforcement, and so forth (Sahoo et al., 2016). A hypervisor runs the virtual machines (VMs) as visitors.

Pools of hypervisors inside the cloud operational framework can bolster enormous quantities of VMs and the capacity to scale benefits here and there as indicated by clients' differing prerequisites. Linux holders run in segregated segments of a solitary Linux bit running legitimately on the physical equipment. Linux groups and namespaces are the hidden Linux piece innovations used to separate, verify, and deal with the compartments. Containerization offers better than virtualization because there is no hypervisor overhead. Likewise, compartment limit auto-scales progressively with registering load, which wipes out the issue of over-provisioning and empowers utilization-based charging. IaaS mists regularly offer extra assets, for example, a virtual-machine plate picture library, crude square stockpiling, document or article stockpiling, firewalls, load balancers, IP addresses, virtual neighborhood (VLANs: virtual local area network), and programming packs. The NIST's meaning of distributed computing portrays IaaS as "where the shopper can convey and run subjective programming, which can incorporate working frameworks and applications. The purchaser doesn't oversee or control the fundamental cloud framework yet has power over working frameworks, stockpiling, and sent applications; and potentially restricted control of select systems administration parts (e.g., have firewalls)." IaaS-cloud suppliers supply these assets on-request from their enormous pools of hardware introduced in server farms. For wide-zone availability, clients can utilize either the Internet or bearer mists (committed virtual private systems). To send their applications, cloud clients introduce working framework pictures and their application programming on the cloud foundation. In this model, the cloud client fixes and keeps up the working frameworks and application programming. Cloud suppliers commonly charge IaaS benefits on a utility processing premise: cost mirrors the measure of assets allotted and expended.

10.4.2 PLATFORM AS A SERVICE (PaaS)

The ability gave to the buyer is to convey onto the cloud framework purchaser made or procured applications made utilizing programming dialects, libraries, administrations, and apparatuses upheld by the supplier. The purchaser doesn't oversee or control the fundamental cloud foundation including system, servers, working frameworks, or capacity, yet has power over the sent applications and perhaps arrangement settings for the application-facilitating condition.

PaaS sellers offer an improvement situation to application designers. The supplier commonly creates toolbox and principles for improvement and channels for dispersion and installment. In the PaaS models, cloud suppliers convey a registering stage, commonly including working framework, programming-language execution condition, database, and web server. Application designers create and run their product on a cloud stage rather than legitimately purchasing and dealing with the hidden equipment and programming layers. With some PaaS, the fundamental PC and capacity assets scale consequently to coordinate application request, so the cloud client doesn't need to allot assets physically.

Some joining and information the executive's suppliers likewise use utilizations of PaaS as conveyance models for information. Models incorporate iPaaS (integration platform as a service) and dPaaS (data platform as a service). iPaaS empowers clients to create, execute, and oversee incorporation streams. Under the iPaaS reconciliation model, clients drive the improvement and arrangement of combinations without introducing or dealing with any equipment or middleware. dPaaS conveys reconciliation and information the board items as a completely overseen administration. Under the dPaaS model, the PaaS supplier, not the client, deals with the improvement and execution of projects by building information applications for the client. dPaaS clients get to information through information representation instruments. Stage as a Service purchasers don't oversee or control the fundamental cloud framework including system, servers, working frameworks, or capacity, however, have power over the conveyed applications and perhaps setup settings for the application-facilitating condition (Tiwary, 2017).

10.4.3 SOFTWARE AS A SERVICE (SaaS)

The capacity gave to the purchaser is to utilize the supplier's applications running on a cloud foundation. The applications are available from different customer gadgets through either a meager customer interface, for example, an internet browser (e.g., electronic e-mail), or a program interface. The buyer doesn't oversee or control the hidden cloud foundation including system, servers, working frameworks, stockpiling, or even individual application abilities, with the conceivable exemption of constrained client explicit application design settings (Tiwary, 2018).

In the product as a help (SaaS) model, clients access application programming and databases. Cloud suppliers deal with the framework and stages that run the applications. SaaS is some of the time alluded to as "On-request programming" and is generally valued on compensation for each utilization premise or utilizing a membership fee. In the SaaS model, cloud suppliers introduce and work application programming in the cloud and cloud clients get to the product from cloud customers. Cloud clients don't deal with the cloud foundation and stage where the application runs. This dispenses with the need to introduce and run the application on the cloud client's very own PCs, which improves upkeep and backing. Cloud applications vary from different applications in their adaptability which can be accomplished by cloning undertakings onto numerous VMs at runtime to meet changing work demand. Load balancers disperse the work over the arrangement of VMs. This procedure is straightforward to the cloud client, who sees just a solitary passageway. To oblige an enormous number of cloud clients, cloud applications can be multitenant, implying that any machine may serve more than one cloud-client association. The estimating model for SaaS applications is normally a month-to-month or yearly level expense per user, so costs become adaptable and customizable if clients are included or evacuated anytime. It might likewise be free. Proponents guarantee that SaaS gives a business the possibility to diminish IT operational expenses by re-appropriating equipment and programming upkeep and backing to the cloud supplier. This empowers the business to reallocate IT activities costs from equipment/programming spending and faculty costs, towards meeting different objectives. In addition, with applications facilitated midway, updates can be discharged without the requirement for clients to put in new programming. One downside of SaaS accompanies putting away the clients' information on the cloud supplier's server. Subsequently, there could be unapproved access to the information. Instances of utilizations offered as SaaS are games and profitability programming like Google Docs and Word Online. SaaS applications might be incorporated with distributed storage or File facilitating administrations, which is the situation with Google Docs being coordinated with Google Drive and Word Online being coordinated with OneDrive.

10.5   VIRTUALIZATION

10.5.1   WHAT IS VIRTUALIZATION?

Virtualization is the way toward running a virtual example of a PC framework in a layer preoccupied with the real equipment (Han et al., 2015). Most regularly, it alludes to running numerous working frameworks on a PC framework all the while. To the applications running over the virtualized machine, it can show up as though they are without anyone else devoted machine, where the working framework, libraries, and different projects are remarkable to the visitor-virtualized framework and detached to the host-working framework which sits underneath it. There are many reasons why individuals utilize virtualization in computing. For desktop users, the most common use of virtualization is to run applications that are meant for a different operating system. Due to this, users can run applications, without switch the computers or reboot into a different system. For chairmen of servers, virtualization likewise offers the capacity to run diverse working frameworks, however maybe, more critically, it offers an approach to portion an enormous framework into numerous littler parts, enabling the server to be utilized all the more productively by various clients or applications with various needs. It likewise considers separation, keeping programs running within a virtual machine safe from the procedures occurring in another the virtual machine on a similar host.

10.5.2   VIRTUALIZATION COMPUTING

Virtualization is certainly not another idea for PC researchers. Memory was the first among the PC parts to be virtualized. Memory was a costly piece of the first computers, so virtual memory ideas were created during the 1970s. Study and examination of different page substitution calculations was a well-known research theme at that point. The present PCs have refined and different degrees of reserving for memory. Capacity virtualization was a characteristic following stage with virtual plates, virtual reduced circle (CD) drives, and prompting distributed storage today. Virtualization of work areas brought about meager customers, which brought about a noteworthy decrease of capital just as operational use, in the long run prompting virtualization of servers and distributed computing. PC organizing is the pipes of processing, and like pipes in every single wonderful structure, organizing is the way to a considerable lot of the highlights offered by new figuring models. Virtualization in systems administration is likewise not another idea. Virtual stations in X.25-based media transmission systems and every single ensuing system enable different clients to share a huge physical channel (Wang et al., 2016).

Virtual neighborhood (VLANs) enables different branches of an organization to impart a physical LAN to disengagement. Thus, virtual private systems (VPNs) permit unique network virtualization (NV) is the way into the present and future achievement of distributed computing. In this chapter, we clarify key purposes behind virtualization and quickly clarify a few of the systems administration innovations that have been grown as of late or are being created in different guidelines bodies. Specifically, we clarify programming characterized organizing, which is the way to arrange programmability. We likewise delineate SDN's relevance with our very own examination on OpenADN application conveyance in a multi-cloud environment. Companies and representatives to utilize open systems with a similar degree of security they appreciate in their private systems. In any case, there has been noteworthy recharged enthusiasm for arranging virtualization powered basically by distributed computing. A few new benchmarks have been created and are being created. Programming characterized organizing (SDN) additionally helps in arrange virtualization. These ongoing guidelines and SDN are the points of this chapter. We talk about a few ongoing system virtualization advancements. Programming characterized organizing is talked about in detail. Our examination of open application conveyance utilizing SDN is depicted. At last, a synopsis pursues.

10.5.3 WHY VIRTUALIZE?

There are numerous reasons why we must virtualize assets. The five most basic reasons are: Sharing: at the point when an asset is too huge for a solitary client, it is ideal to partition it into various virtual pieces, just like the case with the present multi-center processors. Every processor can run various VMs, and each machine can be utilized by an alternate client. The equivalent applies to the rapid virtual machine on a similar host:

1. **Isolation:** Different clients sharing an asset may not confide in one another, so it is essential to give disconnection among clients.

Clients utilizing one virtual part ought not to have the option to screen the exercises or meddle with the exercises of different clients. This may apply regardless of whether various clients have a place with a similar association since various branches of the association (e.g., fund and designing) may have information that is classified into the office.

2. **Aggregation:** If the asset is excessively little, it is conceivable to build an enormous virtual asset that acts as a huge asset. This is the situation with capacity, where countless cheap temperamental plates can be utilized to make up enormous dependable stockpiling.

3. **Dynamics:** Regularly, asset necessities change quickly because of client versatility, and an approach to reallocating the asset rapidly is required. This is simpler with virtual assets than with physical assets.

4. **Cease of the Board:** Last, however, presumably the most significant purpose behind virtualization is the simplicity of the executives. Virtual gadgets are simpler to oversee because they are programming based and uncover a uniform interface through standard deliberations.

10.6 VIRTUALIZATION IN COMPUTING

10.6.1 WHAT IS NETWORK VIRTUALIZATION (NV)?

Network virtualization (NV) alludes to abstracting system assets generally conveyed in equipment to programming (Doherthy et al., 2016). NV can join numerous physical Networks to one virtual, programming-based system, or it can isolate one physical system into discrete, free virtual systems.

10.6.2 WHY NETWORK VIRTUALIZATION (NV)?

NV decouples organize administrations from the fundamental equipment and permits virtual provisioning of a whole system (Yi et al., 2018). Physical organize assets, for example, switches, and switches, are pooled and available by any client utilizing a unified administration framework. NV additionally empowers computerization of numerous regulatory undertakings, diminishing manual blunders and provisioning time. It can give more noteworthy system profitability and effectiveness.

10.6.3 NETWORK VIRTUALIZATION (NV) EXAMPLE

One case of network virtualization is virtual LAN (VLAN). A VLAN is a subsection of a neighborhood (LAN) made with programming that joins organize gadgets into one gathering, paying little heed to a physical area. VLANs can improve the speed and execution of occupied systems and streamline changes or increases to the system.

10.6.4 KINDS OF NETWORK VIRTUALIZATION (NV)

External virtualization: Combines different systems or parts of systems into a virtual unit. Internal virtualization: Uses programming compartments to imitate or give the usefulness of a solitary physical system.

Network functions virtualization (NFV) is an activity to virtualize arranges benefits generally run on restrictive, committed equipment. With NFV, capacities like steering, load adjusting, and firewalls are bundled as VMs on ware equipment. Individual virtual organizes capacities, or VNFs, are a basic part of NFV design. Different VNFs can be added to a standard ×86 server and afterward can be checked and constrained by a hypervisor. NFV's crucial use of production equipment is significant because system supervisors never again need to buy and physically arrange committed equipment gadgets to fabricate a help chain that connections certain capacities to play out an ideal grouping. Each devoted gadget, by examination, should be physically cabled together as needs are, which is a tedious procedure. Since NFV design virtualizes organize works and takes out explicit equipment, arrange supervisors can include, move or change arrange capacities at the server level in a disentangled provisioning process. On the off chance that a VNF running on a virtual machine requires more data transfer capacity, for instance, the head can move the VM to another physical server or arrangement another virtual machine on the first server to deal with part of the heap. Having this adaptability enables an IT division to react in a progressively dexterous way to changing business objectives and system administration requests (Wu et al., 2019).

10.6.5   ADVANTAGES OF NETWORK FUNCTION VIRTUALIZATION (NFV)

The NFV idea was initially exhibited by a gathering of system specialist organizations at the SDN and OpenFlow (OF) World Congress in October 2012. These specialist organizations needed to improve and accelerate the way toward including new system capacities or applications (Riggio et al., 2013). Figure 10.2 illustrates the network function virtualization (NFV) management and orchestration.

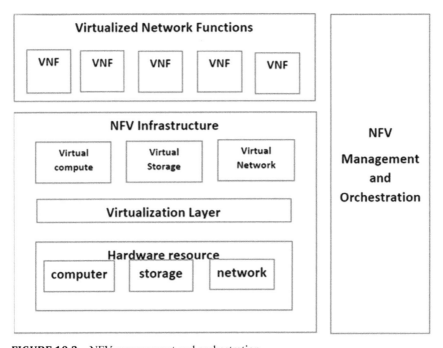

FIGURE 10.2   NFV management and orchestration.

10.7   SOFTWARE-DEFINED NETWORKING (SDN)

Software-defined networking (SDN) is engineering that plans to make systems dexterous and adaptable. The objective of SDN is to improve organize control by empowering undertakings and specialist co-ops to react rapidly to changing business prerequisites. In a product characterized organize; a system specialist or director can shape traffic from a brought together control comfort without contacting singular switches in the system. The incorporated SDN controller (SDN-C) guides the changes to convey organize benefits any place they're required, paying little heed to the particular associations between a server and gadgets. This procedure is a move away from customary system engineering, in which individual system gadgets settle on traffic choices dependent on their arranged directing tables.

10.7.1 SDN ARCHITECTURE

A run of the mill portrayal of SDN design includes three layers:

i.   Application layer;
ii. Control layer; and
iii. Framework layer.

The application layer, as anyone might expect, contains the run of the mill arrange applications or capacities associations use, which can incorporate interruption identification frameworks, load adjusting or firewalls. Where a customary system would utilize a specific apparatus, for example, a firewall or burden balancer, a product characterized organize replaces the machine with an application that uses the controller to oversee information plane conduct. SDN engineering isolates the system into three recognizable layers, associated through northbound and southbound APIs.

The control layer speaks to the concentrated SDN-C programming that goes about as the mind of the product characterized organize (Sahoo et al., 2018a). This controller dwells on a server and oversees arrangements and the progression of traffic all through the system. The foundation layer is comprised of the physical switches in the system. These three layers impart utilizing separate northbound and southbound application programming interfaces (APIs). For instance, applications converse with the controller through its northbound interface (NBI), while the controller and switches impart utilizing southbound interfaces (SBIs), for example, OF-albeit different conventions exist. There is as of now no proper standard for the controller's northbound API to coordinate OF as a general SBI.

It is likely the Open Daylight controller's northbound API may develop as an accepted standard after some time, given its wide merchant support. Figure 10.3 illustrates basic SDN architecture.

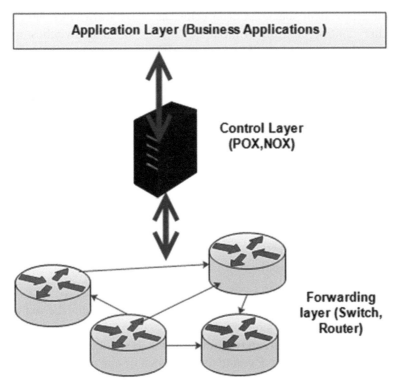

FIGURE 10.3   The generic SDN architecture..

10.7.2 *HOW SDN FUNCTIONS?*

SDN incorporates a few kinds of advances, including utilitarian partition; arrange virtualization and robotization through programmability. Initially, SDN innovation concentrated exclusively on the division of the system control plane (CP) from the information plane. While the CP settles on choices about how bundles should course through the system, the information plane moves parcels all around. In an exemplary SDN situation, a parcel lands at a system switch, and rules incorporated with the switch's exclusive firmware advice the change were to advance the bundle. These parcels taking care of rules are sent to the change from the unified controller. The switch-otherwise called information plane gadget-questions the controller for direction as required, and it gives the controller data about the traffic it handles. The switch sends each bundle setting off to a similar goal in a similar way and treats every one of the parcels precisely the same way (Sahoo et al., 2019a, b).

Programming characterized organizing utilizes an activity mode that is here and there called versatile or dynamic, in which a switch gives a course solicitation to a controller for a parcel that doesn't have a particular course. This procedure is independent of versatile directing, which issues course demands through switches and calculations dependent on the system topology, not through a controller. The virtualization part of SDN becomes an integral factor through a virtual overlay, which is an intelligently isolated system over the physical system. Clients can actualize start to finish overlays to extract the fundamental system and section organize traffic. This microsegmentation is particularly valuable for specialist co-ops and administrators with multi-inhabitant cloud conditions and cloud administrations, as they can arrange a different virtual system with explicit approaches for each occupant (Jha, 2019).

10.7.3 ADVANTAGES OF SDN

With SDN, ahead can change any system switch's principles when fundamental organizing, deprioritizing or in any event, blocking explicit sorts of bundles with a granular degree of control and security. This is particularly useful in a distributed computing multi-occupant engineering since it empowers the overseer to oversee traffic stacks in an adaptable and progressively proficient way. This empowers the executive to utilize more affordable item switches and has more command over the system traffic stream than any other time in recent memory. Different advantages of SDN are arranging the executives and start to finish perceivability (Ge et al., 2014). A system head needs just manage one unified controller to convey strategies to the associated switches, rather than arranging different singular gadgets. This capacity is likewise a security advantage because the controller can screen traffic and send security strategies. If the controller regards traffic suspicious, for instance, it can reroute or drop the parcels. SDN additionally virtualizes equipment and administrations that were recently completed by devoted equipment, bringing about the touted advantages of a decreased equipment impression and lower operational expenses. Furthermore, programming characterized organizing added to the development of programming characterized a wide zone arrange (SD-WAN) innovation. SD-WAN utilizes the virtual overlay part of SDN innovation, abstracting an association's availability interfaces all through its WAN and making a virtual system that can utilize whichever association the controller regards fit to send traffic.

10.7.4 DIFFICULTIES WITH SDN

Security is both an advantage and a worry with SDN innovation. The brought together SDN-C exhibits a solitary purpose of disappointment and, whenever focused by an assailant, can demonstrate negative to the system. Amusingly, another test with SDN is there's no settled meaning of "programming characterized organizing" in the systems administration industry. Various sellers offer different ways to deal with SDN, going from equipment driven models and virtualization stages to hyper-united systems administration plans and controllers' techniques. Some systems administration activities are regularly confused with SDN, including white-box organizing, arrange disaggregation, organize mechanization, and programmable systems administration. While SDN can profit and work with these advances and procedures, it stays a different innovation. SDN innovation rose with a great deal of publicity around 2011 when it was presented nearby the OF convention. From that point forward, appropriation has been generally moderate, particularly among endeavors that have littler systems and fewer assets. Additionally, numerous endeavors refer to the expense of SDN arrangement to be a deflecting factor. Primary adopters of SDN incorporate specialist co-ops, organize administrators, telecoms, and bearers, alongside enormous organizations, for example, Facebook, and Google, all of which have the assets to handle and add to developing innovation.

10.7.5 SDN USE CASES

Some utilization cases for SDN include:

1. **DevOps:** A methodology dependent on programming characterized systems administration can encourage DevOps via mechanizing application updates and arrangements, including computerizing IT framework parts as the DevOps applications and stages are conveyed. (https://www.networkworld.com/article/3253118/what-is-nfv-and-what-are-its-benefits.html).

2. **Campus Systems:** These can be hard to oversee, particularly with the progressing need to bind together Wi-Fi and Ethernet systems. SDN-Cs can profit grounds arranges by offering brought together administration and mechanization, improved security, and application-level nature of administration over the system.

3. **Service Supplier Systems:** SDN helps specialist co-ops improve and computerize the provisioning of their systems for a start to finish system and administration of the board and control. (https:// www.electronicdesign.com/technologies/communications/ article/21799336/whats-the-difference-between-sdn-and-nfv).

4. **Data Focus Security:** SDN bolsters more focused on assurance and disentangles firewall organization. For the most part, an undertaking relies upon a conventional edge firewall to verify its whole datacenter. Be that as it may, an organization can make a dispersed firewall framework by adding virtual firewalls to ensure the VMs. This additional layer of firewall security averts a break in one virtual machine from bouncing to another. Likewise, SDN incorporated control, and robotization permits the administrator to see, adjust, and control arrange movement to decrease the danger of a rupture regardless.

10.7.6   THE EFFECT OF SDN

Programming characterized organizing has majorly affected the administration of the IT framework and system plan. As SDN innovation develops, it not just changes organize framework plan, and it likewise changes how IT sees its job, since IT the executives is all the more vigorously included all through the choice procedure, and rethinks the whole IT foundation. SDN structures can make arrange control programmable, frequently utilizing open conventions, for example, OF. Along these lines, ventures can apply all around mindful programming control at the edges of their systems to get to arrange switches and switches as opposed to the shut and restrictive firmware, for the most part, used to design, oversee, verify, and enhance organize assets. While SDN arrangements are found in each industry, the effect of the innovation is most grounded in innovation-related fields and money related administrations. SDN is affecting how to broadcast communications organizations' work. For instance, Verizon utilizes SDN to join all its current assistance edge switches for Ethernet and IP-based administrations into one stage. The objective is to rearrange the edge engineering, empowering Verizon to improve operational effectiveness and adaptability to help new capacities and administrations. SDN will help Verizon improve organize the board and at last offer better administrations to its clients. Achievement in the monetary administrations' division depends on associating with enormous quantities of exchanging members, low dormancy, and a profoundly secure system framework to control money-related markets around the world. About the entirety of the members in the money related showcase rely upon heritage arranges that, to some extent, are non-prescient, difficult to oversee, slow to convey, and have colossal security vulnerabilities. With SDN innovation, be that as it may, associations in the money related administration part can construct prescient systems to empower progressively productive and successful stages for budgetary exchanging applications.

10.8 NETWORK FUNCTIONS VIRTUALIZATION (NFV)

The job of NFV is to move to organize capacities from committed machines to nonexclusive servers. NFV permits organize administrators to actualize arrange approach without agonizing over where to put the capacities in the system and how to course traffic through these capacities. A typical NFV architecture has demonstrated in Figure 10.4.

NFV moves every one of the capacities as recorded beneath in a typical ×86 design utilizing virtualization.

- Router;
- Firewall;
- Web server;
- Load balancer;
- Switch;
- Media server.

NFV helps in accomplishing the following advantages for the administrators:

i.   Standard equipment;
ii.   Less mind-boggling;
iii. Entirely adaptable;
iv.   Decreased power;
v.   Lower CapEx;
vi.   Lower OpEx;

vii. Test new applications;

viii. Low hazard;

ix. Reduced TTM;

x. Open market to programming providers.

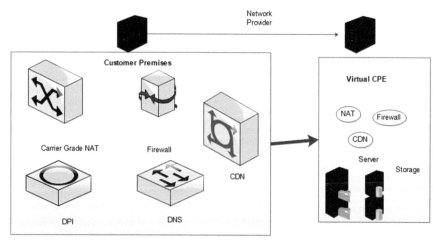

FIGURE 10.4 NFV architecture.

Table 10.1 refers to potential works that could be virtualized.

TABLE 10.1 Network Elements That can be Virtualized

Network Element to be Virtualized	Functionalities
Switching elements	Broadband network gateways, carrier grade NAT (network address translation), routers
Mobile network nodes	Gateway, GPRS support node, radio network controller, various node B functions
Customer Premise Equipment	Home routers, set-top boxes
Tunneling Gateway elements	IPsec/SSL virtual private network gateways
Traffic analysis	Deep packet inspection (DPI)
Assurance	service assurance, service level agreement (SLA) monitoring
Signaling	IP multimedia subsystem components
control plane functions	policy control and charging platforms
application optimization	content delivery networks, cache servers
Security	firewalls, virus scanners, IDS

Both SDN and NFV are highly complementary, but there are few differences between them. Table 10.2 describes the key difference between SDN and NFV (Source: https://www.rfwireless-world.com/Terminology/difference-between-SDN-and-NFV.html).

TABLE 10.2 Key Differences between SDN and NFV

Features	SDN	NFV
Major focus area	SDN focuses on data centers.	NFV focuses on service providers or operators.
Major changes	SDN divides the control and data forwarding planes.	It replaces hardware network devices with software.
Used protocol	OpenFlow	does support OpenFlow
Execution place	Applications run on industry-standard servers	industry-standard servers
Main initiative supporters	Vendors of enterprise networking software and hardware	Telecom service providers or operators.
Customer benefit or end-user benefit applications	It drives down complexity and cost and increases agility.	CDN, WAN accelerators, SLA assurance
Formalization body	Open Networking Foundation (ONF)	ETSI NFV working group

10.9 CONCLUSION

A large industry community already admits that the future networking industry will incline towards software-centric rather than hardware-centric. In this regard, both NFV provide greater performance for networking. Both technologies have some similarities and dissimilarities. The core idea behind NFV is that it virtualizes network services and keeps abstract them from designated hardware. Typically it utilizes commodity hardware, especially servers, for executing the software versions of network services, which were earlier run by dedicated hardware units. On the other hand, Software Defined Network is another emerging technology whose core idea is to separate the CP from the underlying forwarding devices. Centralized network provisioning, lower CAPEX, vendor independence, cloud abstractions are the major advantages of SDN. On the other hand, NFV makes service provider networks easier in terms of security, scalability, and flexibility. A comparative study between these two technologies has been discussed in this chapter, which will provide a clear insight into the technology to the researchers.

KEYWORDS

- **application programming interfaces**
- **data platform as a service**
- **deep packet inspection**
- **integration platform as a service**
- **network virtualization**
- **platform as a service**
- **software as a service**
- **software-defined networking**
- **virtual machines**

REFERENCES

Ageyev, D., Bondarenko, O., Alfroukh, W., & Radivilova, T., (2018). Provision security in SDN/NFV. In: *2018 14ᵗʰ International Conference on Advanced Trends in Radioelecrtronics, Telecommunications and Computer Engineering (TCSET)* (pp. 506–509). IEEE.

Doherty, J., (2016). *SDN and NFV Simplified: A Visual Guide to Understanding Software Defined Networks and Network Function Virtualization.* Addison-Wesley Professional.

Ge, X., et al., (2014). OpenANFV: Accelerating network function virtualization with a consolidated framework in open stack. *ACM SIGCOMM Computer Communication Review, 44*(4). ACM.

Han, B., et al., (2015). Network function virtualization: Challenges and opportunities for innovations. *IEEE Communications Magazine, 53*(2), 90–97.

https://www.electronicdesign.com/technologies/communications/article/21799336/whats-the-difference-between-sdn-and-nfv (accessed on 16 December 2020).

https://www.networkcomputing.com/networking/5-nfv-benefits-trends-driving-them (accessed on 16 December 2020).

https://www.networkworld.com/article/3253118/what-is-nfv-and-what-are-its-benefits.html (Access Date 25-Dec-2019)

Jha, D. N., et al., (2019). *IoTSim-Edge: A Simulation Framework for Modeling the Behavior of IoT and Edge Computing Environments.* arXiv preprint arXiv:1910.03026.

Li, Y., & Min, C., (2015). Software-defined network function virtualization: A survey. *IEEE Access, 3*, 2542–2553.

Riggio, R., Tinku, R., & Fabrizio, G., (2013). Empower: A testbed for network function virtualization research and experimentation. In: *2013 IEEE SDN for Future Networks and Services (SDN4FNS)*. IEEE.

Sahoo, K. S., et al., (2016). A comprehensive tutorial on software defined network: The driving force for the future internet technology. *Proceedings of the International Conference on Advances in Information Communication Technology and Computing*. ACM.

Sahoo, K. S., et al., (2017). Network virtualization: Network resource management in cloud. *Resource Management and Efficiency in Cloud Computing Environments* (pp. 239–263). IGI Global.

Sahoo, K. S., et al., (2018a). A machine learning approach for predicting DDoS traffic in software defined networks. In: *2018 International Conference on Information Technology (ICIT)*. IEEE.

Sahoo, K. S., et al., (2018b). On the placement of controllers in software-defined-WAN using meta-heuristic approach. *Journal of Systems and Software, 145*, 180–194.

Sahoo, K. S., et al., (2019a). ESMLB: Efficient switch migration-based load balancing for multi-controller SDN in IoT. *IEEE Internet of Things Journal*.

Sahoo, K. S., et al., (2019b). Improving end-users utility in software-defined wide area network systems. *IEEE Transactions on Network and Service Management*.

Tiwary, M., et al., (2017). CPS: A dynamic and distributed pricing policy in cyber foraging systems for fixed state cloudlets. *Computing, 99*(5), 447–463.

Tiwary, M., et al., (2018). Response time optimization for cloudlets in mobile edge computing. *Journal of Parallel and Distributed Computing, 119*, 81–91.

Wang, L., et al., (2016). Joint optimization of service function chaining and resource allocation in network function virtualization. *IEEE Access, 4*, 8084–8094.

Wood, T., et al., (2015). Toward a software-based network: Integrating software defined networking and network function virtualization. *IEEE Network, 29*(3), 36–41.

Wu, J., et al., (2019). Fog-computing-enabled cognitive network function virtualization for an information-centric future internet. *IEEE Communications Magazine, 57*(7), 48–54.

Yi, B., et al., (2018). A comprehensive survey of network function virtualization. *Computer Networks, 133*, 212–262.

Index